Mental Health in a Mad World

Mental Health in a Mad World

James A. Magner

Roman Catholic Books

Post Office Box 2286, Fort Collins, CO 80522

NIHIL OBSTAT:
John A. McMahon
Censor Librorum

IMPRIMATUR:
Samuel Cardinal Stritch,
Archbishop of Chicago

April 21, 1953

ISBN 1-929291-09-4

Contents

Mental Health in a Mad World

CHAPTER I

Mental Health in a Mad World

I

NEARLY everyone has heard the story about the old Yankee who pondered the condition of the world and observed to his wife, "Hephzibah, I do believe that everyone in the world is touched in the head, except me and thee; and sometimes I think even thou art a bit touched."

One of the penalties of living in an age of tension is the possession of frayed nerves and a confused outlook. The repeated experience of war in our time, constant apprehension of war with atomic weapons more dreadful than before, and a barrage of disturbing propaganda and psychological warfare on the international front, even in the few moments when guns are quiet — all this has taken a heavy toll of our mental peace and health. The cost of maintaining both peacetime and heavy military expenses at the same time has added to the strain, by requiring what is called stepped-up production, with added work, higher taxes, increased cost of living, and a desperate effort to sustain a high material standard of living.

Rapid urbanization and greater freedom of action, for both sexes, have opened up new opportunities for personal advancement and have served to eliminate many old inhibitions and taboos, which formerly plagued people and made them submissive to ways of life which they secretly recognized as narrow and even unjust. But these factors have also destroyed patterns of family life and community co-operation which gave the individual a sense of security and protected him in fulfilling his duties. As a result, a rather wholesale bewilderment has gripped large sectors of society which have not learned to cope with their new responsibilities or to bring their sense of rights and duties into working harmony.

One need not look far to discover tragic evidence of mental and moral breakdown. The alarming prevalence of divorce is proof, not only of facilities of our civil laws in providing escape from unhappy marriage, but also and more significantly of the fact that too many people have not learned the important art of getting along together. For many people divorce spells freedom; but little is said of the mental anguish that precedes, accompanies, and often follows this action, which might have been averted by more considerate understanding and adjustment. Unhappy homes, children brought up in an atmosphere of dissension or lack of concern, with the increase of juvenile delinquency and crime, are further indications of mental sickness and disorder affecting the community as well as the individual.

It is rather commonly assumed that most behavior problems are solved by the accumulation of knowledge in the normal processes of education, and by improved economic conditions which help people raise their standards of material comfort. To a certain extent these assumptions are correct. But these advantages will not in themselves bring about the desired results. The idea that possession of money, household conveniences, cars, houses, and leisure automatically produce virtue and peace of mind has been disproved over and over again. Quite often they produce the opposite. I am acquainted with more than one instance in which persons in oil-producing regions have prayed that no "gusher" be found on their property, lest the new-found wealth result in the debacle of broken homes, dissatisfied and dissipated lives, and human wreckage which often pursues sudden prosperity. The example of corruption in public life also is frequent enough to convince one that it takes more than a good salary and economic security to make men and women mentally happy and satisfied to comply with their duty.

The accumulation of knowledge, without a directive principle, is no guarantee of mental health. On the contrary, the process has resulted in mental confusion and misdirection for many people. A little knowledge of the more profound problems of existence has brought an end to the simple faith that guided many a life in the past; people find themselves grasping at straws in the wind to produce a sense of direction. Cults of science, beauty, convenience, pleasure, physical health, fraternity, democracy, philanthropy, and personal hobbies have taken the place of religion. Immediate objectives are made to serve in the absence of any final purpose or of a consistent, abiding philosophy in life. With many people, a personal crisis or sense of frustration calls for consultation with a fortune teller, re-examination of one's horoscope, or psychoanalysis, depending upon one's confidence and pocketbook.

2

Whatever the elements of stress or confusion in one's personal life, it is obvious that the problem of safeguarding mental health is intensely real and important. This is true, not only to meet the special challenges of the age in which we live, but also to come safely through the normal crises in the life of every individual — discouragement, disappointment, sickness, death, and the daily emotional disturbances that affect the normal pulses of the brain. The question "What is on your mind?" may refer to a passing thought, or it may denote the presence of a shadow, a burden, or a growing pain that may become chronic and develop into serious proportions unless carefully watched.

On the positive side, it is important to note that clear thinking, sound judgment, fair dealing, pleasant human relations,
efficiency, and enjoyment of life are directly related to mental
health. The reason why many people fail in life is precisely
that they are mentally sick in one way or the other. The success
of others is not simply the result of influence or good luck, but
rather the dividend that comes from the observance of certain
rules that make for the ideal of what the ancients referred to as
mens sana in corpore sano — "a sound mind in a healthy body."
It is true that there are many elements of disturbance and distress beyond our control; but we can, through our own efforts
in the use of right principles, ward off tendencies toward mental
sickness and increase our mental health, vigor, and sense of
well-being.

Mental health may be described as a harmonious functioning
of the various faculties — sensory, imaginative, emotional, and
intellectual — that work together in the human being, to produce the perception of facts, the recognition of truth, and
desire for the good. This does not mean that the healthy mind
is incapable of making mistakes. Normal functioning of the
human mind and senses makes allowance for a measure of
error and deviation. Imperfect conditions, insufficient evidence,
and various forms of deception must be taken into account.
Nor is the healthy mind necessarily brilliant. Persons of all degrees of talent, ability, and intelligence can cultivate mental
health, providing, of course, they are not the victims of an
organic disease which makes normal functioning impossible.

It may be asked whether mental health is the same thing as
happiness. The answer to this needs some qualification; but
they are not necessarily the same. A healthy mind is subject to
various outside pressures which may be anything but pleasing.
The emotional reactions to the experiences of life, such as sorrow,
anger, disgust, indignation, and disappointment, are unavoidable in the average life, and may well be regarded as evidence

of healthy functioning in the mind. An insane man may be a happy man, if he has lost his power of recognizing evil or pain. An opium smoker enjoys his beautiful dreams. Alcoholics seek refuge in drink, which exalts at the same time as it depraves. A healthy mind does not function under false illusions or depend upon artificial stimulation. As a properly functioning mind, it is happy in the sense that it is not only at peace with itself, but also endowed with the power of assembling knowledge in correct relationships and grasping true values.

The healthy mind rises to a view of life as a whole, not merely in single lanes or tracks. It frees itself of psychological complexes and fixations which distort and disturb the relationships between the individual and society. It operates on a philosophy of good logic, realistic optimism, and ethical behavior. It is capable of growth and development; and it can be abused and injured.

3

When we speak of the mind, we refer specifically to the faculties of the intellect, the memory, and the will. Man is described in Holy Scripture as being created in "the image and likeness of God," designating his rational nature rather than his physical body. Nevertheless, as functioning in a human body, the mind depends upon the brain and the sensory and nervous system to serve up the primary materials from which it forms ideas and thoughts. If the brain, the senses, or the nerves become injured in any way, the mind itself becomes hampered in its operations.

While in common parlance, the brain is referred to as a thinking apparatus, it is in reality an organism which receives and interprets in a material way the impressions derived from the senses of sight, hearing, smelling, feeling, and whatever other faculties of perception may be tied into the nervous system. The impact of external objects is registered through the senses and delivered almost instantaneously to the brain, which sets up an image, if the object is perceived by sight; creates the sensation of odor, if the molecular action affects the olfactory nerves; produces a reaction of sound, if the stimulus is received through the pressure of the sonic waves on the eardrums; or of the heat, the cold, the pain, the pleasure, or various tactile feelings if the material object comes in contact with the body surfaces. From these experiences are developed the various kinds of reflex actions which enable the body to protect itself instinctively or to make such adjustments as may be indicated by nature for one's physical well-being. Of the multitude of actions which we perform in adapting ourselves to our environment, the vast bulk are instinctive responses of the brain to sensory and nervous messages.

Perhaps the most remarkable performance of the brain stems from its powers of sensitive memory and imagination. In other words, the brain is able, not merely to register primary impressions, but also to store these up and to re-create them long after the original stimulus has been withdrawn. More than that, it can regroup images and sensations in a fictional sort of way, as in dreams, with all the illusions of an actual experience. In a dream, one has the illusion of actually *seeing* a fire, for example, not merely of thinking about it, of actually greeting friends or of being pursued by enemies, not merely of contemplating the possibility of these situations or of reflecting on their pleasure or pain. To a certain extent, at least, it would appear that the brain of higher animals can perform similar actions. The elephant is said to have a remarkable memory. Dogs bark in their sleep and give other indications of being able to dream.

It is not within the power of the brain, however, to *think*, that is, to form rational ideas and formulate rational judgments. The idea of a thing is universal in scope and goes to the essence of things, which is nondimensional and nonmaterial in nature. Thus, the idea of man may be expressed in terms of "a rational animal," whereas the most that the organic brain can produce is the image of a particular man as projected in space. The essence of this idea is expressed in the terms *rationality* and *animality*, which correspond to no particular image, since neither exists except in the form of an idea. The same observations may be made of other abstractions such as justice, honesty, and goodness, which are universal concepts expressing certain relationships but do not exist in any material or dimensional form. Likewise, the ability to formulate judgments or thoughts, which are in effect the recognition of relationships, is beyond the scope of an organism. An adding machine can produce a total which is the sum of the various numbers comprising it, and the brain of a man, or of a dog, for that matter, can recognize that two apples take up more space than one apple. But the ability to *think* of numbers, without reference to space or particular objects and to consider them in reference to their abstract relationships or in the results produced by addition or multiplication, is clearly beyond a faculty which by its nature is restricted to time and space.

From these considerations, it is concluded that the human mind, that is, the intellectual faculty of thought, is different from the brain, which is the seat of sensory perceptions and imagination. Similarly, the intellectual memory, which can retain ideas, is distinguished from the sensitive memory, which is restricted to sensations and images. And the free will of man, which can choose consciously and deliberately among various courses of action, is, for the same reasons, distinguished from instinctive action, whether of man or of the lower animals, which responds without deliberate action or even conscious reflection to an external stimulus.

We further conclude that the mind, the intellectual memory, and the free will are faculties of a *spiritual* kind and therefore must pertain to a spiritual principle, which we call the soul. One of the most cogent arguments for the immortality of the soul, apart from the aspirations of the human mind and of the human race, and even independently of the teaching of Divine

Revelation, is that, since it is an immaterial substance, the soul cannot have parts which dissolve, corrupt, or disintegrate so as to destroy its identity. The destruction of the soul would seem to require a direct act on the part of the Creator, withdrawing support for its existence as a unit.

This analysis, it may be pointed out, is not acceptable to those psychologists who regard thought processes as only special forms of biochemical action and the soul and the faculties of intellect, memory, and will as without any separate existence from the brain. The implications of this outlook and its effects upon both the theory and the practice of mental health, needless to say, are far-reaching. If one does not accept the principle of the spiritual character and immortality of the soul, it is difficult, if not impossible, to establish a firm basis for human rights and duties. In such a scheme of things, justice, honesty, chastity, and morality generally considered have no absolute values or sanctions. The most that they can claim is a temporary convenience, and the most that one could require in a program of mental health would be a psychological — or, more strictly, a biochemical — adjustment to certain material patterns on the part of the brain.

In a strictly materialistic system, there is no place for a sense of guilt. Psychologists and psychiatrists of this school of thought repeat an ancient error in a new form, and regard the whole problem of good and evil as a kind of molecular or chemical battle going on within the individual. The process of healing consists, not in an admission of guilt with an act of sorrow and atonement to almighty God, whose law has been broken, but rather in a detached and objective attitude in which the warring physical elements within the individual are hauled up into consciousness where they may be recognized as troublemakers. Then, it is assumed, they will eliminate or neutralize each other, and the suffering mind will regain its peace.

Another familiar modern group maintains that the only reality is spirit, that matter is only a kind of projection of the mind, and that the mind can control and adjust the physical body as it pleases. In this theory, pain and disease, whether of the body or of the soul, are due simply to mental maladjustment. All that is required, in this system, to eliminate either sin or disease, is prayerful acceptance of divine truth or reunion with the mind of God. Evil, it is said, is the result of a mental attitude; and all can be healed by faith.

It is true that a great many pains and diseases of the body are imaginary and that the autosuggestion which produces them can be made to banish the illusion. It is also true that a wholesome mental attitude can do much to assist in the cure of real ailments. But it is contrary to the facts established by authentic science to deny the physical causality of disease by germs or viruses or to assert that organic injuries are caused and cured simply by an action of the mind. Medicine and surgery here have a valid and necessary part in the curing of bodily disease and injury; and even the activities of the mind can be controlled by drugs and by surgery upon the nervous system and the brain. Death also is a reality which cannot be removed by any mental readjustment yet discovered by man.

4

The distinction between a spiritual soul or intellect and a material or organic brain within the same individual presents, of course, problems which will probably never be fully solved. Nevertheless, it is only by recognizing the existence of the two, working together as a team, that we can offer a satisfactory explanation of the human personality and of the nature and processes of the human mind. It seems clear that the brain, after receiving its impressions from the sensory and nervous system, presents a material image to the intellect, which then abstracts the essence or universal qualities from the image and proceeds to form ideas and to branch off in its own sphere to think and to reason out things, as we are doing here. It is within this higher sphere that the intellectual memory functions, even while it may be aided or accompanied by images produced by the brain. Here also the will chooses freely, even though the objects may be concrete and dimensional.

This explanation helps us to understand not only the close collaboration of brain and intellect in the operations of the mind, but also the influence and effects which they exercise upon each other. While we speak of a subconscious mind and we can engage in philosophical reasoning which has little if any necessary connection with the material world, it is probable that the intellect does not function naturally in this life without a corresponding agitation in the brain. If, on the other hand, the brain or the sensory and nervous system becomes tired, dulled, injured, or shocked, the thinking and willing processes are likewise affected. To this extent, we may say that a tired mind is the physical result of poisons which have accumulated in the cerebral or nervous tissues. Reasoning processes are largely suspended by the induction of sleep, when the imagination goes on its own to produce dreams, or by intoxication, when the disturbed brain tissues and nerves impede the normal exercise or control of judgment. The mind of an infant functions only in a rudimentary way, since the brain is not fully developed. An abnormal brain, concussion of the brain, cerebral tumor or embolism, similarly, may impede the use of reason and produce insanity in one form or another.

The corrective effect of the mind and of the will on the activities of the senses, brain, and the nervous system may also be noted as an important factor in any sound program of mental health. The mind by its nature endeavors to apprehend truth. It distinguishes between appearances and reality, and can appraise and select from good and sham values, even where the senses and the instincts might be deceived. When a mirror is placed on a bird cage, the bird, deceived by what it sees, begins a mating process even to the point of preening before its own image and building a nest. Such reaction in a human being would indicate a mental defect. Impaired sight or hearing must frequently be subjected to the corrective judgment of the mind. Under certain circumstances, the first reaction of instinct is that of panic and flight, which lead to destruction. Sexual stimulation often results from a passing image. In many crises, the imagination by itself may produce reactions of panic and complete disorder, because of the sensory images thrown on its screen. The mind, however, can step in to correct or control the situation by an appraisal of the facts and cool judgment.

The human will moves toward what is good, at least under some aspect. For this reason, it can control the imagination and, through it, the nerves and physical system. There is no doubt that the will has much to do with determining whether people are calm and collected or just a "bundle of nerves." The individual can do much to steady himself, if he wishes to do so. Wild and disorderly imagination can be encouraged deliberately; it can also be curbed and brought into line with reasonable consideration by an active will. Much sickness — particularly of a nervous character or of fatigue — is induced by a desire to gain pity, to shift responsibility, or to avoid work. Both mental and physical health respond to the whip hand of a vigorous will. And sometimes life and death hang in the balance between the will to live and the wish to die.

5

Whether the soul with its powers of reasoning and volition is subject, in its present state, to sentiments of pleasure and pain, independently and separately from those of the nervous system is not certain. The will can make an act of love of God, because of the recognized supreme goodness of God, without any sentiment attached to the act. The conscience can attach the verdict of guilt against the individual who has violated the moral law. But whether the unpleasant feeling of guilt and the sentiment of sorrow or of remorse should be ascribed to the soul or rather be considered as physical emotions is not entirely certain.

In many ways, the emotions hold a kind of middle position between the intellect and will on the one hand and the body on the other. The emotions, strictly speaking, are a nervous reaction or intensification in response to a specific situation. The emotions may be described as resulting attitudes rather than as sense perceptions. Thus, pain is the result of a sense perception, arising from sickness or a lesion of some kind. Grief is an emotion corresponding to an attitude following the loss of some cherished object or an injury done to one. The higher animals experience a number of basic emotions, such as affection, anger, and grief, sometimes to an amazing degree. Other emotions, however, arise from intellectual perceptions and are special to man, such as those associated with the appreciation of beauty, with religious fervor, or with enthusiasm arising from devotion to a cause, like patriotism, civic pride, or interest in one's business.

While the emotions give added zest to life and serve to stimulate action, they also tend to excite the imagination, disturb good judgment, and gain mastery over the will. Anger, for example, can build up a picture of injustice far in excess of what is warranted by the facts. In persons of strong emotional temperament, it may soon mount into a towering rage, so that they "lose their heads," so to speak, and perform actions of violence, hardly realizing what they are doing. Under the influence of grief or emotional love, the will may be seriously weakened and common precautions be thrown to the winds.

Prolonged emotional agitation tends to affect the entire nervous system, not only disturbing mental health, but upsetting the physical system as well. Anger can upset the digestive processes, possibly leading to ulcers. Fear, stemming from the apprehension of danger or disaster, or preoccupation and worry over responsibility, may cause loss of sleep and appetite and lead to nervous collapse. On the other hand, anger, enthusiasm, and love can strengthen one to endure physical pain and mental obstacles which would normally be far beyond one's capacity.

6

From these observations, it is clear that the secret of mental health is to be found in those practices which serve to blend and harmonize the functioning of the mind and of the imagination with a controlled emotional activity. And because of the reciprocal action of mind and matter in the human system, due regard must be paid to the care of one's body in any sound program of mental health.

Mental health, as already noted, can be radically and permanently impaired by defect, injury, or abnormal growth in the brain. It can be adversely affected by an injury to the nervous system or by emotional shock and collapse, weakening and distorting the messages of the brain to the intellect. It may be impaired, temporarily or permanently, by the excessive use of alcohol or narcotics which dehydrate the brain or eat into the cerebral and nerve tissues, weakening the instruments by which both the mind and the will operate in the human body.

As a matter of fact, whatever tends to debilitate or abuse the physical system has the effect of injuring one's mental health. Fatigue from overwork, overplay, insufficient sleep, and prolonged tension of one kind or the other, produces a run-down condition which automatically weakens the vigor and productiveness of the mental faculties. Faulty diet, insufficiency of vitamins, an anemic condition, insufficient exercise, or injudicious and excessive exercise for one's physical condition and one's age — all these factors enter into the picture and must be taken into consideration by the person who wishes to enjoy mental health and to use to best advantage the greatest faculty which God has given to man.

In prescribing for mental health, we may take note of two general mental types. One is the extrovert; the other is the introvert. The first is concerned primarily with the world around him. He wants to make a display, to produce effects, to get results. He is the life of the party, the candidate for office, the loud speaker, the individual who is out to get results. The introvert looks rather into himself. He is the reflective type, who thinks twice or more often before doing anything because of its possible effect on himself or others. He tends to be timid and self-conscious, wondering whether he will be accepted in society and what others may think of him. He is inclined to probe into his own mind, to diagnose and analyze the dark corners of his soul, and to interpret the mysteries of his emotions.

The introvert is likely to find symptoms of psychological defects and mental quirks where there are none. The extrovert normally rides along blissfully unaware of his defects, which have long since been known to the rest of the world. A compromise or combination of the two types or temperaments may be recommended as producing the best results in any deliberate and planned program in the development of mental health.

Everyone can help himself to avoid mental sickness or disorder and to improve his own mental health, by adopting positive principles of good living, exercising self-control and discipline, at the same time keeping an open eye on the beauty and goodness of the world around him. Self-analysis can be carried too far, leading to a morose disposition and queerness about life. But, within reasonable limitations, this study, combined with the observations of others, experience in human relations, and a desire for self-improvement, can produce much good fruit. Some attitudes and actions strengthen mental health; others weaken and undermine it. It should be our business to study them, with the objective of self-improvement in mind.

A healthy mind is the first requisite for a happy and successful life. It should be used for the enjoyment of God's gifts and for the service and inspiration of others. Through the mind, we come to a knowledge of God, to honor and glorify Him. And in the right use of this faculty, we may reasonably look forward to the fullest contemplation of the infinite truth and goodness of the Creator in the realm of eternity.

CHAPTER II

A Cheerful Imagination

I

ONE of the basic conditions for mental health is a mind at peace with itself, in the conviction that life is fundamentally good. Unless one holds this as self-evident and the keystone to all activity, there is no reason for going on. The great virtues of faith, hope, and charity are intended precisely to strengthen the good cheer of the individual and to provide one with substantial motives of optimism for a life of sharing the good things that we possess. Pessimism as a philosophy of life, not only opposes the principle of the goodness of God, but also nullifies any really constructive action for the betterment of oneself or of mankind.

Undoubtedly, apart from temporary fits of discouragement or moments of great pain, most people are convinced of this. The classic example of the conversion of Old Scrooge in Dickens' *Christmas Carol* shows how thin a veneer even habitual gloom and cynicism can be, over the deep spiritual resources within every human heart. Even the philosophers, poets, and musicians of melancholy — from Schopenhauer to Chopin — have left a message of hope, at least in their tributes to art and beauty. Men and women cling instinctively, even desperately, to life — not because they doubt the existence of an immortal soul — but because they feel that this life is good and worth fighting for.

It is not enough, however, simply to accept this principle, in the assumption that it will go to work by itself. An optimistic outlook on life must be sparked by a cheerful imagination. That is to say, one must learn to approach life in a cheerful and friendly disposition. One's normal reactions to situations should be hopeful, and the strategy and technique used in solving problems should be positive. The mind itself must be conditioned to live pleasantly with itself; and the imagination must be disciplined to picture, as a normal and instinctive activity, what is clean, agreeable, and generous. One might, from time to time, examine his dreams and ask whether they are attuned to a happy life, however unreal and fragmentary they may be, or whether they reflect frustration, fear, and constant conflict.

The color of one's imagination, so to speak, may depend upon a number of factors and influences. Some persons are born with what we call a "happy" disposition. Their first tendency is to think well of others and be trustful, perhaps even to a fault. They show a natural friendliness and radiate a cheer that is part of their personality. Others are not so fortunate. Because of intangible elements of heredity, not yet analyzed by science, they may have a natural tendency to look first on the sad side of life and to be possessed of a melancholy disposition. Some children spend most of their infancy in tears and never seem to emerge completely from this condition. The suffering of bitter poverty, of prolonged poor health, or of an unfortunate experience breeding resentment or disillusion, often sets a pattern for the imagination and shapes the judgments or prejudices upon which people govern their lives.

Still others have basically constructive principles, a sound optimism, and a healthy imagination, but lack the ability to integrate their mental activity so as to give a good account of themselves and share the benefits in return. We are all acquainted with people who are fundamentally fine, but through fear, timidity, lack of tact, or perhaps failure to recognize the importance of externals, leave an unfavorable impression on others. Persons of high spiritual aspirations and religious character are just as prone to this failure as anyone else. There is such a thing as maintaining a very narrow view of the love of God, a view which is disturbed by the intrusion of human considerations. It is possible to imagine that one is cultivating all the supernatural virtues, at the very time when one is losing sight of the natural virtues and the demands of human kindness. Some people may be properly referred to as "pious crabs."

The important thing to recognize in this connection is that one can control, discipline, and direct the imagination. This instrument can become the source of inspiration and strength, of broadened intelligence, of creative activity and service. Or it can serve as a dark and mischievous place for the hatching of plots and the preparation of poisonous potions. It can upset people emotionally and cause them to act rashly and foolishly. It can take the sunshine out of their lives. And it can pull the curtain down on their ability, as Dale Carnegie says, "to make friends and influence people." We can make up our minds as to the line of activity our imaginations are going to take, and we can make a determined and successful effort to bring them under control. Whether the imagination serves us or whether we become slaves to an emotional and deranged imagination depends, in large part, upon our own efforts.

2

In some cases, a gloomy or fearful imagination results from an association of ideas which do not necessarily follow in logical order. I recall, as a newspaper boy, making my Saturday morning rounds to collect for the weekly delivery, and every week receiving a wide variety of receptions, depending on who the residents thought was ringing the doorbell. At one home, I saw a slight stir in the curtains and then heard a heavy thud as of someone falling. After a decent pause and two or three more rings on the doorbell, I decided to push the door open. The lady of the house was lying on the floor, half conscious and groaning. When I asked her what was the matter, she asked whether I had brought a telegram. I explained that I was trying to collect for the newspaper, whereupon she made a rapid recovery and settled with the business. It seems that she had mistaken me for the telegram delivery boy and, being mortally afraid of telegrams, promptly swooned. Many people used to have the idea that a telegram brought only news of death or disaster; they have since learned that it can bring good news as well.

The basis of much worry is precisely the activity of an imagination accustomed to painting alarming pictures. As a result, many people are rendered temporarily unfit to form a judgment or to take action. Very often, the line of action followed is poorly conceived and exactly the opposite of what is appropriate and effective. Perhaps it was for these that the saying was invented, "Cheer up, the worst is yet to come." If, for example, the boss sends for one, it must be to issue a reprimand or to deliver one's walking papers. If one's husband fails to telephone exactly on the agreed hour, something terrible must have happened, or he is up to some mischief. If the children fail to come home on time, they must all be drowned in the river. If I am not invited to a certain meeting, there must be a dark conspiracy against me. If I am overlooked or penalized in some way, or if I fail to get exactly what I want, it must be because of a black and calculated insult or a deliberate attempt to hurt me.

For some years, both as a spiritual guide and as an administrator in a university, I have had the opportunity of observing the reactions of various kinds of minds and imaginations in situations which call for some planning and strategy. And I have often wished that particular episodes could be recorded in preliminary form on motion pictures or on television so that people might see themselves in action and have the opportunity of backing out and trying a different method.

Some people react to a problem as they would to a punching bag. It is there to be punched. They have been challenged to a fight. So they come in swinging and shouting. They see red. They intend to win out on the basis of chopping all heads in sight, leveling and scorching the landscape, and emerging with total victory. Of course, there are times when there must be a showdown and when vigorous action must be taken. Perhaps, under certain circumstances, a good fight has certain therapeutic value in bringing all issues out on top of the table, purging the emotions, and clarifying the atmosphere. Sometimes, when people develop temperamental allergies to certain persons or things, a head-on collision may be the only way to effect a settlement or adjustment. There are times, too, when vigorous action must be taken, and one has to "go to bat," so to speak, to get fair treatment and justice for a person or a good cause that otherwise would suffer.

Nevertheless, an inflamed imagination, overwrought emotions, and a belligerent spirit generally succeed in creating antagonism rather than in disposing others to a favorable view and in winning them over to our side. Emotional reactions have a way of communicating themselves to others. Hot words create hot heads. Bad tempers and angry moods have a tendency of arousing others to a similar state, so that in a short time everyone is swinging fists and shouting. Under these circumstances, the man who wins is usually he who manages to keep his temper; and this is not always an easy task.

There is an old saying to the effect that a drop of honey catches more flies than a barrel of vinegar. The meaning, of course, is that we are instinctively drawn to what is pleasant, cheerful, agreeable; we are repelled from the bitter, and no quantity of the latter can make it more attractive. People who are giving orders, as well as those who are looking for favors, will do well to keep this in mind. Persons who are called upon to act as "trouble shooters" or conciliators in any capacity must act upon this principle as basic to their trade and technique, even under the most difficult conditions, if they are to succeed.

The more one examines this principle, the more its validity and strength shines forth. To a certain extent, disagreeable people can command attention above those of good manners and patient consideration. "The wheel that squeaks the loudest gets the grease" is often advanced as a principle to show the value of a nuisance. But a wheel that continues to squeak the loudest or to squeak regularly is likely to be removed as defective and to be replaced by one that can function without annoyance. The same is true in human relations.

Some people tend under the stress of emotions to excel in the arts of invective and sarcasm and in various ways to tell others "where to get off at." This may serve the temporary purpose of relieving one's feelings and of deriving a sense of triumph; but it leaves, not only wounded feelings in others, but regrets in oneself. Many a lifelong friend has been lost in a moment of inconsideration; and many a life enemy has been created over the rapier exchange of wit pointed with poison. Abraham Lincoln offered shrewd counsel for those tempted to vent their bitter emotions because of some wrong, real or imaginary, or in reply to a sharp communication. Sit down and write a strong, sharp, and mean letter, he advised, and then tear it up.

3

Perhaps lurid imaginations and violent emotional reactions may be typed under high blood pressure. There is another type that corresponds more to a low blood pressure condition. This is the gloomy imagination, already described to some extent. This kind concentrates on what is wrong with self, with others, and with the world in general. No matter what the problem may be, the solution is difficult. Any kind of exertion seems fruitless and doomed to failure. As one is never appreciated or thanked, what is the use of trying to please? Whatever way one turns, the outlook is dim. People cannot be trusted. Good times are but a snare and a delusion. As the children say, there is nothing left except "to go out and eat worms."

In some instances, this kind of imagination is morose and introspective. The individual chews away on his grievances like a cow upon a cud, and takes a secret sorry pleasure in the endless process. Some people, with what is called the persecution complex, rather enjoy the feeling of injury. They meditate on the wrongs which they believe others are doing to them or planning to do. This is like scratching a mosquito bite, getting relief at the same time as one makes the bite worse. Some wives think that they are persecuted by their husbands, neglected by their children, despised by their neighbors. Some people are always getting a bad deal from their employers or employees, as the case may be. Discouragement, which follows failure or lack of confidence in self, can plague youth as well as old age and may color with various shades of gray and black every opportunity for enjoyment or advancement. With some people this form of diversion is only fleeting or occasional. They recognize its folly and make the necessary effort to arise from it. With others it becomes chronic and takes the sunshine out of life.

In other cases the symptoms are those of a person looking for attention or sympathy. This follows a perfectly natural pattern. Babies cry for attention. When there is no other way of interesting people in our case we can always appeal to their sense of pity. With many people the handiest implement is poor health, a theme capable of endless variations and one which can easily bend the ear of others eager to get their turn in reciting their own particular aches and pains.

I remember the little drama which occurs every time I meet a certain housekeeper at the home of a friend of mine. After the preliminary exchange of greetings, I always inquire for her health. Her first reply is: "Fine; I never felt better in my life, that is, except for a bump that I got yesterday. Of course, this caused a little flare-up in my rheumatism, from which I have been suffering for years, especially in my back. Every time I get this, it seems to bring back my migraine headaches, which, as you know, are terrible. These seem to affect my whole nervous system, so that sometimes I wonder how I keep going at all. . . ." From this narrative which gathers momentum as it proceeds, there is only one retreat. While she is catching her breath, I always hasten with the observation, "Well I am certainly glad to know that you are looking so fine and feeling as well as you do," and then hurry on.

Despite the comfort that comes from the unfolding of one's physical disabilities and the exchange of symptoms, the person striving for mental health will be on his guard against this habit. With many people, it becomes an obsession. Their conversation, like their medicine cabinets, is filled with remedies, doctors' prescriptions, and home cures. Their interests are centered in personal ailments, diagnosis, prognosis, and all the atmosphere of the operating room, the hospital, and even the morgue.

A little of this goes a long way, particularly with people who are trying to live normal lives and to keep their interest on vital things. Everything has its time and place. Poor health and pain have theirs, as does the important work of medical skill, alleviation, and cure. But there are times when we must learn to laugh at our troubles, conceal our sufferings with a smile, and pass over in silence the pains which we should so much like to share with others.

At the conclusion of an extended illness, some people develop what is called "hospitalitis." This may be described as the sickroom feeling of dependence upon others, a timidity about getting out into the world again, and a desire to remain in the status of a semi-invalid. There is also a mental "hospitalitis," a kind of morose imagination, dwelling on one's ills and crying out for the sympathy of others. We must resist this tendency, when it appears, and make vigorous efforts to bring our minds and imaginations out into the fresh air and back to healthy, vigorous exercise in useful tasks.

People who are advancing in years should also be on their guard against any tendency to feel sorry for themselves because they are growing old and because they cannot indulge in all the activities they once knew. Every stage of life has its own special privileges and drawbacks, its characteristic activities and its limitations. It is just as silly for mature and for elderly people to act like children, as it is for children to despise the joys proper to their years and to sulk because they cannot do the things that are reserved for their elders. To imagine that one has been "put on the shelf" because the procession of younger people passes by, or to brood over the thought that our children no longer love or care for us because they wish to go out by themselves, with their own friends and in their own age group, is to waste energies which might be put to good use.

Persons in the prime of life and beginning to face toward the west, as well as those nearing the twilight, may take comfort and strength from the words of Browning's *Rabbi Ben Ezra*:

> Grow old along with me!
> The best is yet to be,
> The last of life, for which the first was made.
> Our times are in His hand
> Who saith, "A whole I planned,
> Youth shows but half: trust God: see all, nor be afraid!

4

There are a number of fundamental principles in the technique of developing or maintaining a cheerful imagination. Prime among these is the determination to concentrate on the brighter side of life. In other words, the will must be brought into action, so that the individual controls the imagination and is not simply the slave of every passing fancy, or suspicion, or mood that may cross the mind. There must be a deliberate decision to keep away from certain subjects and to turn the imagination into other fields of endeavor. If the thoughts of certain people, situations, experiences, or problems move one to disgust, anger, feelings of depression, or to desperate action, the sensible thing to do is to turn the page, so to speak, and direct one's mental activity into other fields, more pleasant to contemplate and deal with. This is not an escape from reality; it is rather a recognition of the fruitlessness and even danger of playing with dynamite or of wasting one's time in unavailing grief. Better to get over to the sunny side, where one can achieve something useful or at least derive some comfort and inspiration for positive action and service.

If, for example, one is inclined to rehearse mentally the quarrels of the past, or the rebuffs received from others, or to plan strategy for "getting even" with others, the proper action indicated is to shift over into remembrance of pleasant things, of favors received, and of plans to please others. As a general rule, it is far better to concentrate on one's friends and to improve one's friendly relations and activities, than to be concerned with one's enemies and to be worried with thoughts of what they may do next. Life is too short to be fighting windmills.

In times of discouragement, when one is feeling tired and "blue," it is refreshing to be able to turn the mind to sunny days, vacation places, and happy times, or to plan ahead for such. At times, when I am overworked and pressed too hard by business, or by the demands of insistent people, I like to imagine myself on a certain little beach in Florida, listening to the blue and white surf breaking on the sunny sands, or in an enclosed garden, watching the shadows of the palm trees lengthen in the long afternoon. I can draw on the memory of other happy times and the picture of many lovely places as a welcome relief and relaxation when the going becomes rough and I am tempted to become slightly mad. I recall as a student in Europe writing back enthusiastically to my brother about the wonderful places I had seen. His reply was "See and enjoy all the beautiful places you can now, and store them in your memory. You may have occasion to draw from this treasure chest in dark days ahead."

It may have been with just such a need in mind that Browning wrote his song:

> The year's at the spring
> And day's at the morn;
> Morning's at seven;
> The hillside's dew-pearled;
> The lark's on the wing;
> The snail's on the thorn;
> God's in His heaven —
> All's right with the world!

There are times when an effort to direct the imagination into these channels may seem incongruous and even ridiculous. Sometimes the effort is only partially successful or satisfactory. But even then, some good is achieved. Pain is relieved. The mind is cleansed and refreshed and perhaps given new strength and courage to proceed with God's help.

Another exercise which may be recommended, particularly when one is inclined to resentment over a situation or to self-pity for one's lot, is that of rationalization. In effect, this amounts to turning one's attention from the debit to the credit side of the ledger. The unhappiness of a great many people and the reason for their failure in life is due to the fact that they concentrate, not on what they have or what they can do, but rather on what they do not have and on their shortcomings. One must learn to make the best of a bad situation, to discover that things are not as hopeless as they seem. What might be a great disappointment for one person can appear as a prize or privilege to another. Much depends on the point of view. We set our hearts on certain things. We are left with empty hands or forced to take a less desirable substitute. So what? We could fare worse. Many people go through life happy with much less than I have. Perhaps an affliction which has so bowed my spirit may turn out to be for my own good.

In application of this philosophy, Shakespeare put these words into the mouth of the banished Duke, forced to leave his palace by his evil brother and to wander in the woods:

> Sweet are the uses of adversity,
> Which, like the toad, ugly and venomous,
> Wears yet a precious jewel in his head;
> And this our life exempt from public haunt
> Finds tongues in trees, books in the running brooks,
> Sermons in stones and good in everything.
> I would not change it.[1]

Sound advice for those confronted with a bad situation and inclined to blame certain people or to impute evil motives is to suspend judgment until all the facts are in hand and carefully checked. With one thread of evidence, some people can construct a whole suit or dress. The trouble is that it may not fit. A runaway imagination can do much damage. Reputations may be ruined before we know it, and our own eager and evil sleuthing may bring us no end of embarrassment.

Where there is a tendency to chronic suspicion and moroseness, one cannot do better than to seek relief in outside activities. People whose noses are too close to the grindstone, or who seldom leave the house, would do well to circulate more among their friends and make it a point to engage in more social activities. Solitude has its benefits; but it can also lead to strange mental quirks. For some people, to develop a hobby may mean the difference between mental health and sickness. Stamps, embroidery, carpentry, music, books, the theater, photography, charity, or even an awareness of the importance of one's work — any one of these may serve a therapeutic value and at the same time enrich the cultural life and reserves of the resourceful person. A life with interests is usually a happy life and one which serves as a beacon light to others.

---

[1] *As You Like It,* ii, 1.

The cause of a gloomy imagination and low spirits is often to be found in a physical condition. This may result from lack of fresh air, insufficient exercise, indiscrete eating, excessive drinking or smoking, or insufficient sleep. As noted elsewhere, mind and body exercise a mutual influence. One cannot abuse the one without suffering in the other. This is fundamental. For many people, Monday is "blue" because they fail to go to bed on time Sunday night. For others, every day is blue because of the careless abuse of their physical and nervous systems.

If the trouble is more deep-seated, a physician should be consulted. There is no sense in dragging oneself through life, if the proper physical care can correct the condition. There may be need for additional vitamins. The difficulty may be a matter of diet, relative to a high or low blood pressure condition. It may require an operation, or it may respond to vigorous common sense rules about activity. In this connection, a word of caution may be offered against taking dope, particularly of a habit-forming character. Many people develop a dependence upon various forms of barbiturates and other readily obtainable sedatives, not merely to relieve pain and nervous tension, but even to guard against it. The results in many cases are not good. Sedatives and painkillers have their place if used in moderation, under direction, and as necessity indicates. But it may be better, at times, to endure a little pain and to suffer a little stress rather than to become a slave or addict to drugs which can create mental dullness and a feeling of helplessness without them.

To a larger extent than we realize, the maintenance and functioning of a cheerful imagination depends upon the human environment and atmosphere in which we live. Living with people who are constantly complaining, criticizing, worrying, and crying makes it difficult to maintain one's own tranquillity and mental peace. On the other hand, we can create our own atmosphere and shape our own environment by the personality which we reveal to others. Some people seem to go through life, having things easy, with gracious poise and command. The reason is not that they have softer living than others or that luck always breaks their way. Rather, they have learned to smile, to speak kindly, to treat others with courteous interest and consideration. They get what they want because they endeavor to act tactfully and to handle problems on a calm and reasonable basis. Their inner cheer communicates itself to their manner, and this in turn influences and attunes others to a favorable reaction.

There is an old saying "Laugh and the world laughs with you; cry and you cry alone." Like most generalizations, this is subject to some modifications. Nevertheless, it contains much practical truth. A cheerful imagination and a friendly exterior produce a chain reaction in diffusing cheer and promoting a spirit of co-operation among others. A gloomy personality bogs down in its own grief, because others resent its creeping influence upon themselves; and they lose no time in getting out of its radius if they are able to do so. To a large extent, by the application of these principles, we can make the world in which we wish to live.

There is nothing "Pollyannaish" in the development of a cheerful imagination. It may, as we have observed, call for stern discipline and constant vigilance. There are times when it is far easier to sink to the depths. Nor does it involve a blindness to the harsh aspects of existence. On the contrary, it calls for a realistic view of suffering, hardship, sin, and death. But it draws deep spiritual strength from an abiding sense of divine watchfulness and love. In the words of Christ: "Behold the birds of the air, for they neither sow, nor do they reap, nor gather into barns: and your heavenly Father feedeth them. Are not you of much more value than they?"[2] It rests in the confidence and serenity of Christ upon the cross, with the prayer: "Father, into thy hands I commend my spirit."[3]

---

[2] Mt. 6:26.
[3] Lk. 23:46.

CHAPTER III

Learn to Relax

I

THERE is an old Spanish toast used by friends to clink glasses on convivial occasions: *Salud y pesetas y tiempo para gastarlas.* Which, being translated, means "Health and prosperity, and the time to enjoy them." The old Spanish greeting contains a world of common sense.

One of the great problems of the mad world in which we live is precisely to take time out to relax, to think, to enjoy. Modern technical advance has devised a great many timesaving devices — automobiles, refrigerators, washing machines, and gadgets without number — but they all cost money, which takes more time and energy to earn. The forty-hour week is supposed to give people more leisure, more time to rest and enjoy themselves. Sometimes it has the opposite effect.

Nervous disorders and mental cases resulting from the tensions of modern living have multiplied. There has been a notable upsurge of what are generally called "strokes" and "shocks." Heart disease and attacks constitute one of the most serious threats to life, particularly among men in middle years. All of this indicates a general need to slow down in the pace of living. It is possible for the mind as well as the body to push too far and too fast, within a given time span, crippling real efficiency and unduly shortening the span of existence for many people. One of Europe's outstanding dictators during the tragic era leading into World War II adopted as a motto "Better to live a day as a lion than one hundred years as a lamb." The results of his experience would seem to call for a reappraisal of this program.

Men and women of energy and action are always inclined to think that their case is different. They think that they can go on and on without a break — until the break actually comes. The fact of the matter is that all living resources are limited. Even the trees drop their leaves or suspend some of their activities of growth and reproduction, to go into periods of rest. All animals require sleep in one form or the other. Beasts of burden, if pushed beyond their strength, become permanently disabled or die, sometimes in their tracks. Mankind is no exception. If mental, nervous, and physical exhaustion is to be avoided, one must pause for relaxation and allow sufficient time for change of pace, appropriate recreation, and sleep.

There are some people who are willing to take the chance, with the devil-may-care sentiment of the lines:

> I burn my candle at both ends.
> I know it will not last the night
> But Oh, my foes, and Oh, my friends,
> It gives forth such a lovely light.

Others try to postpone the inevitable by drinking black coffee to keep awake or by inhaling benzedrine to sharpen their wits. But these are only temporary expedients, and, when followed too regularly, can develop into dependence upon stronger stimulants and the formation of narcotic habits.

Science has not given us a complete understanding of the connection between mental and nervous tendencies and exhaustion. That there is such a connection, however, and that it ties into the various organisms of the body, no one can doubt. Experiments with animals, involving attention at an object, such as food, or the solution of a problem, such as escape, definitely bring out the symptoms of frustration, exasperation, and complete nervous breakdown. With human beings there is a wide variety of symptoms; but most of us can detect our own without too much difficulty.

With some, the danger signal comes in the evidence of irritability. Problems and situations which normally would be handled with ease and good humor become a source of great annoyance. Every demand upon one's time or attention appears as an imposition; every disturbance is a calamity. We begin to shout and to insult our most inoffensive and loyal associates and helpers. We start arguments or lose control of ourselves during a discussion or difference of opinion. Our facility for sarcasm becomes more pointed; and we imagine that we are surrounded by surly, stupid, slow, impudent, and unco-operative drones.

With others the sign is a tendency to dejection, if in a man, and to ready tears, if in a woman. The world is against us. We are not appreciated. All that we have done for others has gone for nothing. People are conspiring and scheming against us. There is no use trying to go on. Admission of failure, self-pity, and escape seem to be the only things left. Our energies are low, and the outlook is dim.

Particularly in the case of mental fatigue, our judgment becomes impaired. Objects lose their normal importance and relationships. Matters of no consequence suddenly assume great proportions, so as to stagger and alarm us. Matters of conscience which we thought we had settled or which we regarded as of venial character now start to crackle with the odor of fire and brimstone. Details which would regularly be taken care of in routine become major preoccupations. On the other hand, we are too tired or too disinterested to be bothered with things that really count. We are unable to concentrate sufficiently to see the point; and if something dawns on our consciousness, it is simply to go around and around without ever coming into focus and being settled. The tired mind does not necessarily lose its activity; on the contrary, it may increase its dynamism, so as to make sleep fitful and even produce insomnia. But it loses control over itself, much as in night dreams, which may become highly fantastic with little relation to reality.

In some cases the signs are more directly of a nervous character. Little sounds "get on our nerves." The sounds of certain voices become unbearable. Colors, odors, the physical appearance of people, the arrangement of furniture, heat and cold, become a source of nervous suffering. Music must be turned off. Any rattle in the plumbing drives us crazy. The drip of a faucet is enough to keep us awake all night. The honking of horns, the sound of a typewriter, someone laughing and talking next door, become like cannons and the jungle roar. The prattle of children is maddening.

At times the indications break out in physical disturbances. Surgeons, executives, and others called upon for exacting work or decision sometimes develop small cracks in their hands or little sores on their ears, when the tensions begin to mount. I have known people to develop red streaks almost like those caused by poison ivy, on their arms or necks or other parts of the body, as a result of hypertension. Many skin diseases are the result of fatigue and nervous strain. A great amount of stomach trouble and other internal disorders are undoubtedly due to the same causes, and may well serve as a danger signal. The several garden varieties and special forms of headaches, with which most persons are afflicted at one time or the other, are the most familiar barometer of psychic and nervous strain.

These various symptoms, however painful they may be, serve the useful purpose of a warning to stop, look, and listen. Better still, however, is a balanced program of work and rest, activity and relaxation, which will conserve one's energies and avoid these penalties of nervous excess. Why wait until stomach ulcers have made their painful inroads before easing up on mental tensions? Why drive one's mind and nervous system to the edge of a breakdown, with all of the physical distress, from which one may never recover? The time to "ease on the vigil" and to spare the whip is when one is enjoying mental health, not after one has lost it. Day by day consideration and self-discipline are the answer.

2

There are various causes of psychological tensions, some of them rooted in the human constitution or personality itself. Some people are naturally "high strung" and full of nervous energy. They tend to drive themselves and others as by inner impulse. Like children, they seem to be full of tireless motion. They are inclined to walk fast and to bury their heels in the pavement as they move. They work hard; and, if they play, they play hard. These are the people who must be particularly on their guard against excessive expenditure of energy and make a special effort to relax in good time.

Others are naturally phlegmatic. They are in no particular hurry, and not too much distressed if they do not arrive at their destination. Their whole personality is designed along the lines of the flat-bottom boat, safe but slow, and always easy to stop.

Nevertheless, external appearances are often deceiving. Some persons of apparently easygoing disposition may be intensively active internally, the more so for the reason that they do not possess the ready co-ordination or ability for external expression. If such is the case, their relaxation may take the form of activity rather than rest. Still others shift from high to low energies. For a period they are full of energy, enthusiasm, and exaltation; then comes a reaction which causes them to sink to exhaustion and depression of spirit. These people need a steadying influence.

All these types should come to recognize themselves for what they are and make the appropriate adjustments of mental outlook and habits, both mental and physical.

The immediate cause of tensions arises from some situation which puts a strain on the powers of attention or arouses the emotions to a high point of activity. Tension may arise from an unpleasant situation which causes worry, such as passing an examination, paying bills when no money is available, concern over the health or safety of oneself or others, a problem of conscience, the security of one's position, or the activities of one's enemies. It may spring from a sharp word or insult, an argument or quarrel, or the undertaking of a difficult and unpleasant task. It may also be identified with agreeable excitement. The excitement of lovers in each other's company or in pleasurable anticipation, the nervous energy consumed in watching a horse race, the thrill of travel in beautiful or interesting places, the competition of a game of cards, or simply reading a mystery story — all produce special tensions, sometimes, with the "shivers" that run up and down one's spine. Some tensions are the result of a constant stream of work and of demands upon one's time, so that it seems one more visitor, or customer, or telephone call will break the camel's back.

From this analysis, it is obvious that tensions are not necessarily bad or even disagreeable. They serve different functions and purposes. In some cases they are the emotional by-product of a situation which calls for caution and control. In others they serve as an agreeable stimulant. In still others they serve as a signal that it is time to close up shop.

A distinction should be made also between tensions and fatigue. Tensions may bring on fatigue, if they are particularly intense or prolonged; but they can occur when one is rested and at the height of his powers. Fatigue can produce tensions, and even make mountains out of molehills. People snap at one another when fatigued and become extremely bothered over matters to which they would not give a second thought if they were rested. But fatigue in itself is being and feeling tired, and is not a tension as such. It should also be noted that neither tension nor fatigue is bad in itself, either physically or psychologically. On the contrary, both are evidences of the wisdom and adaptability of nature in bringing one's power to a point of focus and intensity, when required, or of indicating that the time has come to "level off" and recuperate one's forces. A tired feeling may be just as healthy and beneficial as a feeling of freshness and an eagerness for excitement.

The problem with which we are confronted in dealing with mental health is that of *controlling* tensions and fatigue, so that they do not distort the mind or produce a debilitation or exhaustion of the nervous system, with the consequent physical disturbances already outlined. Danger lies in excessive tension or excessive fatigue; and, since one is the cause and the other the effect of disturbance, they both respond to the same general observations and treatment. What we are concerned with here is the establishment of practical directives which anyone can apply to avoid danger. The treatment of sickness or pain resulting from mental or nervous exhaustion is another matter, calling for the ministrations of a physician or psychiatrist.

3

The basic rule of control is to learn to relax and to practice the art of relaxation as a matter of principle and regular program.

With some people, the problem is one of mental readjustment. Certain conceptions which are responsible for excessive or needless tension must be replaced with others which open a more objective and tranquil view of life. The idea, for example, that one is indispensable and that the world will fall to pieces unless one is there to do the job and hold it together, plagues many a good man and woman and brings them to an early grave. The fact is that the world is well over a billion years old; mankind has been muddling along for probably a million years and it probably will go on just the same the day after we are dead.

I may be very helpful in a given situation; but someone else might do as well, or even better. It is remarkable how resourceful other people are. Sometimes, they wish that we would step out of the picture so that they might take command.

Everyone would do well, even those of the greatest abilities and most important responsibilities, to keep these correlative thoughts in mind. There is no sense in killing oneself or in bringing oneself to the edge of a breakdown, or even of living in a state of hypertension, because of a false assumption. Moreover, many people would do well to prepare themselves for the time when they can retire from active duty and, in the role of elder statesmen, watch the younger generation come up and assume some of the burdens.

Akin to this mentality is what is sometimes referred to as the "fuss budget" type. This is the person who must always be busy about something. In the gospel story of Christ with the two sisters Mary and Martha, the Master chided Martha for being "busy about many things" and praised Mary who sat with Him as having "chosen the better part." It is perhaps difficult to understand this, particularly as Martha is represented as getting the meal and taking care of the house. Possibly, however, Christ's remarks were intended, not as a rebuke to the fulfillment of daily duty, but rather as a warning against that kind of ceaseless preoccupation with business which allows no time out for thought, social amenities, or even personal rest and relaxation.

Some people never sit down. Nothing is ever finished or ever quite right. Everything in the house may be perfect, except for one grain of dust, which is enough to keep the place in an uproar. There is always something to be taken care of at the office, in the barn, out in the yard, or some place. There is no letup, except in the tranquillity of the grave. And, of course, the dust will again accumulate, the correspondence will continue, new demands will be made and pressure exerted, the scythe will have to be sharpened, the grass will have to be cut.

People with a perpetual motion complex would do themselves and their associates a great favor by tolerating a little dust, so to speak, and by sitting down quietly with themselves and their friends from time to time, while the work piles up and the grass grows. "Remember the lilies of the field."

Another assumption that leads to sleepless nights, frayed nerves, and upset stomachs is the idea that everything must be done at once. As a general rule, it is best to take care of obligations daily. The procrastinator either proves his incapacity for a position of responsibility, or he triples work for himself in the complications that follow upon delay of things that should be done. But the other extreme is to attempt to do everything at once. From a physical standpoint, this is impossible, and the attempt usually ends in confusion, partial completion, and loose ends. Moreover, there is a certain appropriateness of time for doing certain things. There are certain things that call for careful consideration. Hasty action may be harmful. Sometimes calculated delay has the desired effect of bringing others to a keener sense of their obligations. The person who has to do everything right now so as to get it off his mind, usually finds something else coming along immediately to take its place.

An effective way of meeting this problem is to write things down, as a reminder of what is to be done later at an opportune time. Persons whose minds become particularly active after they retire for the night may be advised to keep a memorandum pad and pencil at the side of the bed; and when some item of agenda pops into the agitated mind, the thing to do is to turn on the light and make a note. Eventually all the troublemaking remembrances and brilliant ideas will be fixed where they can be reviewed in the broad daylight; and the tired mind, relieved of this encumbrance, can sink into restful sleep. During the day, likewise, a memorandum pad on one's desk or in one's pocket will serve the same useful purpose of preserving in handy form the things to be done at the proper time. Meanwhile, one can proceed calmly with the business in hand. As an interesting observation, one will find that many of these mental tortures take care of themselves and can be scratched off; others are revealed as impractical or of no importance; and the remainder can receive the attention they deserve.

Another source of tension is the opposite tendency of waiting until the last moment before taking action. Some people alternate between periods of dormition, like bears in winter, and rushed action, like squirrels in a cage. They sleep late, rush through breakfast, catch the train from the rear platform, and arrive at work out of breath. Preparation for almost all events consists of a mad scramble at the last minute.

With others, the difficulty arises from an attempt to do too many things. Nothing gets the attention it deserves; everything is given short, quick attention in the hope that it will turn out for the best. The results may be wondrously, almost miraculously successful; but this is taking too much of a chance and is the pace that kills.

4

It is important in life to plan ahead. There is too much uncertainty in waiting for the last minute, and too many disappointments. The last-minute rush, as well as the constant push, leaves no time for real comprehension or enjoyment. A life spent in rushing is a life without dignity. It will not secure the respect of others, no matter how much merit or credit we think it should command. It leaves too many important things forgotten or overlooked. There is a proper tempo or pace for all things. If everything we do has been crushed, crowded, pushed, and rushed through at breakneck speed, the time has come for a radical reappraisal of what we are doing and how we are doing it. If we are the victims of our own poor planning or of our own nervous energy, we should pause from time to time to ask ourselves some pertinent questions or to take sound advice from others. If we are tyrannized and imposed upon by others, we may have to exert real moral courage to rise above a situation which makes us little more than puppets jumping and dancing on a string.

This involves, not only the question of allowing adequate time for a particular task, assignment, or project, but also the proper disposition of one's time. Busy people are not always those who accomplish the most. Many people complain that they do not have time to do the things they wish. Often, the trouble is not with lack of time, but with a disordered schedule, or no schedule at all, or with a tendency to be thrown off of one's plans and schedules by various distractions. Some people are always doing something; but it never seems to be exactly the thing they would like to do or had in mind; and the sum total never seems to mount up to anything. Fifteen minutes a day, according to Prof. Charles Eliot, will enable anyone of intelligence and persistence to read all the great classics. How many people plan fifteen minutes a day for any project of their own with a cumulative value?

5

Rational planning of one's time must also make provision for divided periods of work, relaxation, and sleep. In a day of twenty-four hours, most people put in a period of eight hours in what may be designated, at least roughly, as work. The average person needs approximately eight hours of sleep. Some need more; others can get along on less. Different age groups have different requirements. But there is no worse delusion than the idea that sleep is a waste of time or that one can pass it up for a good time or for any other consideration. No amount of entertainment, study, or work can compensate the loss of necessary sleep; and no amount of black coffee or other stimulant can take its place. Lowered efficiency in work, lessened resistance to disease, increased tendency to irritability, and other symptoms of impaired vitality as well as of weakened mental health, all follow a regime of insufficient sleep.

With some people, one night off is enough to produce these

disorders; others can skip a full night's sleep from time to time. But no one can ignore the necessity for sleep, over an extended period of time, without paying the penalty. It is said that the great Thomas Edison needed no more than three or four hours of sleep each night; but this can hardly be advanced as a general pattern, and even he made up the difference by taking frequent "cat naps" during the day. This is a luxury which few people can afford. A rested mind is the foundation of mental health. To repeat, there are no short cuts to this. The answer is sufficient, continuous, regular nightly sleep.

Some people have considerable difficulty in going to sleep or in staying asleep. There is no experience more annoying than that of insomnia. A number of causes may be responsible for this; and if the experience is prolonged, one should consult a physician. A few rules, however, may be suggested. At least some exercise in the open air every day is advisable, and if possible one should take a few good deep breaths of fresh air, so as to "oxidize" the system, immediately before retiring. Any kind of strenuous mental exercise, excitement, or concentration should be avoided within at least one-half hour before going to bed. Light reading or conversation or listening to a light radio program may be suggested as a means of lowering pressure upon the brain and preparing it for sleep. With some people, an aspirin helps to relax the system when necessary; but one should beware of falling into the habit of using any drug to produce sleep, except when urgent and under the direction of a physician. Apart from the undesirability of dependence upon drugs as a regular thing, one can expect what is called the "hang-over" or mental depression which so often follows.

Even during the day an occasional amount of relaxation from work is indicated. Better still, a short recess in the morning and again in the afternoon, similar to the program followed by elementary schools, compels one to take time out for a change of subject and pace. A nationally advertised beverage refers to "the pause that refreshes," and undoubtedly there is much merit to this thought even apart from the drink which furnishes the occasion. The English have a delightful custom of serving tea in the afternoon, even in business establishments, which gives the personnel not only tea, but an opportunity to relax. This time off is more than repaid in the increased efficiency and morale of the organization. "All work and no play makes Jack a dull boy," according to the adage. The reason is that Jack becomes tired after a while; and fatigue makes him dull.

As a teacher for some years, with the difficult task of trying to keep students awake in class immediately after lunch, I resorted to the following formula, as suggested by a friend, and found it very successful. The class was asked to close its eyes and to stroke the forehead lightly with the finger tips, moving several times from the center toward the temples, at the same time shutting out all thoughts and letting the mind subside to a point where it was conscious only of the combined distant sounds of the city. At that moment, each student was asked to whisper the following prayer several times:

> I breathe the light and life of God
> Who fills me now with strength and peace,
> Strength and peace . . .

At the end of this, the hands were taken down, the eyes were opened, and the class was asked to remain calm. The effects, in establishing an atmosphere of tranquillity and alertness, were remarkable. This same exercise may be recommended to all, particularly when nerves are jumping and one needs spiritual calm.

6

The assumption, sometimes made, that after deducting eight hours for work and eight hours for sleep, the average person still has eight hours for play, is hardly borne out by the facts. The process of cleaning and dressing oneself, of eating, of transportation to and from work or equivalent preparation, and similar incidentals, are not generally considered as entertainment. Nevertheless, while circumstances differ, much depends on the attitude that one brings to these various functions and the spirit of relaxation with which one engages in them.

The morning shower, for example, can be either a hateful thing or a bracing experience. Breakfast and lunch can merit a literary description, such as one finds in the magazine advertisements of country bacon and eggs, or it can be a hurried and disagreeable gorging of food supplemented with bicarbonate of soda. The trip to work can be an ordeal of nerves, or it can be an opportunity to catch up on one's reading. One's dinner may be a grand occasion when the family assembles to enjoy together the experiences of the day; or it can be an opportunity for everyone to torture the others and break up in stormy silence or in tears. Our going out to a party or to the theater can be an occasion of relaxation and joy, or it can be an impossible chore preceded by complaints and recriminations.

So much depends on whether one is prepared to relax and enjoy, or whether everything is an effort and an afterthought. The lives of two people doing exactly the same thing can be completely different — one full of enjoyment and happiness, the other tied up in muscular and mental knots. I have watched people traveling on luxury cruises, with every convenience and all the time in the world at their disposal. One person is relaxed and having a wonderful time. Another is thoroughly miserable; nothing pleases; and the only thought is of some silly worry, such as whether the kitchen plumbing is working properly back home. I have seen two people doing the same work in the same office. One is joyous and radiates good will. The other despises the whole business, suffers during the working hours, and can hardly wait until the afternoon gong sounds the signal to leave.

I have always preached the doctrine that the greatest joy in life comes from doing one's work well; but, at the same time, I think that all holidays and vacations should be seized upon and enjoyed, particularly with a change of scenery, if possible. Almost any kind of change is a form of relaxation. When someone in the family loses his or her temper or cannot stand things any longer, a good walk around the block works wonders. The housewife who begins to scream at the children or at the dishes in the kitchen sink should go out to the afternoon motion picture or card party. The businessman should go fishing or take a trip or work in his garden on his day off. Husband and wife should go their separate ways, from time to time, so they can appreciate each other more and exchange some fresh, new experiences on the reunion. Those who can take a vacation make a mistake if they do not do so when they have the time, energy, and money — the *salud y pesetas y tiempo para gastarlas*. For what is more relaxing and refreshing than a beautiful memory, the echo of a wonderful experience?

But there are other pleasures, more available and inexpensive, yet equally profitable and enriching. A pipe and a good book, a quiet evening with congenial friends, a Sunday walk in the park or in the woods, a surprise party or anniversary commemoration — all these add to the joy of existence, refresh the weary mind and body, and help to maintain sanity and an even keel. Even the exchange of pleasantries and humor helps to break the tension of a situation and bring out the laughter that helps people to get along in peace and harmony.

Learn to relax. Relaxation lengthens life. Plan to relax, and practice the arts of relaxation. Nothing pays richer dividends in life in enjoyment of what we are doing, in the cultivation of good health — mental and physical — and in the solution of many a difficult problem.

CHAPTER IV

Conquering Fear

I

A VERY extensive literature has developed on the subject of
fear in relation to mental health. There seems to be a common
supposition that fear is to be avoided at all costs, that it arises
from a fabric of ignorance and produces nothing but useless
pain. The healthy mind is represented as the mind which has
liberated itself from fear; and various methods are indicated as
to how this may be achieved.

The question, however, is not quite so simple. Fear is a
natural mental and emotional reaction, and it serves a fundamentally useful purpose. Like pain, it indicates that something
is wrong, and it alerts the individual to take corrective measures,
if possible. The person whose nervous system has deteriorated
to a point where he can no longer suffer, has lost a vitally necessary guardian of health. The child pulls his hand from the fire,
because it hurts; otherwise, the hand might burn off without
notice. In the same way, fear indicates that there is evil or
danger in a certain situation; without this warning, one might
be caught unaware. Fear arouses one to take the necessary
measures of protection or precaution.

For adequate understanding of this problem, we will have to distinguish between fear as a mental apprehension of danger, fear as an instinctive reaction to a situation, and fear as an emotion. Mental fear may be called rational or irrational, depending upon whether there are good reasons for sustaining it or not. Instinctive fear is a kind of nervous reaction, which serves to put animals as well as man on guard. In the case of man, it can pour over from a mental fear. If it arises instinctively in him as an animal reaction, it may work in reverse to affect his thinking processes. Emotional fear extends all the way from a simple tension to panic and paralysis. Because of its physical effects, therefore, emotional fear may serve a useful purpose of alerting the individual or it may produce the harmful effect of both mental and emotional disorder and vulnerability. Hence the importance of controlling fear and, where necessary, of conquering it.

It is sometimes questioned whether mental fear, as a source of concern or action, may be considered worthy of a self-respecting person, or whether every effort should be made to dismiss it as a motive. In other words, should the fear of evil consequences be regarded as an intelligent and honorable stimulus to observance of the law, the performance of duty, or compliance with some directive? Or is it an unworthy consideration? The answer to this is very simply and forcefully given in the words of Sacred Scripture: "The fear of the Lord is the beginning of wisdom. Fools despise wisdom and instruction."[1]

Recognition of divine wrath and punishment as a sanction for divine justice and law would appear to be a rational fear and a worthy motive for observance of the Commandments. The first stimulation of conscience, as the intellectual power of distinguishing between moral good and evil, comes from an inborn understanding of the absolute nature of the moral law. The individual understands that, if he chooses to disobey the

---

[1] Prov. 1:7.

dictates of his conscience, there still remains a reckoning with the Creator who has made the law. It is certainly as rational to be governed in one's practical judgment by this consideration as it is with reference, in the material order, to the consequences of putting one's hand in a fire or in a buzz saw. To conquer one's moral apprehensions by deadening the conscience, through the development of vicious habits or a process of false rationalization, is as irrational as ignoring a physical infection or sickness by cultivating a narcotic habit or taking a sedative. Sooner or later, the penalty must be paid.

The same observations may be made in reference to fear as a motive for observing civil laws and social usages. There is certainly nothing cowardly about paying attention to traffic speed laws or "no parking" signs for automobiles, for the reason that one may be arrested, be forced to pay a fine, and lose one's driving permit. It may be convenient to speed in excess of the legal limits or to park in forbidden zones, at times; but fear of the penalties is an entirely rational motive for not doing so.

Similar considerations help to keep in check many an unruly and violent impulse. Many an unkind word is withheld for fear of losing a friend. Many an insult remains unuttered for fear of losing a customer. Many a brash act is stifled for fear of losing one's position. In this sense, rational fear may be regarded as the friend and counselor of prudence. Many good thoughts and sensible reflections have been generated by a wholesome fear of unpleasant consequences. Even the observance of the rules of health is assisted by the fear that comes from the knowledge of what happens to people who eat and drink intemperately or expose themselves needlessly to drafts and disease or who fail to take precautions in seasonal dress, in exercise, and in rest.

2

It is a mistake, therefore, to eliminate rational fear either from educational and formative processes in the formation of personality or from the motives that guide one's daily judgments. Children should be taught to respect rational fear and to experience practical forms of punishment, administered consistently and considerately, for failure to obey or behave. I have never been a strong advocate of physical punishment for children, in the form of whipping; but I would not deny that in particular instances this might be the only efficacious way of making a child understand what is meant by an order.

The important element in making fear serve a constructive purpose is precisely that it backs up a principle of what is right and wrong and serves to direct one in making a prudent choice, in acting temperately, in avoiding certain pitfalls, and in living wisely. Fear is rational only when it is based on at least an elementary understanding of what is involved. For this reason, the punishment of children, or the threat of punishment, serves no useful purpose, unless the child has been made to understand that there is a good reason for requiring a certain obedience. Civil or institutional authorities soon learn that the imposition of penalties for the violation of various statutes simply has the effect of infuriating the public or of creating rebellious subjects, unless there is a sound reason for the enactment and the penalty is proportioned to the crime of violation. Fear as a motive for discharging any social obligation or for complying with any particular code of amenities falls flat the moment it is revealed that the obligation does not exist or that the code has become defunct. Even the fear of God is no directive norm, unless one admits that there is a God and sees the reasonableness of the moral law, both in general and in specific pertinent detail.

In a word, fear is rational when it is inspired by what is known and understood. Fear is irrational when it has been demonstrated that there is no sound basis for the apprehension of danger or evil. If fear, as a form of mental and emotional agitation, is to be controlled, it must be by pursuit of the truth or acceptance of the consequences. If it is to be conquered, it must be by recognition that the obstacles or the dangers and evils are nonexistent, or that they are of such small significance that they can be overcome by an act of the will.

3

One must not, however, allow fear to become a mainspring or principle motive of action in life. Health is not maintained simply by combating pain and sickness, but by regular nourishment and sane living. Happiness and security are preserved, not by dodging and outwitting dangers or by knight-errant feats of courage, but by positive action, sustained by motives of interest, love, and gain. The normal question to ask is whether a particular object or course of action is good and worthy in itself and whether there is any sound reason for desiring it or pursuing it, even though there is no pressure of fear.

In this connection, a familiar formula for sorrow for sin, or act of contrition, may be adduced as an example of the ascending motives, from fear of punishment, to the recognition of divine justice, and thence to love of God and resolution to positive virtues:

O my God, I am heartily sorry for having offended Thee, and I detest all my sins, because I dread the loss of heaven and the pains of hell, but most of all because they offend Thee, my God, who art all good and deserving of all my love. I firmly resolve, with the help of Thy grace, to confess my sins, to do penance, and to amend my life.

This prayer may be recommended to persons who live in the shadow of fear and indecision, as it opens the whole soul to God in complete reconciliation and in the purging of fear through the crucible of love.

Action which is motivated by fear alone is seldom of permanent value. Such action generally consists of a series of evasions. A person dominated by fear either withdraws into his shell, so to speak, or develops a cunning mentality calculated to outwit, deceive, or dodge a world which is viewed as in one vast conspiracy to hurt him.

In many cases, fear is confused with other reactions of a completely negative character, including laziness. Sometimes the trouble is a matter of distaste for an object, disinclination to undertake a task, a tendency to worry, difficulty in coming to a decision, a matter of chronic suspicion, or simply an affectation of fear. These reactions are allowed to dominate the mind and to offer various excuses to oneself or to others for not doing certain things, for refusing to participate in certain endeavors or to contribute to certain causes, or for hesitating to accept certain invitations or take certain risks. In these cases, the problem is not one of fear but rather of making an effort, of sustaining a little discomfort, of co-operating with others, of broadening one's tastes, of making some sacrifices, and of learning to like and to do things.

4

Special consideration should be given to the difference between physical fear and moral fear. Some people have no hesitancy whatever in engaging in acts or situations that demand considerable physical exertion or risk, but tremble at the thought of undertaking tasks which call for leadership or responsibility. I recall the instance of a structural steelworker, whose work carried him on the slender girders high in the air within the view of the gasping inhabitants of the community. But when he was asked to address a meeting of these same citizens, he almost fainted with fright. The opposite is equally true. Physical cowards often have no hesitancy in facing a situation that calls for great moral courage. I have seen women who are frightened out of their wits at the sight of a mouse bravely face the prospect of raising a family with nothing more than their determination to rely upon.

Very often, the problem of fear, whether physical or moral, arises from a deficiency of experience or from an unfortunate experience which remains to create a pattern of bashfulness, timidity, and reticence. Many life patterns are set by what happens in childhood or by some casual act. Some persons hesitate to express themselves or to give any kind of public performance for fear of being laughed at. It is possible that, as children or adolescents, they were never taken seriously in the family circle but had to endure a regular program of being "kidded" or made the butt of jokes. Perhaps they forgot their lines in a school program or succumbed to stage fright in their first and last appearance at a piano recital. They may have been brought up on a steady administration of the principle that children are made to be seen, not heard. They may have been given a great fright while learning to swim. The recollection of a tyrannical parent or strict schoolmaster, or even of a brush with a clergyman, sometimes carries over into adult life, so as to set patterns, not only of social reactions, but also of deep personal convictions.

Natural timidity, as well as acquired fears, can be remedied, sometimes by the force of personal initiative and persistence, sometimes with the aid and encouragement of others. The methods may have to differ in each case, but the general process consists of a building or rebuilding of self-confidence. Sometimes a sudden shove, so to speak, is sufficient to break the complex and to bring about or to restore a personal feeling of mastery. As a rule, however, more certain results are obtained by the process of gradual progress and recovery.

For some years I taught in a preparatory school, where everyone was required to participate in some form of athletics. There was a rotation of activities, and everyone was required regularly to report at the swimming pool. Many of these boys went through the shower as a matter of routine and then stood shivering on the side of the pool until the period was over, when they returned to the locker room and dressed. These "sideliners" never learned to swim. They were afraid of the water. They saw no point in plunging into it, no fun in swimming, no sense in taking the risk of drowning. From time to time some of their more frisky companions would push them into the pool, which simply increased their distaste and terror as they threshed about trying to catch their breath and get out.

Then, someone in authority decided that everyone should learn to swim. A competent instructor was engaged, and classes were organized to put the process on a scientific basis. For many of these lads it was an agonizing experience to lower themselves into the water. For some, the first dive was like saying farewell to life. Nevertheless, the fact that learning was placed on a systematic basis, that it was made gradual with every reasonable assurance of help and vigilance, with horseplay and practical jokes eliminated, made all the difference. The boys actually learned to swim and to dive. They came to see the value and importance of knowing how to swim, and, having conquered their fear, they came to enjoy swimming as a sport.

Systematic training and practice, encouragement, and patience are undoubtedly the ingredients that make it possible to overcome fear, where fear is the obstacle to achievement. Most people can learn to speak in public without nervousness or embarrassment. It is very probable that, with some coaching and a few trials, the young structural steelworker to whom we referred could deliver a speech as easily as he was able to walk from girder to girder. With the spirit of willingness to try and with supervised instruction, there are few things that the average person cannot learn to do proficiently. One must be willing to take the first step, to co-operate, and not to become discouraged by an apparent failure. One can learn much from the training of animals, which are first coaxed from natural fright and suspicion into confidence and friendliness, and then into readiness to learn.

Fear has a way of building up mental phantoms, hazards, obstacles, difficulties, and reasons which magnify the problem or distort the picture. Even without the help of others, one can do much to overcome these phantoms, to place things in proper balance, and to secure a correct perspective on life and its sundry challenges. The first step consists in quiet reflection on what is involved and in consideration of what others have done and are doing. Each one has his own problem or problems to face. Everyone has a different kind of fear to cope with. Personal recognition of this must come first, before appropriate action can be indicated or taken.

Moreover, it must be recognized that some types of fear or by-products of fear, such as nervousness, cannot and need not be completely overcome for success. I have known distinguished public speakers and concert artists to break out in sweat and to develop other symptoms of nervous fright before mounting the platform or facing their audiences. These are manifestations of constitutional tensions which must be endured. But they are not sufficient to defeat determination or to interfere with trained ability to produce and perform in masterly fashion. Some types of fear should not be overcome, for there is such a thing as overconfidence or a brash disregard for caution and right order, or even for one's actual limitations.

5

The personal treatment of fear, therefore, must be worked out in three stages. The first must be a response to the question: "What am I afraid of?" The second consists of an examination of the question: "Why am I afraid of this?" The question in the third stage is: "What must I do to turn this fear into a practical advantage or, if it serves no good purpose, to get rid of it?" In other words, this involves a practical coping with fear, which may result in taking measures to deal with a situation of real responsibility and danger, in sharpening one's powers to whittle down the challenge, or in dismissing the fear as unfounded in reality.

In some cases there is a real pleasure in fear, for example, in the simulated and comfortable fear of people who read mystery stories, and in the affected fear of persons who like to command sympathy and find a haven in someone's strong protecting arms.

The kinds of fear which upset the mind and disturb mental health may be divided into four general groups — fears about health or physical safety; fears as to social position and reputation; fears for financial or material security; and fears in the moral order, particularly with reference to the future life. Of course, all of these fears may be transferred as apprehensions for the safety or well-being of others.

Fears relative to health or physical safety take various forms with different people. We are referring now, not to a normal solicitude and proper care of the body, which is only reasonable and proper, but to a morose preoccupation or obsession. Some persons are burdened with a concern for disease, and excessive fear of suffering, or a constant apprehension of physical danger. These keep the mind in a state of agitation, which leads to all kinds of eccentricities. Some individuals are so conscious of germs that they will not touch a doorknob except with a handkerchief. Others are constantly taking medicine, pills, and lotions to kill pain or to prevent the possibility of an ache. Some women are so terrified at the thought of the pains of childbirth that they refuse to get married, or, if married, refuse to become mothers. Many men are great cowards at the prospects of any pain. Some people postpone necessary operations indefinitely because they have a mortal terror of hospitals, as the result of the death of certain relations or friends in a hospital. Others refuse to permit any kind of physical examination or checkup, in the fear that something wrong may be discovered. A considerable number of people have such a dread of death in any form that they refuse to attend the funeral services of a friend. They go out of their way to avoid the sight of a funeral procession.

These and related fears affect different people in different ways and in different degrees. To some they represent an obstacle which can be overcome by pressure of the will and perhaps of some friendly persuasion. To others they become a very serious matter, to the point of obsession or phobia. At the root of each fear of this kind, however, there is either an unfortunate experience or an idea which crystallizes into an attitude. Only when the experience has been shown to be an isolated item or the idea is proved to be without validity as a general rule, can the fear be dispelled or brought under control. In some cases, there may have to be a fundamental revision of one's philosophy of life, to include a more ready acceptance of the uncertainties of existence, the inevitability and values of suffering, and the logical place of death in a faith which trusts in almighty God.

Certain fears of a physical character are of a specialized nature, arising from the nervous system rather than from any particular idea or unfortunate experience. Such, for example, is claustrophobia, or the fear of small or narrow places which bothers some people. Most people experience a certain sense of dizziness in high places; for this reason, some refuse to ride in mountainous country or to look out from the roof of a sky-scraper. Some people have a deadly fear of flying; others cannot bear to enter a larger body of water than a bathtub. There is no particular reason to be distressed by these fears. Forcing oneself or being forced into a situation which disturbs the entire nervous system produces no good results. On the other hand, if one must tolerate a situation to which one is allergic, the tension can sometimes be lessened by turning the mind to other thoughts. Otherwise, there is nothing to do but suffer the regular reaction. Some people cannot stand the sight of blood or undergo a vaccination without fainting. Under these circum-stances, the only thing to do is face the inevitable — have a good faint, and get over it.

Many people devote needless fears and fretting in the antici-pation of ills and anguish which never materialize. Nature has a marvelous way of adapting us to changed conditions; and it is wonderful what we can endure when we have to. When I was a boy and even in my twenties, I had the idea that anyone over forty years of age had one foot in the grave. I have subse-quently revised my views. The terror of old age which afflicts some persons is exaggerated and is generally needless. As a result of medical science, improved habits of living, and increased alertness due to education, what used to be called old age has largely disappeared. Every period of life has its own particular joys and advantages as well as its limitations, including so-called "old age," as Cicero pointed out many centuries ago. There is much truth in the adage "You are as old as you feel."

Of course, the wonder of death never ceases; but everyone should become reconciled to the idea. It can come to the young as well as to the old, and in the twinkling of an eye through an accident or an embolism, as well as through a lingering sickness. But there is no reason to fear it, if the state of one's soul is satisfactory.

6

Fears as to one's social position and reputation generally stem from lack of self-confidence. This may result from a physical defect, from unfortunate social experiences, possibly in childhood, or from certain erroneous ideas. No one can afford to ignore all consideration for what others think or to act as though there were no such thing as social responsibility. On the other hand, there is an exaggerated preoccupation with the reactions of others. We all must lead our own lives, and we must take risks no matter what we do. This is particularly true of persons in administrative or executive positions. No matter what we do, someone is not going to like it.

Fears of this category cover a wide range, often resulting in a personality fixation or mannerism. One of the most frequent manifestations is a display of self-consciousness or bashfulness. People with this reaction do not feel at ease in the company of others. They are awkward in their social manners with equals or obsequious in a display of deference, particularly to social or organizational superiors. Internally, they may be ferociously angry with themselves and may deeply resent their reaction or the situation which reveals their weakness or inferiority. Others have a morbid self-consciousness or fear in reference to the opposite sex. This likewise may be the result of a maladjustment between desire and expression.

Some persons are never quite certain whether they are accepted by others. If of sensitive temperament, they are quick to sense slights, insults, and sundry forms of neglect and embarrassment. They fear that they may be disliked by members of their family or by friends; they feel dejected and rejected if others receive more attention or honors or invitations than they do. They may even fear that others are in a conspiracy against them and that their reputations and their future are at stake.

In many cases, the problem revolves around a fear to accept or assume any form of social responsibility. We feel unequal to a task. We fear to make commitments that we should later regret. Perhaps something more attractive might turn up, and we might like to change our minds. One thing often leads to another, and one can never tell what this responsibility might lead to. Lack of self-confidence, which is implicit in all these fears, may arise from several sources; but it must be replaced before the fears can be successfully coped with.

Sometimes, the difficulty arises from faulty training or instruction. Children must be encouraged in a certain amount of self-expression and be permitted to gain a reasonable assurance of their own powers. The old theory of fright, employed by some parents, teaching boys and girls and growing adolescents that everything which parents disapprove of is a sin, must also be subject to critical re-examination. Youth should be encouraged to meet both sexes on a social basis and learn the meaning of normal, friendly, taken-for-granted social companionship. Shy, backward persons must compel themselves to mix in with social groups. If they are uncertain or confused as to proper procedures or if they are disturbed on matters involving sex, they should confer with competent counselors whom they feel they can trust and who will take them seriously. An occasional rebuff should not be a permanent discouragement.

It is true that there is such a thing as assuming responsibility beyond one's capacity; but there is also such a thing as developing a sense of responsibility and of expanding one's powers. One must learn the art of give and take. The pendulum swings both ways, as everyone must learn. Even a physical defect will not stand in one's way to success, if one has something to offer and does the best he can. One of the most successful lecturers I have known was a man with badly crossed eyes. He was determined not to let this stand in the way of his ambition. After the first minute on the platform, the audience promptly forgot about his eyes and concentrated on his readings or his message.

7

Fears for one's financial or material security, like many other fears, are sometimes well founded. Obsession on the subject, however, can drive a person away from a happy life, into a narrow groove where making and saving money becomes his only object. No matter how much one possesses, the fear of insecurity may loom up like a vast and terrifying specter. Some people have what is called the "poor mouth," that is, they are always complaining about being poor. No matter how much or how little they possess, the present appears to be very lean and the future outlook, very discouraging.

To carry this burden of fear through life is indeed a great mistake. Better far to enjoy what one has, with reasonable frugality, living within one's means, and to let the future take care of itself. It is remarkable how few people, at least in this Western hemisphere, die of starvation or are lowered into a pauper's grave. Most of us manage to save something. We have friends, families, pensions, and our own resources to count on; and, if worse comes to worse, we can always look for help from the many public agencies. No matter how dark we wish to paint the picture, there is always a ray of hope, a way to solve our problem with decency. Rich men, suddenly confronted with a financial loss of millions, have committed suicide. Poor folk, with little more than one room and a geranium plant, have known how to love life, to raise families, and to survive, these countless generations.

Contentment with one's blessings and an abiding trust in the Providence of God are the richest of all treasures. In the words of Christ, "Consider the lilies of the field, how they grow: they labor not, neither do they spin. But I say to you that not even Solomon in all his glory was arrayed as one of these. . . . Be not solicitous, therefore, saying, What shall we eat: or, What shall we drink: or, Wherewith shall we be clothed? . . . Seek ye, therefore, first the kingdom of God and his justice: and all these things shall be added unto you. Be not, therefore, solicitous for tomorrow; for the morrow will be solicitous for itself."[2]

8

Fears in the moral order are generally concerned with matters of conscience. As we have already observed, these fears are not to be summarily dismissed, any more than other fears. Rather, they should be carefully analyzed, with the view of reaching a satisfactory conclusion. The mental disturbance that comes from a sense of sin, from the consciousness of an obligation unfulfilled, from an injustice that needs to be righted, cannot be laughed out of existence, drowned in dissipation, or simply forgotten. The sensible way to eliminate such agitation — which is in reality the voice of God calling for retribution — is through an honest confession of guilt before God, with an act of sorrow and a determination to comply with one's duties. If a debt is owed, pay it. If a lie has been told, correct it with the truth. If a harm has been done, make amends. If decency has been violated, purify the situation. There is no other way: and there is no point in delay.

---

[2] Mt. 6:28–34.

In some tender souls, fear may arise from brooding on what is past or from confusion of moral values. There is also a morbid fear of hell or divine wrath in one form or the other, which leads to no good. True religion should be a source of comfort and strength to the sincere person. When the mind becomes upset with "scruples" and worries about matters in the order of conscience, without coming to a satisfactory solution, the best thing to do is to consult a competent guide or confessor and then humbly abide by his directives. Fear and pride travel hand in hand, more often than is apparent. The person of humility will never hesitate to seek and follow good advice, and learn to restore his or her peace of soul through the love of God.

In this connection, an important distinction must be drawn between religious guidance and dependence upon superstition. It is an amazing fact that many persons who are inclined to look with contempt upon religious practices allow themselves to be guided and frightened by various cabals, numbers, practices, fortunetelling, dream books, and the like, which have absolutely no connection with science, religion, or common sense in any form. I must admit that I know little about the validity of astrology as a science; but it is a cause for wonderment to observe the number of people who guide their daily lives on the indications of astrology magazines and related forecasters of future events.

Mental health cannot thrive in an atmosphere of constant wonderment about the future, as though one had to tread lightly to avoid waking evil forces. Even making allowance for a measure of truth in the "science of the stars," it is evident that one cannot achieve freedom from fear or triumph over the forces of opposition in life simply by mechanical devices. Hitler had his astrologers, and others before him; but history tells a sad story of their miscalculations.

The secret of conquering fear is to look within ourselves, in the words of Cassius to Brutus:

> Men at some time are masters of their fates:
> The fault, dear Brutus, is not in our stars,
> But in ourselves . . .[3]

Fear is conquered, not by escape, but by crystal-clear honesty with ourselves, a willingness to be ourselves, the courage and faith to accept our responsibilities and to leave the rest to God.

---

[3] William Shakespeare, *Julius Caesar*, i, 3.

CHAPTER V

Accent the Positive

I

ONE of the first principles in the development of mental health is to accent the positive. The mind should be regularly directed toward what is constructive. According to an old Chinese proverb, "It is better to light a candle than to curse the darkness." An understanding of this principle, together with its regular practice, in outlook and in action, means the difference between success and failure in life.

For a number of years I have conducted travel groups to Latin America, to Europe, and around the world. When the group has been assembled, immediately prior to departure, it has been my practice to brief the members of the party on what to expect and in general how to conduct themselves. My first point is to emphasize the importance of the positive outlook, in terms which may be summarized as follows:

"Why are you taking this trip? It may be for pleasure, recreation, education, or companionship. Keep your eye on these objectives. Do not allow petty annoyances to spoil your trip. Perhaps you will be given a room, somewhere along the line, with only one window, while your neighbor has two windows. Such things are incidental and unavoidable. Do not allow these details to interfere with your enjoyment. If you really have cause to complain about a condition which should be corrected, let me know about it; but do not allow yourself to pout or to become melancholy.

"It is inevitable that, in the course of time, people traveling together will 'get on each others' nerves.' Be on your guard against this and make up your mind that nervous tensions will not change your outlook or tempt you to make sharp or sarcastic remarks that you will later regret. Take a walk around the block, or give yourself a little change of scenery or companionship. Remember that you also annoy others, perhaps even more than you realize. Keep alert for the *important* things. I want you to return home better and happier than when you started out. You will do this, if you *accent the positive*."

I have seen people on delightful, interesting vacations, losing the full benefit of their opportunity simply because they allowed themselves to become peevish about things of small consequence. Under a tropical moon, with palm trees swaying, and the music of an orchestra against the gentle swish of the southern sea, husband and wife may engage in a continual round of nagging because one or the other has been late for dinner, or has slept over two minutes, or smiled sweetly at someone else. The beauty of many a mountain view, the joy of many an artistic masterpiece, the pleasure and inspiration of many an unforgettable moment has been lost forever, because someone preferred to concentrate on an imaginary slight, a small hurt, a grudge, or an irritated feeling of righteous indignation.

My own experiences have convinced me that, with determination and practice, everyone can achieve a "positive" mentality and improve upon it. The results in joyous living, straight thinking, and conservation of energy are tremendous.

Some people are born with a native ability to look straight

to essentials and to group facts and situations so that the items of different importance fall into their relative positions. These people manage to get things done with a minimum of noise and fuss. They take life pleasantly and cheerfully and somehow manage to retain a youthful outlook and to remain young. As a rule, they are socially successful and sought after, even though circumstances may not permit them the time or even the inclination for social activities. Their advice is solicited as sound and constructive, precisely because it is positive, stripped of the nonessentials and negative considerations that serve to confuse issues and to distress and irritate most people.

Too many of us, however, waste our time and the patience of others, in shadowboxing with real or imaginary troubles, arriving at no positive decision. It is possible to spend one's entire life in a disagreeable atmosphere of conflict, with nothing to show in the end except a sense of futility. Carping, criticizing, and "letting off steam" may, of course, bring some emotional relief and produce the illusion that an important matter has been disposed of. Some persons feel better after a session of this kind. But, generally speaking, those who face life with these methods lack a real desire or the courage to solve their problems. Their only desire may be to feel sorry for themselves, or to engage the attention and promote the agitation or misery of others. While there are different schools of thought on this matter, it is my conviction that, as a general rule, "letting off steam" is a poor way of gaining emotional relief or of asserting one's importance. It usually succeeds only in arousing the pity, contempt, or enmity of others who may have to put up with it.

2

This negative reaction toward life and its problems takes various forms. But none is more frequent or more easily recognized than the tendency to grumble and complain. It may be about the other members of one's family, or it may involve the disagreeable qualities of the neighbors. It may extend to a chronic dissatisfaction with one's school, church, or club. It battens on the bad service received from housekeepers, waiters, janitors, clerks, banks, and stores. It may be the weather, which is always too hot, too cold, too dry, or too wet. It may be one's migraine, sinus, or rheumatism. It may be the world in general; but whatever it is, it is always about something *wrong*. As the old man said in the play *Juno and the Paycock* — "The world is in a state of chassis!"

This mental slant on life often sets the tone of comment in stores, offices, and factories, as well as in what are sometimes referred to as back-fence conferences. The boss complains about his helpers — it is impossible to secure honest and reliable workers. The latter complain about the boss — he is an impossible slave driver, always in a bad humor. It may shift to a critical attitude toward the manners or mannerisms, the stupidity, the bad conduct, scandals, the neckties, the clothes, or simply the existence of one's fellow workers and associates. From this social atmosphere come the frequently heard expressions — "Who does she think she is?" "Just wait until I give her a piece of my mind!" "Did I tell him where to get off at!" And "You can't do this to me!"

Retreat from this position and the formation or strengthening of a positive outlook on life and its problems are not always easy. Complaint is a rather natural and easy form of expression. To criticize and point out what is wrong with people and things is far easier than to suggest means of correction. The development of a positive outlook requires an alert mentality and an expanding range of interests. There is always material at hand for grumbling. Readiness to take a negative outlook may be the reflection of inner, personal conflicts, which have little or nothing to do with the matters of open complaint. Sometimes the tendency has a physical background which inclines one to become morose or excitable. In other cases, it seems easier to go along with the current of common misery and antagonisms than to strike out boldly to find out what is *right* with the world.

The first step in the right direction is self-examination. A number of questions may be asked, and each one should be given an honest answer. The first question is: "What am I criticizing or grumbling and complaining about?" Strange as it seems, the answer may often be "nothing." Children whine when they are tired or looking for attention, with no definite object in mind. Many adults act in the same way, and for the same reasons. The chronic grumbler grumbles as a matter of inclination or habit, without having anything to grumble about. If pressed for an explanation of his attitude, he can find something. Perhaps it is the food he has to eat, or national politics, or modern youth, or the way the grass is cut — anything will do to grumble about. If one can recognize the fact that there is really nothing substantial or tangible to justify his grumbling, perhaps he can examine the reason for his ticking away in this fashion and take measures to correct it.

In some cases, it will be found that there is a real object of complaint, but that it is none of our concern. Many persons busy themselves with problems and situations which, properly speaking, do not pertain to them at all. Whether my neighbor takes one drink too many or owns a Cadillac when all he can afford is a Chevrolet may be of great concern to his wife; but there is no good reason why I should be agitated by it. The fact that some people waste their lives, beat their children, wear outlandish clothes, or come late to work, may be of vital concern to someone. But if it is none of my business, why should I become disturbed or indignant about it or complain to the world at large? To the extent that such matters occupy my attention, they may be crowding out positive considerations and responsibilities to which I should be giving some analytical thought and constructive action.

The second question to ask oneself is: "Why am I grumbling or complaining or criticizing?" If it is just to make conversation, then I should make a strenuous effort to get out into the sunshine and find more agreeable topics for discussion. If it is to relieve my feelings, I should make sure that the person to whom I am unburdening myself will lend a sympathetic ear and not serve as a sounding box which may later do me harm. Even with persons sympathetic to me and my gloomy stories, there is a limit of endurance. A constant program of this kind is enough to try the patience of a holy Job. Am I criticizing maliciously, to cause mischief and harm to others, for revenge or a similar motive? If so, I may have to make some radical changes in my ethical standards and practices. To this end, it may be helpful to know that nothing makes one so socially dreaded as the reputation of an evil or dangerous tongue. Can I honestly say that my purpose in formulating complaint is to seek advice; or in offering criticism, to suggest improvement? If so, then I should be prepared to carry through with the necessary action and adjustments or to co-operate with others to this extent.

The trouble with many people is that they lack the courage or tact to bring their complaint to the person or the department that can really do something about it. If the goods they have purchased prove to be shoddy, they complain to the neighborhood instead of taking them back to the merchant from whom they bought them. If their working conditions or salaries are not up to their expectations, they grumble to everyone except to headquarters. If they think they have been given a bad deal by a friend, they air their grievances to everyone except to that friend, who should at least be given an opportunity to explain. If they are dissatisfied with a service, they are vocal in their soreness to everyone except the responsible party.

Most of us have had the experience of dining with people who are difficult to please. The soup is too hot or too cold; the meat is too rare or overdone. I recall such an experience in a restaurant with a person who was satisfied with nothing. "Why don't you speak to the waiter when he returns?" said I. "I am sure that he will have things done to your taste."

"Shh," replied my friend, lowering his voice to a whisper. "I wouldn't want to cause trouble. Here he comes now." As soon as the waiter had departed, the barrage of complaint started up again.

We are all guilty at times of this kind of performance and, in the process, waste much time and energy. If we really feel that a condition is unsatisfactory and should be remedied, we ought to speak up to the right persons or hold our peace. Getting satisfactory results is comparatively easy, as a rule, if we use a tactful approach. Most human beings have natural limitations and eccentricities; but if given a friendly opportunity, they are glad to co-operate with us. If we have a complaint to make, it is always advisable to begin with a comment on something good rather than to launch on a complete denunciation; and others will understand.

There are some unpleasant conditions which cannot be remedied. As Mark Twain once remarked, "Everyone talks about the weather, but no one does anything about it." We have to learn to adjust and adapt ourselves in a cheerful spirit, instead of shedding tears and fraying others' nerves.

3

Everyone with any sense of responsibility is naturally concerned with difficult situations which must be faced and solved. It is only natural and right that one should be preoccupied with such matters as involve one's personal interests, or those of one's family, one's business, one's friends, or the community in which one lives. We are all interested also with much larger issues, such as the solvency and safety of our nation and the peace of the world. Some of these concerns are susceptible of an immediate solution. Others call for continued thought, and perhaps will never be permanently solved. Eternal vigilance, as the old saying goes, is the price of freedom.

It is important, however, not to confuse worry with a genuine sense of responsibility, vigilance, or endeavor to solve a problem. Worry is an emotional and mental disturbance, arising from a combination of indecision and fear.

I have a problem to solve or a situation to face. It involves unpleasant and even dangerous possibilities or prospects. Somehow I cannot find the solution for my problem. I cannot come to a decision on the matter. I cannot reconcile myself with what may be inevitable. And I am afraid. Perhaps my fear is precisely in facing the problem, from which I should like to flee. Or it may arise from the contemplation of a scene, real or imaginary, over which I have no final control. So I worry, and my mind goes around and around like a squirrel in a cage looking in vain for some kind of escape. Meanwhile, my emotions become agitated. My nerves are affected. And if this situation is sufficiently severe or prolonged, my physical and mental health may become impaired.

Worry of this nature may concern itself with problems that range from the insignificant and even silly to the vitally important. It may lead to suicide or insanity, or it may simply have the effect of interfering with one's sleep, or of leading to eccentric activity, sapping vital energy that could be better employed on useful purposes, and creating an atmosphere of tension and gloom for all within its radius.

Many wealthy men, during the financial depression of 1929 and the 1930's, met the shock of a deflated stock market by jumping out of windows. Persons who suffer the pains of unrequited love, or face a future of impaired health or great physical pain may worry themselves into taking desperate, lethal measures. Men and women who are saddled with responsibilities greater than they are equipped to carry are likely to develop symptoms ranging all the way from peevishness to a nervous breakdown, as a result of worry over the problems confronting them.

The cure for worry differs with the cause and the nature of the problem, as well as with the temperament of the individual. In general, the best advice that can be given to people who worry is to seek and to take counsel and advice from a competent friend or guide. Since one of the elements of worry is indecision, it is helpful to secure the opinion of another who is capable of evaluating the issues involved in the problem and of assisting in coming to a solution or decision. Where the element of fear is involved, the sharing of one's apprehensions undoubtedly increases one's courage and, in some cases, may serve to reveal the fear as groundless.

The only end for a train of worry is a solution or decision. Nevertheless, it is a curious fact that persons who are given to worry and who find it difficult to arrive at any conclusion by themselves are often extremely proud, sensitive, and stubborn in seeking or accepting advice and direction from others. There are some people who go to a physician and then pay no attention to his diagnosis or prescription. There are others in mental distress who apply for aid, only to reject it. Sometimes the difficulty arises from a lack of complete honesty and frankness in explaining the problem. In some cases, one knows in advance that the solution offered will be incorrect or only partial. In other cases, the individual knows that the counsel is right, but he or she lacks the courage to face the truth and the consequences. There is also the type of person who enjoys the morose pleasure of mental doubt and distress. Persons of this kind are comparable to those who are out of a job and are in distress but really not eager to go to work, or are like others with pains and aches who would feel just lost without them for lack of a subject of conversation and complaint.

The person who really wishes to get out of the habit of worrying, or to be delivered from a particular worry, must make up his mind to examine the facts so far as they are available, with or without counsel, then to come to a decision and to stick to it. This calls for determination — an act of the will — as well as conviction, and willingness to risk being wrong. This is not always easy; but it is the only way.

Take, for example, the case of a man who goes to bed, and then wonders whether he locked the door. There is only one way to find out. He arises, tries the door, and finds it locked.

He returns to bed and is about to fall to sleep, when the thought occurs to him that, in testing the door, he may have unlocked it. There is only one way to dispel the doubt. He gets up and tries the door again. This time again he finds the door locked; he flips the lock to make sure that it checks and returns to bed. It is only a matter of minutes before the awful doubt arises in his mind that, perhaps, in rechecking the lock he may have opened it.

There are two ways of facing this problem. One is to continue getting in and out of bed to test the door — just to make sure. The other is to examine the facts, give oneself the benefit of the doubt, come to a decision, stay in bed, and go to sleep.

A similar situation arises in the case of the mother whose daughter has gone out with a young man of recent acquaintance and has failed to return precisely on the agreed hour. Maternal concern turns to anger, and then to apprehension, as the imagination begins to take command of the anxious mother. The lonely road, the woods, the struggle . . . all these flash through the mind in gruesome detail. What to do? Of course, the mother may argue with herself that the girl is sensible and resourceful, that there is no good reason to suspect the young man has foul designs upon her, and that there may be perfectly legitimate reasons for this delay. Possibly the car broke down. Perhaps the party was so enjoyable that they decided to remain a little longer. The latter line of reasoning would normally seem to be sensible. It would help to maintain peace of mind and secure a friendly greeting and understanding spirit for the girl when she finally returns. She should be given the opportunity at least to tell her side of the story. The worrying habit, in a situation of this kind, changes nothing, and produces nothing except frayed nerves, family arguments, and disgust. An enjoyable evening is ruined with endless explanations that satisfy no one, and everyone goes to bed in tears.

In many instances, the habit of worry stems from a faulty

philosophy of life and from a lack of confidence in permanent values. One can understand the panic of the men who took their own lives during the financial crash. Undoubtedly, many of them became temporarily insane because of the impact of emotions as they viewed the melting away of their life's savings, the humiliation to themselves and their families, possible loss of social position, and the agony of having to start all over again. One can understand the mentality even of the Nazis who committed suicide at the end of World War II rather than risk capture, trial, imprisonment, and execution, with the attendant shame. But in practically all such cases there is at least a temporary suspension of faith in God and in Divine Providence. Men lose confidence, not only in themselves, but also in their families and good friends, who certainly would stand by them in their hour of need. The hunted man, or the man who thinks he is being hunted, may feel that he can block or defeat or retreat from justice by the negation of his life. And self-pity — the most dangerous and deceptive of all the emotions — may be all that is needed to complete his ruination.

So long as a person keeps his grasp on the positive elements of life — faith in God and in himself, confidence and trust in at least some friend, and an assurance that somehow justice will prevail and a solution will be discovered — mental health and peace can be preserved, and reasonable hope can be held out even in the most gloomy and confused of dilemmas.

To repeat, the only way to get rid of worry is to examine the positive factors involved in the problem, then come to a decision and hold firm. The element of worry consists in going over the same old ground. Of course, if something new of an important substantial nature appears to reopen the subject and possibly to alter one's judgment, it should be considered. Otherwise, the matter should be closed, and one should proceed on the reasonable assumption that worry will add nothing helpful to the course of action determined upon.

4

Ability to make a positive decision and to stand by it, even in the face of opposition, is absolutely essential for anyone who aspires to an executive or administrative position or to carry responsibility of any weight. When one steps into a family, an office, or an organization of any kind and finds the members at sixes-and-sevens, constantly quarreling, scheming, and conniving, he may well surmise that the authority is weak, unable to face issues on a positive basis, and to make decisions which will be respected and enforced. Worriers and those who are inclined to be disturbed change their minds with the least criticism and do not make good leaders; and the probability of their holding a position of responsibility is slight.

These considerations are equally important in the spiritual and moral problems of the individual. Peace of soul, which is the greatest of all gifts, even above physical health, cannot exist where there is a constant sense of guilt or a profound uncertainty as to one's moral responsibility in a matter of importance, whether this importance is real or imaginary.

Many people carry the consciousness of guilt, like a hidden wound, with them through life to their deathbed. Sometimes the problem is a silly incident of no consequence which happened in childhood; sometimes it arises from a situation of great importance. There are definite areas of stress over which the individual can exercise control, sometimes alone and sometimes with counsel. Some attempt to rationalize a course of conduct which they know to be wrong, with various falsely comforting arguments as convenience may supply. Others struggle, or flounder, with moral problems of a personal nature, because of a delicate conscience or lack of courage to discuss the matter with a competent guide, or inability to come to a decision.

In all cases, it is folly to carry this kind of mental baggage around, with the accompanying worry and hurt. The remedies are honesty with oneself, frankness and the desire of reconcilia-

tion with God, and humble readiness to take the advice and
follow the orders of a good spiritual guide. Competent counselors
have long realized the therapeutic value of the Catholic con-
fessional, even apart from its sacramental character. "Honest
confession is good for the soul" is an adage that carries meaning
for persons of all faiths. To be of value, of course, any type of
confession must be regarded in a positive spirit, with conditions
in which dignity and confidence are respected and sound advice
can be expected.

During recent years, advanced studies have been made in
psychology and psychiatry, to probe the hidden causes of mental
and emotional distress and to apply a remedy. Various theories
have been developed both as to diagnosis and cure. It is obvious
that in so delicate and complex a field the greatest caution must
be exercised, and only competent and approved experts should
be allowed to function.

5

In the development of a positive outlook on life and a positive approach to its problems, whether of a personal nature or
in the world around us, it is important to recognize the close
connection between our physical condition and our mental
powers. Very often, a disposition to complain or criticize or
worry, rather than to take a bright and constructive view, is the
result of a physical ailment or of a run-down condition. Intemperance in drinking or smoking, insufficient sleep, irregular habits
in eating, lack of exercise, failure to observe sensible routine in
one's daily program — all of these can enter as factors into a
picture of frayed nerves, foggy thinking, and a retreat from
reality. Dependence on drugs as the first aid for sleeplessness,
pain, indigestion, or "jitters," is unfortunately the pattern in
too many lives. One cannot neglect or abuse the physical system
without at the same time doing injury to the mind which it
houses.

Mental health and physical health are closely connected. Just as worry is capable of producing stomach ulcers, so an upset stomach may result in a dim and bleary outlook on life. It is a fact that some persons go along from day to day, complaining, criticizing, and fretting, without the least apparent effect upon their health. Nevertheless, the general rule is sufficiently operative to make it worth while to practice self-discipline of mind and body to make them better working partners.

Some of the grandest and most serene characters have lived in pain or have suffered from physical handicaps that are discouraging even to contemplate. Sufficient to recall the inspirational life of Helen Keller, born deaf and blind. All of us are acquainted with some brave man or woman who has been crippled by an accident, or is stretched out in permanent pain, yet spreading cheer and making a living in some useful occupation.

The dividends from any effort to face forward, to look upward, to see life positively, are so rich that one cannot afford to lose them. The world is full of people who are *against* something, people standing on the side lines of life while the procession passes by. It is easy to find those who can tell us what is wrong with us and with the world in general. What we need are more people who can tell us what is *right* and what to do to make things better. It is the people who stand *for* something, who know what they want, and who go after it that shape the world. This is the secret of advancement in knowledge, of enjoyment and of the art of sharing, of contentment and appreciation with the least of gifts, and of considerate restraint under all circumstances.

In the words of the poet:

> Hast thou named all the birds without a gun?
> Loved the wood-rose, and left it on its stalk?
> At rich men's tables eaten bread and pulse?
> Unarmed, faced danger with a heart of trust?

And loved so well a high behavior,
In man or maid, that thou from speech refrained,
Nobility more nobly to repay?
O be my friend and teach me to be thine![1]

A rule of life for everyone should be: "Sublimate the negative; accent the positive."

---

[1] Ralph Waldo Emerson, *Forbearance.*

CHAPTER VI

Dynamic Appreciation

1

IT IS important to stress the fact that mental health is not merely
a passive state of mind. Like physical health, it requires activity
and exercise. For this reason, passive contemplation of what is
good is not sufficient. A *dynamic* appreciation is necessary, an
active, vocal, and fruitful recognition of what philosophers call
the true, the good, and the beautiful, if the mind is to maintain
its health and discharge the mission implanted in it by the
Creator. The health and the strength of the mind may be
gauged by its powers of recognition; and in exercising these
powers, it is only natural to expect external evidences of
appreciation.

There is nothing which gives such satisfaction and brings
such rich rewards as the expression of thanks. Whether it be
the spoken word, a note of appreciation, or a token or gift
following a visit or a favor, the friendly recognition of a benefit
received not only discharges a debt, but opens the way to
renewed and enlarged reasons for gratitude. The success of
many people in authority can be traced directly to their thought-

fulness in giving a friendly pat on the back, a word of commendation, or some tangible evidence that they are not only open to support and co-operation, but aware of it when it comes. There is not too much that children can do to repay parents for the years of struggle and often pain that they go through to provide food, clothing, education, and opportunities for their youngsters; but even the little remembrance of birthdays, anniversaries, and other occasions, with a greeting card, an affectionate letter, or a gift is a reward richer than gold. Friends may say to one another, "Please do not bother to acknowledge," and lovers may wave aside the formalities of gratitude for favors that come from the heart. All the same, it is the expressed recognition or acknowledgment that keeps alive the bonds of affection and renews the confidence upon which true love is nourished. One cannot say "thanks" too often.

Most people are long on expectancy of favors, but short on gratitude. This corresponds to the trend of instinct rather than intelligence. The activity of animals works toward the fulfillment of an appetite or need; and in the training of animals, a bait of reward is held out for the performance of a certain routine. But once that need has been satisfied or the reward has been given, the animal's interest in the subject drops. One of the primary problems in the education of children, and one which by no means ends for the individual at any stage of his existence, is precisely the recognition of a benefit as such and the expression of thanks.

Among the many apt and eloquent lines of the immortal Shakespeare, none are more pointed than his reference to ingratitude:

> Blow, blow, thou winter wind
> Thou art not so unkind
> As man's ingratitude;
> Thy tooth is not so keen
> Because thou art not seen,
> Although thy breath be rude.

Freeze, freeze, thou bitter sky,
That dost not bite so nigh
As benefits forgot:
Though thou the waters warp,
Thy sting is not so sharp
As friend remember'd not.[1]

From the standpoint of mental health, the pangs of resentment for ingratitude can be severe and work considerable harm. The resentment of parents for what they regard as lack of understanding and ingratitude in their children may become a preoccupation and has been known to hasten death through grief. Friendships are often broken off because of the failure of acknowledgment or reciprocity in gifts and favors; and some of the most bitter enmities arise from the fact that someone has taken unfair advantage of a friend. Many lives are blighted to a greater or less degree, because people carry with them the feeling that they are not appreciated, that their efforts and their contributions have been wasted on selfish or stupid people, and that the recognition to which they are entitled has been withheld.

2

Fundamentally, appreciation means the ability to form a conception of values, qualities, relationships, and even possibilities. In the world of human relations it means the recognition of effort, expenses, consideration, and contributions on the part of others. It means an evaluation of one's own abilities and shortcomings, of the opportunities before one, and of one's responsibilities and obligations before God and men. In the world of things, it means the perception and distinction of good and evil, of beauty and ugliness, of what is appropriate and what is improper, of what is substantial and sincere and of what is sham and fakery, of what is cause and what is effect, of what is important and what is incidental, of what is quality and what

---

[1] *As You Like It*, ii, 3.

is inferiority. One of the basic purposes of all true education is not merely to convey information, but to develop this sense of appreciation and to put it to work.

In the processes of cultural development, the sharpening of one's perceptions and powers of appreciation is essential. The joy and richness of life that come from the appreciation of art, music, literature, the theater, and beauty in its many forms depend upon the growth and application of one's native powers. The difference between slovenly, mediocre, and gracious living is not merely a matter of finances; rather it is found in an alert imagination and a judgment which is educated to tell the difference. The degrees of success which a person achieves in life itself, or in the various endeavors and tasks to which he puts himself, is due in large part to the processes of appreciation from interest to analysis, discovery, invention, production, and service. This is the meaning of dynamic appreciation, as distinguished from simple acceptance of benefits without positive reaction or evidence of evaluation.

The place to start in the exercise of dynamic appreciation is in one's own setting — home, work, and community, however humble it may be; and the time to start is at once, whether one be young, middle aged, or old. The principal reason for frustration in life, which is a sense of failure and perhaps the worst of mental troubles, is that kind of mental escape or romantic dreaming which sees opportunity or value only in the otherwise and the elsewhere. People addicted to this outlook never seem to get their feet on the ground, a position which is necessary to secure traction and make progress. Many children, for example, hate the idea of school. They long for the day when they will be free, on their own, and have a real chance to make good. Meanwhile, their studies suffer. With some people, this attitude carries through life. They are dissatisfied with their homes, their friends, their jobs — nothing that they possess seems to amount to anything. If only they lived in some other place, knew more exciting and important people, or were in a position to show their real ability, life would take on a true luster. So, at least, they think.

Of course, everyone is entitled to a certain amount of dissatisfaction, which in itself may be a form of appreciation and lead on to improvement. But the negative outlook, of contempt for what one has or where one is, particularly if indulged as a regular thing, is bound to result in mental sterility and complete stagnancy in life. There are few situations so hopeless in appearance that they do not offer real possibilities for an alert and appreciative mind.

Perhaps I can illustrate this with an imaginary scene in Sangamon County, Illinois, which, let us say, happened many years ago. Two young men were seated on soapboxes on the front porch of a small country general store. From their appearance, it was evident that both were close to the soil, born and reared in a rural community. Both were whittling on sticks, in the manner of small-town philosophers. As they whittled, one of them remarked. "This is a dead place. Nobody here knows anything and nobody cares. Nothing ever happens. There's no chance to learn anything here and nobody here ever will. If you're from this neck of the woods, you may as well give up."

It is probable that this young man fulfilled his prophecy, from his analysis of the static condition in which he found himself. In any event, we have no record of his having made any mark in the world.

The other young man said nothing on this occasion. It is probable that he also had recognized the meagerness of opportunities, for education, experience, and personal advancement in the community. But somehow, he made the most of what he had. He managed to borrow books and to improve his store of knowledge. He studied character in the simple people he knew. He watched nature and drew wisdom from the soil, the woods, the streams, the seasons, and crops, as he chopped down trees and prepared the ground for farming. In the quiet of his cabin and as he went about his tasks and chores, he came to know himself better; and he developed a strong sense of personal relationship with God. In later years, men were to call him "Honest Abe." He came to be one of the greatest presidents of the United States, known and respected as an epic figure throughout the world. His writings have passed into the depository of the world's greatest literature; and his decisions and his deeds held firmly to the union of the United States of America at one of the most critical points in its history. His name was Abraham Lincoln.

This story might be retold in a thousand forms for every community in the world. Not that one may look for an Abraham Lincoln to emerge in every instance, nor can one expect such personal development without an extraordinary natural capacity. The point is rather that in every setting there are elements of universality, which permit everyone to achieve maturity and relative greatness. Even if Lincoln had never become president or moved far from his orbit in Illinois, he still would have been a great man, for he made the most of what he had and determined to improve upon it with a view to giving service.

One might, with ample documentation, transfer the story of frustration to great metropolitan centers and to the homes of the rich, without altering it in any essential. The world is full of privileged young men and women who fritter away their opportunities in boredom and cynicism and make no genuine contribution to the world in which they live. They accept what they have without appreciation of what it has cost in terms of planning, working, saving, and even suffering on the part of others; and by their own lack of imagination, their selfishness, and their stupidity, they create an atmosphere of personal stuffiness in which any achievement of value seems impossible. Even with all the advantages in the world, one needs a dynamic appreciation to recognize opportunities and to put them to work.

This scene and situation might be re-created in innumerable factories, offices, organizations, homes, and institutions, where people sitting across from one another or working side by side entertain totally different outlooks on themselves, their work, and their future. For some it is a hateful daily grind, and a burning desire to escape into something else, only God knows what. For others it is a matter of dull routine in a kind of mental fog and a nameless discontent with where one is at the moment and with what one is doing most of the time.

There are times, of course, when one can and should make a radical change. But for most of us the answer is nothing more radical than a change of attitude and outlook within ourselves. The trouble is usually not with our surroundings or with what we are doing; it is rather with ourselves and the way we are doing things. One can be joyous in a cottage and miserable in a palace; or the other way around. One can bring a professional attitude to the digging of a ditch and take pride in his work, and one can approach the most responsible position in the world with listlessness or distaste. The joy we take in our lives and, to a large extent, the success we achieve in our fields depend upon the effort that we make to become aware of the importance of what we are doing and to render ourselves able and worthy to do the task well. When we have reached a certain point of competence, we shall know whether to move on or to broaden and intensify our activities where we are.

In the home, the alert housewife will look about her and manage to keep busy and happy, appreciative of the opportunity to improve herself in cooking, designing, entertaining, inspiring her husband, and providing for the domestic needs of her family. More than that, the attitudes and social qualities of a wife profoundly affect the habits, aptitudes, and abilities of her husband, and may make the difference between his advancement or stagnation, success or failure. Many a lost week end, spent in alcoholic excesses, can be chalked up against a complaining or nagging wife and an unattractive home. And many a man, in line for promotion, may be passed over, unaware of the factor of a wife who has failed to appreciate the social graces and tact that mean so much at critical times.

In any office organization, a recognition of the importance of one's work, an attitude of responsibility, and a desire to improve professionally make all the difference in the world. Some people see things to be done, find ways and means of effecting improvement, of making savings, and of contributing to greater harmony and co-operation of effort. Others are interested in only one thing — the pay check. This difference of outlook and capacity is evident in all lines and ranks — secretaries, typists, file clerks, receptionists, switchboard operators, messengers, supervisors, and managers. As in charge of an office organization for many years, I have seen them come and go — good, bad, and indifferent — hard workers and clock watchers, people who thought they were too good for their jobs, people who were interested only in the pay, people who remained long enough only to criticize and complain; and people who saw what was to be done and put their shoulders to the wheel.

The same is true on the top level of administrators and executives. Some never stop growing in appreciation of their work and in study of its problems and possibilities. They know the people in their organization. They are willing to learn from the janitors as well as from their desk associates. They can be counted on for loyalty, because they understand its importance. They are not afraid to think about their work and to put to work what they think. Others remain forever in the category of what are called "stuffed shirts," contributing to their position little besides their time.

In some ways, these considerations are most pertinent to fields of scientific research or creative work of any kind. Discovery, or, what is more important, the recognition of discovery, and the advancement or application of any kind of scientific knowledge, call for awareness of a problem or of a need, with energy and patient resourcefulness in finding the answer. Creative work and interpretation, in teaching and writing, in music and in art, likewise require an active application of the powers of recognition and appreciation.

Generally speaking, there are no short cuts. Intuition cannot solve mathematical problems, or put paint on a canvas, or roll the notes on a piano to sound like a Beethoven sonata, or even fill one page with words in logical sequence. All of this takes planning, at long and short range, and the passage of time filled with effort. There is no sense in thinking that we are producing something so that we may take the credit for it, when we are doing only wishful thinking. We have all heard children banging away at the piano, trying to give themselves the illusion of great proficiency, when they should be practicing the notes on the music before them.

3

The reason many people fail to meet the challenge of dynamic appreciation and to produce anything outstanding, even to their own satisfaction, is the lack of some ingredient essential to success. It may be a question of sufficient time. It may be the need of proper tools. Perhaps one is not in the right place for the work. The atmosphere may not be conducive. Or if one has all these things, one's energy may suddenly give out. One cannot question the validity of these arguments. But in their application, they may serve as a form of self-deceit.

No one can question the importance of time. When an eminent president of Harvard University was asked by a student how long it would take to get an education, he replied that nature can produce a pumpkin in one summer but that it will work one hundred years to grow an oak tree. In the disposition of the limited time at one's command, one may have to decide what is more important and concentrate on that. In many cases, the problem is the proper organization of time. "How do you find time to do this or that?" friends sometimes ask. It is amazing how much one can accomplish over a period of time by the dedication of fifteen minutes, a half hour, or an hour daily to the task. This calls for determination and self-discipline and sometimes sacrifice. Of such ingredients is time made productive. One needs time for reflection, appraisal, mental absorption, and for the formulation of the appropriate appreciative action. In the hectic rush of the mad world in which we live, however, time seems to be the most difficult thing to lay hands on. People receive courtesies and special considerations, but are too much hurried to say thanks. We accept gifts and hospitality, but cannot find time to make the proper acknowledgment. We are surrounded with wonders of science and art on every side, but the average person is confused by the rapid procession.

In some respects, the situation has become really absurd. I have seen escorted groups rushing from room to room in art galleries, as if they were running to catch a train. On Sundays, the traffic of automobiles carrying people out to see the wonders of the country is so crowded that the net result is nervous strain. People talk about reading two and three books a day. How is this possible if one is to derive any substantial meaning and flavor from an author? Magazines are designed, not only as digests of articles, but also as digests of digests, becoming smaller and smaller in size and content, with the idea of making cover to cover reading *quick*. Everything is designed to save time for something else; but it is not clear just what happens to the time that is saved.

Suitable tools are also necessary. But many a task goes by default and many an opportunity is seized by others, because we fail to use what we have and instead spend our time envying the fine equipment and technical superiority which someone else possesses. I would suggest that everyone memorize the following poem by Edward R. Sill, in answer to this temptation:

> This I beheld, or dreamed it in a dream:
> There spread a cloud of dust along a plain;
> And underneath the cloud, or in it, raged
> A furious battle, and men yelled, and swords
> Shocked upon swords and shields. A prince's banner
> Wavered, then staggered backward, hemmed by foes.

A craven hung along the battle's edge,
And thought, "Had I sword of keener steel —
That blue blade that the king's son bears — but this
Blunt thing!" — he snapped and flung it from his hand,
And lowering crept away and left the field.

Then came the king's son, wounded, sore bestead,
And weaponless, and saw the broken sword,
Hilt buried in the dry and trodden sand,
And ran and snatched it, and with battle-shout
Lifted afresh he hewed his enemy down,
And saved a great cause that heroic day.[2]

In too many cases, people foster a sense of frustration and
injure their mental health by resentment and complaint against
lack of facilities. The typewriter is an old model, the piano is
out of tune and is only an upright, the studio is too small, the
laboratory is antiquated, the tools are dull, the pen will not
hold ink, the stove is old fashioned . . . if it is not one thing,
it is two. But the finest book binding in my library was made
by a friend with tools fashioned from a kitchen knife and spoon.
Good poetry can be written with a pencil on the back of an
envelope as well as on fine bond paper with an expensive machine, perhaps better. Some very fine art has come out of
garrets. And while modern technical equipment is required for
most advanced scientific research, some highly significant contributions have been made by men whose ingenuity made up
for laboratory deficiencies. Great music has been composed on
spinets. And some of the best cooking I have ever enjoyed
came from my mother's coal-burning Majestic range.

Similar observations may be made regarding other conditions
requisite to making benefits acceptable to us and a creative reaction possible. One of the most fruitless and positively dangerous mental activities is that of envy for the real or imaginary
advantages of others. Almost equally corrosive is the sulking
mentality which stunts appreciative growth and activity under

---

[2] Edward R. Sill, *Opportunity*.

the delusion that one is not in the proper atmosphere, or in just the right setting or locale, for satisfactory performance. The people we are with do not seem quite up to our standards. The community we are living in does not seem to enliven the divine spark within us. It may be the house, the color, acoustics, the arrangement, the lights, the furniture, the noise . . . there is always some disturbing element to keep us from producing. Under certain conditions, this affectation is called artistic temperament; but a large number of people possess it without specific reference to art. They are impossible to please, and no matter what one does to draw them out, they cannot be satisfied.

It is true that others may have certain advantages over us; and often the conditions we are expected to approve and to work under are not ideal. It is senseless, however, and sometimes downright ungrateful to spend one's time and mental energy in resentment when the application of a little effort and sportsmanship could work wonders. Most gold, it should be remembered, is extracted from barren and desert places. I can imagine that it would be wonderful to have a villa overlooking the sea, where one could think, and write, and plan great things, amid the songs of birds, and with the odor of jasmine and orange blossoms blowing in through the windows. But one of the most productive writers I have known did his work in his study, from five to eight o'clock in the morning, with a candle on the table as a warning to his family that he did not wish to be disturbed, should anyone be about at those early hours.

4

The trouble with many of us is that we have too many activities and too widely diversified interests. As a result, our energies are spread too thin, and nothing worth while is accomplished. There are certain values in diversification, but the process, if carried too far, ends in fragmentation and superficiality. We become jacks of all trades, masters of none. This is true, not only of piling too many things together, but of constantly changing one's interests. The lives of some people, in this respect, are like a constant chasing after the will-o'-the-wisp. No solid interest is developed, and no depth of understanding, appreciation, or skill is ever reached in anything.

With others, the problem is that of becoming so deeply involved in one's work and so totally consumed in its details, that no time is left for leisure or for an appraisal of the value of what one is doing or where one is headed for. In some cases, work is piled on to such an extent that valuable people are put into the position of drudges. They never find time for any of the things they would really like to do, for which they may be best equipped. When a situation reaches this point, it is time to stop, look, and listen. Neither the mind nor the physical system can stand this pace. This is the beginning of mental distress, nervous breakdown, shock, and heart failure. Too many people, in this modern age, recognize the symptoms when it is too late.

There is an old saying that if you wish to get anything done, ask a busy man. There is much truth in this. People with nothing to do, in many cases, do nothing; and every effort at thought or action is a tremendous strain. Busy people, as a rule, know how to organize their time and can always take on something else. But there are limits to which the prudent person should extend himself. When one is pushed to a point where there is no time or energy left for appreciating the good things of life, discharging the functions of gracious acknowledgment, doing at least some of the creative things for which one's talents are inclined, and for viewing one's life in the light of eternity — the situation needs correcting definitely and even radically.

In a very true sense, mental health and dynamic appreciation are synonymous. The exercise of vital appreciation means, not only life, but also growth, and to the same extent the elastic and vigorous qualities of youth. It requires, not only a disposition and willingness to learn, but also the humble recognition that there is more to be known and that others can teach us. To be willing to listen, to consider, to meditate, to sit at the feet of the small as well as of the great, to be alert to add to one's store of knowledge and wisdom — to keep *growing* mentally and spiritually — this is the sign of true greatness and of comprehension of the purpose of life and the meaning of salvation.

CHAPTER VII

A Sense of Direction

I

I RECALL an experience while a small boy on a shopping tour
with my mother, which I have often had cause to remember.
We were in a department store, and in the process of looking
at dress material, all of which was very boring to me, when
suddenly my mother took me by the hand and said, "I must
get out of here."

With no further explanation, I was hurried to the elevator,
down to the street level, and out to the sidewalk.

"What is wrong?" I inquired. "Are you sick, Mother?"

"No," she replied. "It may sound strange to you, but I lost
my sense of direction. I simply had to come out here to get
my bearings. Now we can go back."

There may be something hereditary in this trait, as I have
never felt comfortable in a location until I have ascertained
which direction is north. By a rather peculiar throwback of
memory, I find myself lining up things with the street of my
childhood home, with the location of the schoolhouse, and the

river beyond. Sometimes, the compass directions do not seem to be right with the plan in my mind; and a certain mental rotation of the land takes place until I have effected a reconciliation. Having achieved this, I can feel comfortable and happy again.

Once or twice I have been lost in the northern woods for a short time; and I can appreciate to some extent the feeling of loneliness, panic, and even shock that overcomes those who are lost and wander about for days before they recover the trail or are rescued. Without a map or compass, directives, stars, or landmarks, to point the way, it would be impossible for mariners, aviators, or explorers to establish any certainty of direction. Without this assurance, disaster, or the vision of disaster, is almost inevitable. Everyone who drives an automobile knows the anxiety of the motorist on a strange highway until he recognizes some sign or indication that he is on the right route and headed in the desired direction. Even moving about in an unknown city, one can become totally exasperated with diagonal streets, circles, dead-end streets, and blind alleys, unless he knows just where he wishes to go and has the assurance that he is on his way.

However important a sense of physical location and direction may be for peace and security of mind, a far more important and basic need for mental health itself is that of a sense of direction in life as such. There is nothing more disturbing and depressing than the feeling that one is simply drifting in life, without aim or purpose; and nothing is more demoralizing than the realization that one has lost his way and does not know where to turn.

It may be noted that aimlessness and dissatisfaction with life are by no means confined to the ranks of those who have little of natural endowment or of this world's goods. Some of the most unhappy, lonely, and aimless of people are to be found among those who seem to have everything. Fine houses, cars, fancy clothes, and opportunities for travel and leisure are not essential for happiness; nor do they necessarily produce a sense of peace, direction, and security. The possession of talent and ability is no guarantee of satisfaction and achievement. Many highly gifted individuals are hopelessly confused in their outlook and thinking, and, despite their talents and even apparent success, are filled with interior distress and frustration. The supposition that education as such is sufficient to assure contentment and progress is one of the great fallacies of this age. The accumulation of knowledge, without basic co-ordinating principles, can simply create a vast mental miscellany of confusion and increase the number of unsolved riddles. Only through the unifying effect of a pattern, and with the wisdom that comes from a sound standard of judgment and sense of purpose and finality, does the mind gain repose and strength.

2

This need for a sense of direction is required in a number of levels. It ranges all the way from the assurance of satisfaction and security in one's daily activity, to a profound, basic pattern of faith in the meaning of life itself and of one's personal career as related to that pattern and purpose. From the dawn of reason, every individual ponders these problems, and he endeavors, with the help and guidance of others, to adjust himself to the challenge.

In an elementary way, this challenge is indicated in the question asked of children by older relatives and visitors in the home: "What are you going to be when you grow up?"

"A policeman or a fireman or a cowboy," may be the answer of a boy. "A nurse, an actress, or a mother," may be the ideal of a girl.

These ambitions may be modified as time goes on, but they point to the fact that everyone feels the need for certain objectives in life, a definite place in society, a sense of importance and security, and a goal of achievement. Happy and fortunate is the young man or woman who knows what he or she wishes to do in life and who sets out in a systematic way to prepare for this vocation or career. The young man who is determined to become a lawyer, a doctor, an engineer, or a member of one of the other professions, an artist, a businessman in definite fields, an accountant, a clergyman, or a civil servant, to mention but a few of the ambitions of youth, has already laid the foundations for an alert and orderly mind and a life of successful endeavor. The young woman who thinks in terms of teaching, nursing, secretarial work, religious vocation, or any one of the numerous careers now open to women, or in terms of preparation for marriage and homemaking, likewise has opened the way to a definite and forward view of life for which one can plan and prepare and to which one can devote useful and continuous energy.

Within recent years, notable advances have been made in the development and administration of various psychological and aptitude tests, in connection with counseling services, in schools and other agencies. These serve to help people recognize their capacities and particular talents with reference to the selection of a career, and to correct such defects as may stand in the way of success. The practical application of this service as an implementation of education is certainly to be encouraged. In many cases, it may mean the setting of a definite ambition in life for which the individual is fitted, where otherwise he or she would be launched to drift in an open sea.

But the principle of seeking competent advice and of following it when it is offered extends far beyond the techniques of psychological testing and the selection of a career. The trouble with many people who have a serious problem to face is that, instead of confiding in someone whom they can trust, they become secretive and carry the mental burden of doubt and indecision until it is too late to avoid disaster. One cannot get the benefit of advice unless one is willing to seek it and to listen with a humble and honest mind.

3

A number of causes or reasons may be assigned for the lack or loss of a sense of direction in life, but they all narrow down to one principle — that of escape. Just as many persons build their lives on a pattern of fear, others find their actions dominated by a pattern or urge of escape. This takes various forms. It may be an escape from work, escape from decision, escape from reality, escape from responsibility, escape from self. This is not to say that the person who tries to solve his problems by escaping from them is necessarily to be blamed for taking this way out. The solution may be false or erroneous; but is not always culpable. The tendency to face life on the strategy of escape may be an evidence of mental or physical sickness rather than of deliberate choice. But in any case, it is only through an honest diagnosis of our own problems, or of the problems of those whom we wish to help, that we can build or rebuild a positive program of life and start our way forward in the right direction.

This is particularly true where aimlessness and lack of ambition arise from the desire to escape work. This is known as sloth, or more familiarly as laziness. Sloth has been designated by moralists as one of the capital vices, along with pride, envy, avarice, lust, and gluttony. As the source of a cultivated distaste for personal effort and useful enterprise, it carries a moral responsibility for the great mischief of idleness. As the old saying goes, "An idle mind is the devil's workshop." The evasion of one's rightful share of work and responsibility, moreover, may work a positive injustice upon one's family and friends as well as a personal deterioration.

Sloth takes a variety of forms. In some instances it appears as a lack of vigor sufficient to look for a place in society and for a definite use for one's ability. Some people hate to go to work; nothing pleases them more than to "hang around the house," in a familiar expression, or to sit and think, or just sit. With others the difficulty is not a lack of vigor, but rather of a dim view toward useful activity. They like to play, to enjoy social activity, to engage in the pursuit of pleasant hobbies, and to offer elaborate alibis for their failure to produce work, to assume responsibility, to find a place in life and make a definite contribution to society. In other words, they are willing to work, but not at the kind of work they should be doing.

If sloth takes the form of listlessness, it may be important to examine one's physical condition. Mental attitudes are often the result of anemia, faulty diet, sluggish metabolism, lack of vitamins, or organic troubles. The answer to this problem may be a tonic, more fresh air, and habits with better regard for one's physical needs and limitations. Medical direction may be required to uncover and to cure the cause of debility. It may be that one's "extra" activities, so to speak, are sapping vitality that should be reserved for primary duties, leaving one in a state of chronic fatigue and mental distress. We can go only so far. We all have our limitations, and must make a choice.

Many persons are dissatisfied with their jobs and generally exasperated with the whole prospect of work for the reason that they are physically exhausted from too much social activity at night. During the day, they go about in a kind of mental fog, and express themselves as confused and "all mixed up." The question then is what is more important. Something must give way under the strain, unless we discipline ourselves and ration our energies in accordance with the rules of common sense.

Sometimes, the symptom of aimlessness stems from a Peter Pan outlook, a failure to grow up and mature. Some people prefer to remain playboys and playgirls and to act as if the whole world were a toyland. There is a period during adolescence when it is smart to regard one's elders as "old fogies." This is the age of high school and college pranks, a kind of devil-may-care time, when one can criticize others and be undependable oneself, without having too much to lose. Parents pay the bills and will always come to the rescue if there is trouble. But there is such a thing as being too completely dependent upon others. The time arrives when we must cut loose, take ourselves seriously, and stand on our own feet. It may be true that our parents are obliged to support us as children and to put up with our whims as youth; but to carry through life the idea that the world owes us a living and that we can continue as irresponsible infants is bound to end in disaster.

Parents die. Indulgent friends move away, grow tired of imposition, and become disgusted with irresponsible associates. Opportunities for advancement pass to others who know what they want and are willing to pursue it. Centuries ago, the Greek storyteller Esop taught this lesson in his fable of the ant and the grasshopper.

Lack of ambition, which is often synonymous with sloth, is sometimes not so much a form of escape as an evidence of lack of understanding. We do not like to do things for which we see no good reason. Children dislike going to school if they see no purpose in education and no sense in study. Students fail, not always from lack of ability, but from failure to comprehend the reason for the subject that gives them trouble. "What good is Latin?" they ask. "I don't intend to speak Spanish." "Who has any use for algebra or geometry?" And unless they enjoy the challenge of learning a language or working a problem, it may be difficult to explain just what is meant by training the mind to think in an orderly way, to analyze, and to organize one's knowledge.

As one passes through slum areas of a city or looks at the shacks of the poor in the outskirts or in the country, the same defect of understanding and imagination becomes evident. Slovenliness and dirt are not necessarily the product of poverty. One can be poor and still be neat and clean. Lack of interest in one's premises is often the result of an attitude which says, "What's the use?" Or it may be the natural transmission of a low level of understanding and appreciation, which can be corrected by education and encouragement. The filth and squalor of poor Negro sections might lead to the easy conclusion that the Negro is naturally lazy and without the native intelligence and ambition to improve himself. But this conclusion is proved incorrect by the fact that, with education and opportunity, the Negro produces artists, professional and business men, jurists, and statesmen, capable of distinguished action and self-improvement. The same observations may be made of other groups which have to make a start in depressed circumstances.

Basic to a sense of direction, of course, is personal determination and self-confidence. One needs both courage and persistence. Some people become frustrated and give up too easily. "If at first you don't succeed, try, try again," was the theme of a song we used to sing in grammar school; and it is certainly an important rule to keep in mind in a world full of competition and distraction.

There may be something desperate in the idea of working simply for the sake of working. And yet it is only in the attempt, at least, that one finds what he is looking for. In a way, life is like a fisherman who throws his baited hook into the water. If he does not get a strike the first time, he throws the line back again to better his luck. Good luck, in any consistent and continued form, is the result of persistent effort and hard work.

The dangers of idleness are too well known and too often demonstrated to need elaboration here. Dullness, boredom, mischievous habits of intemperance, and moral deterioration, all come easily with inactivity. The first rule for a sense of direction in life is to keep busy.

4

The difficulty which many people have to face and to overcome is that they never know what they want. Their lives lack aim and program because they cannot make up their minds. They move in an atmosphere of indecision; or it may be said that their direction is always a retreat from decision. If they could be perfectly certain what is the right thing to do, there would be no problem; but, of course, there are few things about which we are perfectly certain.

This difficulty confronts not only those who have limited talents and means at their disposal, but those also who have many abilities and are especially gifted. As a matter of fact, there are disadvantages in having too many talents. One may be torn perpetually among aptitudes and preferences and end up by being a jack of all trades and master of none. It is possible to spread oneself too thin by trying to cover too wide an area of activity, and to end in total confusion like the man who jumped on his horse and dashed off in all directions.

The reason why some people hesitate to make a decision is that they are unwilling to assume the responsibility, the work, and the sacrifice that it may entail. If we set our eyes on a definite objective, we must take the means to gain that objective; and this may not be so easy as we should like. Many people would like to play the piano if they could learn quickly, without practicing. We should have many more doctors if medical students could secure professional information and skill without studying. Many a fine book would be written if just dreaming and talking about it would produce the result. Many a happy marriage would be realized if the parties concerned did not have to settle down and live together as man and wife with all the responsibilities that this involves. Many young men and women would devote their lives to religious service, if they did not have to sacrifice certain worldly advantages and pleasures as a result.

Inability or unwillingness to make a decision may be the result of other considerations as well. Some people have no confidence in their own judgment. Others are afraid of doing anything that might give offense. Still others entertain the curious idea that by never making up their minds, they are always in a free and independent position. None of these attitudes, however, comes to a grip with reality or solves the problem of daily living and direction in life. One must decide what he wants to do, as his own preference, or with counsel from others if necessary. The next step is to hold fast to this decision and give it a reasonable opportunity to prove its worth. One must take risks. There is no complete guarantee of success for anything in this life, and no positive assurance of perfect happiness and satisfaction; but there are rich dividends for those who make up their minds to something definite and who pursue this with determination.

Failure to adjust to reality is perhaps the most frequent cause of disappointment, confusion, and drifting. Too many people never appreciate properly what they have, and as a result fail to make the best of it. They do not see the opportunities at hand; they do not recognize the importance of their work; they sell themselves short in what they are capable of doing. The grass looks greener on the other side of the fence; what others are doing seems to be so much more interesting and productive. As a result of these dreamy attitudes, they remain in a state of mental suspense. They move about in a fog of mediocrity, with a feeling of personal inferiority and various degrees of resentment for the imaginary advantages of others.

Many people go to their daily work, with no professional attitude toward what they are doing. They make no effort to understand their jobs and improve themselves on the job. They do the minimum required to collect their pay checks; and they spend the remainder of their energies complaining about the place and about the shortcomings of their associates.

Others, with the "never-never land" complex, have high ideals of what they should like to do; but they never seem to be in the right place to work them out. If they seem to follow a line of ambition, it is a kind of will-o'-the-wisp chase — just as they are about to grasp the object, it turns out to be another illusion. Irwin Cobb illustrated this point, some years ago, in a short story of a girl who wished to become an artist. This girl happened to live in a small town in a setting of rural beauty, but she had an eye only for the big city. So she went to the city to pursue her art; but here she had an eye only for mountain and jungle scenes, which she copied from others. The greatness of the city and interest of its human parade somehow escaped her. This girl failed as an artist, for the simple reason that, whether in the country or the city, she never learned to live in the world of reality and to recognize the beauty around her.

To those who are inclined to despise their work or who feel that what they are doing is of no importance, I like to recommend a reading of Hawthorne's famous story *The Great Stone Face*. It may be recalled that Ernest, the hero of this story, grew from boyhood to manhood and to old age in the valley of the New England mountain where nature had carved out the profile of a noble human face on one of the overhanging cliffs. Like the others in his village, Ernest had heard the local legend and looked forward to the stranger who would some day appear, bearing the features of the great stone face and exemplifying the character and virtues written into the stone. But as time moved on, the stranger never came. It was Ernest himself who lived to fulfill the prophecy through his life of humble goodness and greatness.

How many times is this story repeated in real life! The world is full of people unknown except in their own communities and unimportant except for the great and good work they do in the fulfillment of their duties, in their charity toward others, and in their shining example of the richness of life when it copes courageously with reality.

Everyone is important, with the supreme importance that God has attached to His creative act in producing an immortal soul. All life is important, as the field for every man and woman to work as the image of God and in the presence of God. The character and glamour of one's career have little to do with the case. Whether one is called upon to spend days in the classroom teaching youth, or in the home at the end of a broom or over a stove, whether one fixes rivets or sells insurance, drives a taxi cab, heads a banking system, preaches the Gospel, plows the earth, or lies on a bed of pain, one can face up to the call for action and see in the task an important challenge and an opportunity to do something genuinely useful, to make a pattern of life, and to advance to the full extent of one's ability.

From time to time, everyone should ask himself the question: "What have I been brought up to do, trained and educated for?" What has been my choice in life? Am I fulfilling that preparation, decision, and expectation? Am I facing reality, with its "ups" and "downs," its fulfillments and disappointments, its glamour and its meanness, in a spirit of acceptance and adjustment? Or am I living in a shallow make-believe world of evasion and escape, trying to do things for which I am not fitted or qualified, and failing to fulfill my duties at hand? Am I trying, at least, to come to terms with the here-and-now, or am I living on the moon or in some imaginary time and place which never quite comes into focus? Am I producing, or am I just dreaming?

5

Many people who fail in the struggle with reality adopt a form of escape which relieves them of personal responsibility and reduces the world to a gigantic joke and fake. This is the mental attitude of the cynic who has lost his sense of direction in life because he has lost his confidence in the existence of sincerity, honesty, and finality. For the cynic, "things are not what they seem"; people do not mean what they say and cannot be trusted. In his view, there are no honors but those that are bought and paid for. Virtue is only a pretense, and religion is a sham. There is no point in making an effort, because the winner has already been determined. In the parlance of the gamblers, everything is "fixed," and only the gullible and simple-minded think otherwise. Such is the philosophy of cynicism. It is a deadly thing.

A cynical attitude toward life may arise from an unfortunate experience, or it may develop from a variety of causes. It may be the result of repeated efforts and failures, ending in the final expression of disgust, "I give up." It may develop from disappointment in one's expectations or disillusionment in one's heroes. It may be the aftermath of bitterness and resentment for an injustice, whether real or imaginary. It may be a refuge for disappointment in one's ambitions. It may be a camouflage for one's personal limitations, a rationalization to justify one's immaturity and inner sense of insecurity. Or it may be an outlook of bewilderment adopted from listening to older and more seasoned cynics, who are always on the lookout for ready listeners to their tales of woe and for apprentices in the art of cynicism.

The treatment of cynicism, as the symptom of a mental hurt, differs with the nature of the cause itself. If it is only a pose or an affectation of adolescent smartness, it will probably wear off by itself as one reaches maturity and attains a deeper appreciation of the true and solid values in life. If it is induced by association with a cynical set, the best procedure is to move out of this atmosphere into more wholesome and positive company. If it serves as a sedative for a troubled conscience or justification for a bad moral situation or a lapse in the performance of a recognized duty, the only cure is a return to moral honesty and a resumption of what one knows, deep down, to be right. If it comes from the shock of disillusion, one may have to reach into one's reserve of faith and hold fast to a sense of principle as against living examples of weakness, corruption, and hypocrisy. This is particularly true when one is exposed to scandal involving religious faith and morals. The mental shock of an unfortunate experience may reach deep and require more vigorous self-steadying efforts, sometimes with the assistance and encouragement of good friends and counselors.

Cynicism from disappointment in their expectations or from the rebuffs that greet their honest efforts is a familiar and frequent temptation for young men and women who are freshly launched upon their careers. They may find their zeal rapidly cooled by supervisors, superiors, or older associates on the job, who have become complacent or somewhat soured with the years, envious of young blood, and jealous of their own security. They may be asked to compromise their youthful ideals with practices of a questionable nature and to serve as a cover-up for questionable practices and unethical deals. They may discover that their living models, at closer range, are in reality persons of flesh and blood, with feet of clay, and perhaps not the paragons of strength and virtue they were once thought to be. Repeated efforts to do a good job may be sabotaged in subtle ways; and repeated failures may cause one to wonder whether he has not been deceived from the beginning.

Under these circumstances, one needs a strong will to persevere, much patience and watchful waiting, and a basic philosophy of what is right and wrong, to keep his sense of direction. Many people go down in the struggle. Only those who keep their faith in abiding values emerge from the experience, stronger than before. Those who succumb to cynicism take the tortuous path of escape from responsibility and from self. Those who survive take the path of leadership and hold aloft the torch of truth for others to follow.

6

In this age of confusion, the need for a positive, enduring philosophy of life and for a firm spiritual faith becomes more and more imperative. It is basic to the maintenance of mental health. Success is often confused with material gain. Progress is confused with the accumulation of knowledge, technology, and gadgets for amusement and comfort. Importance is confused with noise. Greatness is confused with power, however acquired. Significance is confused with mere agitation, motion, excitement, and mechanical work piled upon work, to such an extent that society itself is in danger of going mad. It is no exaggeration to say that, without a return to a pattern of life which is related to eternity, our civilization may collapse.

We all need to pause, from time to time, and meditate prayerfully upon the reason for our existence — where we came from, where we are going, and how our program of life conforms to the accounting which we must give all one day to almighty God. There are intermediate motives which help to steady and inspire us. The strong love of man and woman, of husband and wife, is often enough to give a person reason to carry responsibility and move ahead, under difficulty and tension. Devotion to duty or to an inspiring cause, whether it be one's home, friends, community, church, or state, can produce a forward thrust of energy that gives zest to life and justifies one's early hopes. But, in the final analysis, it is love of God that gives life its fundamental pattern and sense of direction. With this faith and love, human activity becomes genuinely important and serves a dedicated purpose that is substantial and permanent. Life has a meaning — every part of it — if we hold fast to God.

CHAPTER VIII

Righteous Indignation and Mental Peace

I

Some years ago I undertook to deliver a lecture under the title "The Pillars of Friendship," endeavoring to outline certain basic principles which effect the making or losing of friends. Among other points, I stressed the fact that friends are not made by quarreling with people, held by arguing and giving offense, or regained by continuance of a feud or attitude of resentment. I thought that my presentation was quite convincing, until the question period which followed.

At that time a gentleman arose from the audience to advise me that I had completely missed the essential. The important thing in life, he maintained, is that of upholding right principles and defending justice. If others recognize this obligation, there can be no reason for dissension among people. If they do not, they are unworthy of our confidence and friendship. We should not, he concluded with some emphasis, just to make ourselves popular or to maintain peace, overlook the demands of righteous indignation.

I have thought a great deal since that time about these observations. There is no doubt about the importance of maintaining truth and justice and of deploring wrongdoing and the propagation of error, no matter where or how it is advanced. But it has also occurred to me that righteous indignation has often served as a cloak for much mischief. The man whose anger mounts to a towering rage so as to affect his better judgment, the person who nurses a grudge and plans revenge, the individual who feeds on religious prejudice or political partisanship to such a point that it becomes an obsession, the poor loser, and the sharp mind that can detect an evil eye or sinister motives in others whose ideas or interests do not happen to coincide with his own — all these people tend to justify their attitudes and actions as righteous indignation.

People whose lives are dominated by a desire to suppress or exterminate others who have given them offense in any form, who cannot tolerate a difference of opinion or belief, and who seek to take justice into their own hands, can become a menace to the community. The individual who nurses hate and plans revenge is doing damage, not only to others, but to the health and integrity of his own mind and soul as well. The person who prizes peace of mind and mastery over his own soul will do well to practice the arts of tolerance and forgiveness and of learning to live as if offense had never been given or received. Among the words of wisdom preached in Christ's name, none carry more practical value than these: "Be angry and sin not; let not the sun go down upon your anger."[1]

2

One of the most frequent causes of mental disturbance is personal sensitiveness, which is quick to take offense and to see an insult in every jest or remark of a personal and pointed nature. From childhood days, we can all remember the boy or girl who cried and ran home to mother if he or she was not given

---

[1] Eph. 4:26.

preference in the games or happened to be the loser. Some children, it is true, get more than their share of hazing, whether because of a physical defect, a mannerism that provokes ridicule, or an extra talent or achievement that arouses the envy of others. But some imagine that they are being "picked on" all the time, and take refuge in the lowest and most dangerous form of consolation, self-pity.

I recall an experience that happened while I was in third grade of school and which has served me as a good lesson ever since that time. The teacher blamed me for a trick in which I was partly involved, but failed to catch or punish the boy who planned it and who drew me in as a secondary accomplice. My righteous indignation drew tears and then a quick flight home, where I was sure of parental comfort and speedy justice. Unfortunately, my explanation of what had happened did not satisfy my father that I was entirely innocent in the affair.

"Go back to school without any further delay or nonsense," said he. "Apologize to the teacher and take your medicine. And let this be the last of your complaint."

There was nothing to do but follow his command. As a result, I was soon restored to a normal place in the class, and life went on as usual. Undoubtedly, similar episodes have happened repeatedly since that time, but they have taken care of themselves without reference to a court of appeals, and have consequently been forgotten. A good thick skin, a quick facing up to facts, a ready acceptance of penalties, and an early dismissal of unpleasant episodes from the realm of one's mind — these are the blessings of childhood, which may well be carried over into adulthood against mental soreness and much ado about nothing.

I recall a similar incident in the life of an attractive girl who decided one summer to work in what was then referred to as an "ice-cream parlor." Her first day on the job, three or four local figures, who may have stopped at a tavern before deciding on a sundae, dropped in for refreshment. Exactly what happened — whether they used some profanity at the slowness of the service, or referred in some rough way to her feminine beauty, or even pinched her arm — was never made clear, but this early disaster was enough to effect her immediate resignation with the announcement that she would never work again, at least not in an ice-cream parlor where men would come in. It required a certain amount of persuasion and explanation to alter this decision; but finally she returned to the scene of her early disillusionment and prepared to face life on the same basis as most other mortals.

To allow unpleasant incidents to rankle in the mind is a great mistake. It makes no difference whether others have been at fault or we should share the blame. The tendency of everyone is to disengage himself or herself from guilt. A long reasoning process follows, particularly if we have been embarrassed by others, or if we have been caught in a culpable act and feel that we should justify ourselves. The natural and easier thing to do is to shift the blame to someone else. The more we think about it, the more indignant we become. Then begins the plotting for revenge, so that we may secure justice by penalizing others and squaring things for ourselves. Sometimes, children who have been punished slap back at their mothers. Boys and girls who feel that they are not understood at home like to imagine that they are dead, with the family in tears around the coffin, or they run away, with the idea of bringing distress to an unappreciative family.

Companions and brothers and sisters, old enough to know better, go on a program of silence to evidence their indignation over some slight, real or imaginary. "I'll never speak to her again as long as I live," is an expression frequently heard in offices and homes. People smitten with this strange form of insanity often work at the same desk or eat at the same table for days, months, and years, without referring to each other, except as "that individual" or through a third party.

In flight from an unfortunate incident, an imaginary wrong, or from a command to an unpleasant duty, people leave their homes, their work, their clubs and organizations, their church and religious faith, sometimes to spend the rest of their lives arguing with themselves, painting black and ugly pictures of those whose friendship they have lost or of the responsibilities and associations they have abandoned.

When sensitiveness to injury becomes chronic, it may develop into a psychological complex, interpreting all actions of others as a conspiracy of evil. This is what is known as a persecution complex. This tendency likewise may show itself early in life, and should be nipped in the bud, lest it develop into a mental pattern. Children who fail in their studies or regularly get into mischief, for which they are punished, like to attach the blame on the teacher. "She is always picking on me. The teacher is down on me. Nothing I do seems to be right," says the child who comes home with a poor report card or an unsatisfactory record of conduct. It is, of course, possible and sometimes true that a teacher may discriminate against a certain pupil. But the chances are rather that the child is at fault. With a little intelligent inquiry and assistance from the home and an honest attempt at readjustment, this situation can be remedied. Parents who assume that the teacher must be wrong and who encourage the child in the view that a vicious campaign is being waged against him, by the teacher or the school authorities, are doing no good. Sometimes these grudges are carried through life; and the mind of the child is carried over, with its baggage of infantile and juvenile complexes and resentments, into an adult atmosphere of muddy thinking.

Many adults are troubled with the haunting fear of being pursued by malignant spirits, in one form or the other. They get the idea that their parents do not love them; or, as old age comes on, they feel that they are not loved by their children, and that they are being neglected and persecuted. People who fail to forge ahead in life as they had hoped often find an easy explanation in blaming their bosses and superiors, as the big bad wolves in the way. "What is the use of trying," they ask, "when you know that you are going to be blocked at every turn?"

There are undoubtedly instances in which these reactions correspond to the facts. Perhaps some people are badly treated, betrayed, or discriminated against by someone in control. But in most cases this is an illusion or a lame excuse for failure and personal fault. It is easy to magnify a rebuke into the expression of tyranny, to interpret the refusal of a permission as evidence of personal dislike, and to consider a difference of opinion as an example of opposition. Before deciding that one is being "picked on" or persecuted, it may be well to check the facts. Even if such is the case, there are other solutions besides retirement into a brooding mind. The mind that broods on persecution may be close to collapse. If a bad situation cannot be remedied, it may be better to withdraw from the scene and look for new fields of endeavor.

3

One of the soundest rules for mental health, and one that should be applied every day in our lives, is to forgive and forget. The mind that carries a baggage load of resentment, soreness, or brooding sense of foul play and injustice is a sick mind. Such a mind becomes a dark labyrinth for all kinds of imaginings, assigning devious motives to others, developing a persecution complex of its own, and planning various forms of revenge. Time that should be given to useful activity is consumed with morose meditation, and energy that might be devoted to constructive and happy living is consumed in regurgitating and chewing cuds of self-pity. Remnants of old and unpleasant incidents are allowed to parade back and forth across the imagination, with only one end result, that the individual becomes the victim of his own hallucinations, more miserable as time goes on.

From a moral standpoint, the act of forgiveness calls for nobility of character and often the exertion of great effort and self-conquest. Nevertheless, it must be exercised if one is to live comfortably with oneself or with others. Moreover, it is essential if one is to appeal to the mercy of God in his own behalf. Its importance is such as to merit a leading place in the teachings of Christ, who identified it with the practice of charity and exemplified it in His own life to a heroic degree. Hanging upon the cross in His death agony, He prayed for His enemies, "Father, forgive them, for they know not what they do."[2] In His great prayer which He formulated for our daily utterance, He taught us to say, "And forgive us our trespasses as we forgive those who trespass against us."[3] The practice of forgiveness and reconciliation, He pointed out, is basic to the friendship of God and is the first condition of worship which is acceptable to God: "If therefore thou offer thy gift at the altar, and there remember that thy brother hath anything against thee, leave there thy offering and go first to be reconciled to thy brother; and then coming thou shalt offer thy gift."[4] This injunction He made imperative whether the fault is ours or others' and whether those involved remain our enemies or not. "You have heard," He declared, "that it hath been said: 'Thou shalt love thy neighbor and hate thy enemy.' But I say to you: Love your enemies: do good to them that hate you: and pray for them that persecute and calumniate you: that you may be the children of your Father who is in heaven, who maketh his sun to rise upon the good and bad and raineth upon the just and the unjust."[5]

The ability to forgive can be cultivated if one starts by making a distinction between a wrong and the person who has done that wrong. In a very true sense, it may be said that God never forgives sin but is constantly forgiving sinners. The reason for this is that while a thing which is wrong can never be made right, by an act of forgiveness or by any other means, the person who has performed the evil act is not bad in himself. He may have been subject to certain influences which would

---

[2] Lk. 23:34.   [4] Mt. 5:23, 24.
[3] Mt. 6:12.   [5] Mt. 5:43–45.

lessen or even remove the element of personal guilt; or, if actually guilty of the sin or wrong, he may be moved later to regret and to genuine sorrow for his evil deed and thus become eligible for pardon.

With regard to the first possibility, we must all be aware of having given offense to others without realizing or intending to do so. In other cases we have acted on the spur of the moment, without reflection or under the impulse of excitement or emotion, and without averting to the fact that we are causing distress or injury to others. In many instances, what appears to be an inconsiderate word or deed is performed under a misapprehension or misunderstanding. Sometimes reports of what others have done or said against us remain unverified and serve only to arouse suspicion and ill will. For any or all of these reasons, the admonition "Judge not that you be not judged" contains much practical wisdom.

With regard to the second consideration, we should be prepared to accept the apology of others who have hurt us, and to open up avenues of approach which will make it easier for them to apologize. When people stop speaking to each other because of some difficulty, someone has to make the first move, to say the first word, and to help restore good relations. Someone has to give or accept the peace offering. One must have patience and above all humility, which is a mark of greatness, to re-establish good understanding and friendship. Silly pride and obstinacy serve only to continue and to deepen feud and resentment. If we find it hard to offer pardon, because the offender gives no reasonable explanation or refuses to offer even an implicit apology, we can still formulate forgiveness in our hearts and leave the rest to the judgment of God, with a prayer for better understanding and divine mercy.

A distinction may also be made between insult and injury. An insult is an offense against our dignity or sensibilities. An injury is harm or loss inflicted on some person or possession. An injury may be in the moral or spiritual order, such as a damage to one's good name or reputation; physical injury may be in the nature of a theft, damage to one's property, or harm resulting from assault upon one's body.

From this explanation, it seems obvious, that one may forgive another for an insult, upon the rendering of an apology or satisfactory explanation, or even in the charity of one's heart, without such apology, and at the same time rightly require in justice a restoration or repair of the injury involved. Thus we may demand that persons who have circulated lies about us should now endeavor to retract those stories in satisfactory form. The thief who has tearfully admitted his guilt is still under obligation to return his loot or make restitution. The motorist who has damaged my car because of reckless driving may offer profuse apologies, if his responsibility is clear; but he may still be called upon to pay the bill.

In the rendering of justice for injury after pardon has been rendered, it is, of course, prudent and advisable for the person in the "driver's seat" not to demand restitution which is beyond the power of the other to give or reparation in such form as exhibits a spirit of revenge. Whatever good is done by an apparent pardon is often nullified by the exorbitant terms of the settlement. In the days of the debtors' prisons, many a man died in wretchedness and prison chains before he could raise the money to repay his righteous and forgiving creditors. The terms of reparation imposed upon nations defeated in war, even in modern times, have sowed the seeds of new wars and destruction more dreadful than before. If forgiveness is to serve a mollifying, reconciling, and constructive purpose, it must be kind and considerate also in establishing terms of restitution where injury has been involved.

Persons who are inclined to demand their "pound of flesh" in settling their differences and grievances with others will do well to meditate upon the eloquent plea of Portia in Shakespeare's *Merchant of Venice:*

The quality of mercy is not strain'd,
It droppeth as the gentle rain from heaven
Upon the place beneath: it is twice blest;
It blesseth him that gives and him that takes:
'Tis mightiest in the mightiest: it becomes
The throned monarch better than his crown;
His sceptre shows the force of temporal power,
The attribute to awe and majesty,
Wherein doth sit the fear and dread of kings;
But mercy is above this sceptered sway;
It is enthroned in the hearts of kings,
It is an attribute to God Himself;
And earthly power doth then show likest God's
When mercy seasons justice. . . .[6]

The problem facing many persons with respect to forgiveness is a tendency to dramatize slights, insults, and injuries. Some seem to be on the lookout for trouble in a challenging kind of way. They take a morose pleasure in telling their friends how often they have been ignored, mistreated, insulted, and injured by others. Women of this type often identify themselves by frequent use of the expression; "My dear, I was never so insulted in all my life!" Men of a similar mental outlook become belligerent and dare others to repeat insulting phrases so that there may be a showdown. Some persons, as already noted, resort to silence as their form of indignation and refuse to speak to their real or imaginary offenders. Such individuals may even create a kind of social vacuum around themselves for lack of sympathy or with the multiplication of insults and injuries.

From the standpoint of mental health, it is foolish to elevate every clash of rights, temperaments, and sensibilities to an incident of importance calling for adjudication and formal settlement. It is far preferable to overlook or quickly forget most disagreeable incidents before they reach proportions which call for apologies and formal pardons. Many harsh words, sarcastic remarks, and inconsiderate actions are the result of thoughtless-

[6] Act iv, 1.

ness or passing irritation rather than of design and purpose.

If we were to allow ourselves to take seriously the jokes that are made at our expense or the criticism directed against us, even by our best friends occasionally, we should soon be in a state of nervous frustration and collapse. If we were to erase people from our affections because of their selfish blunders which hurt us, we should find ourselves without friends. Everyone makes mistakes. This is all part of life. We ourselves give offense to others, sometimes wittingly and sometimes unaware of the fact, more often than we realize. Rather than to read evil motives into the deeds of others who offend and hurt us, or to plan ways of securing revenge for every little irritation, it is much better policy to smile, pay no attention, be indulgent and understanding, laugh the matter off, and get back to work.

People in public life, or in a position of responsibility where the requests of others may have to be denied, know how important it is to maintain an even disposition in this respect. The person who cannot tolerate criticism, who is hurt by being made the butt of jokes and cartoons, who fears any kind of opposition, who regards difference of opinion as a personal affront, and who lives in an atmosphere of constant uneasiness and suspicion regarding his associates, will not last long in such a position. No one should go into a political contest or run for office of any kind unless he is prepared for disappointment, "to take a licking," in the popular phrase, and be a good loser.

Being a good loser calls for considerable character and self-restraint in any field of endeavor. It means that one is willing to concede defeat, bind up one's wounds so that they do not continue to fester and hurt, and to greet one's victorious opponents and their backers in a civil, kindly way. One of the truly great things about the United States of America is that political opponents have learned to live together in peace. After the national presidential elections, for example, the country settles down to work together. This spirit is what has made the country strong and progressive.

Some persons cannot tolerate the idea of losing. As a result, they give themselves high blood pressure and everyone else a rough time whenever they enter a contest. They cannot discuss a subject calmly and dispassionately but must argue about it as if personal honor were at stake. The argument grows more furious and becomes highly personal, far from the basic issues. Voices rise, fists are clenched, tempers explode, insults are hurled, and friends are parted.

We can usually remain calm on subjects in which we are competent or in fields in which we are reasonably sure of ourselves. The hard winner or the poor loser is furious with himself quite as much as with others, because he secretly recognizes the relative weakness of his position, and he vents his spleen to gain relief. Persons who are high-strung to the degree that any kind of contest or contention is likely to end in violence should remind themselves of this and observe the danger signals. What a wonderful thing it is to be able to recognize that one is wrong, that his arguments are weak, that his skill is mediocre, and that others with whom he is contending are really more competent, better prepared, more highly favored, or in a stronger position!

To make this discovery and be able to live comfortably with it brings wonderful relief, particularly to those who have been unable to play cards without cheating or accusing their opponents of doing the same, or to those who would ordinarily throw or break their golf clubs, curse, and leave the course, if they made a poor stroke or lost a game. With the conscious recognition and acceptance of one's personal limitations, a great calm descends upon one's life. One becomes a better listener and learns to play for the fun of playing, whether one wins or loses.

To reach and maintain this state of being, we should make definite rules for ourselves and engage a monitor, if necessary, to remind us when our righteous indignation is beginning to rise to the danger point. Some persons should resolve never to argue, but to cherish their opinions in silence. Those who cry or stamp off in high dudgeon if they lose in a game or contest should, perhaps, confine their competitive activities to the side lines. Even from this position, there are some who cannot tolerate defeat. Many a football game is fought over by the spectators far more vigorously than by the players on the field.

Some people make a compromise with their righteous indignation in the expression "I shall forgive, but I shall not forget." There are times when an unhappy experience teaches us to be more cautious. Sometimes we say, "I shall forgive you this time, but do not let it happen again." Then, through the dictates of prudence, we set up certain safeguards lest it happen again. Very often, however, these expressions indicate that forgiveness is but partial and that one's mind is serving as an active file for past grievances. To keep the mind in a state of nervous agitation of this kind or to continue the accumulation of old resentments is a mistake. If one is inclined to this, there should be a determination to have a "spring house cleaning" from time to time, when this mental rubbish can be swept out and disposed of much in the manner of the old magazines and junk that accumulate in the attic, closets, or basement of one's home.

If forgiveness of others and dismissal of ancient rancors produces a cleansing effect upon one's mind, when others have been at fault, the same wholesome effects follow as the result of apology and amends to others when the fault has been ours. There is nothing so powerful in disarming enemies and regaining friends as a sincere, open apology. The words "I am sorry" carry sweet music to ears eager to find a way for reconciliations and wonderful relief to the mind of the individual who has been suffering in the consciousness of guilt and alienation.

We are taught — notwithstanding the theories of materialistic psychoanalysis to the contrary — that sin is forgiven and moral guilt is lifted only by honest acknowledgment to God, with a contrite heart and firm purpose of amendment. Honest acknowledgment and expression of regret is good for the soul, whether the aggrieved person is God or man. True, the offended person may refuse to accept the apology or demand more in the way of proof for our sincerity or repair of injury. Nevertheless, we must run this risk and be prepared, even by humbling ourselves, to make amends by any method which is reasonable. The attempt in itself will restore peace of mind.

4

These principles should not be overlooked when we are forming our attitudes toward others — individuals or groups. Even at the cost of considerable effort and the revision or sacrifice of some of our most cherished opinions and prejudices, we must learn to make allowances for a measure of error, in others as well as in ourselves. It is remarkable how rapidly we can adjust ourselves to an act of stupidity or mischief which we have energetically blamed on others, when it is shown that we ourselves were responsible for it. Then, of course, the whole thing can be explained. There was a completely logical reason for it; or if not, then we were really not thinking, and the incident is laughed off. We would do well to be more tolerant of others, to suspend our judgment for further evidence, and to make allowance for human error, instead of seeing malice and evil when others differ with us or from us in one way or another.

One of the most frequent and misleading forms of intolerance is what I may call the "personal allergy." There are some people whom we do not like, the first time that we meet them. Perhaps it is the physical type that displeases us — too fat, too thin. The voice may be on the raspy side or too saccharine. There is a strange look in the eye. We do not like the way they part their hair. Whether such reactions are physical or psychological is not certain. Dogs growl at some people and are friendly toward others. We are inclined to do the same, sometimes for a reason which we can analyze, sometimes not. In the words of the familiar jingle:

> I do not like thee, Dr. Fell
> The reason why, I cannot tell.

These first impressions may be right. But, often as not, they are wrong. Persons who appear to be most charming at first sight may turn out to be only good actors, with no depth of personality to sustain the outward show. Others whom we regard with suspicion and dislike may prove to be of sterling character, of deep qualities, loyal and lasting friends. We must allow time and experience to develop the facts. Hasty judgment may be unfair to others and a source of deep embarrassment to ourselves. Some people are always making new friends and losing old ones, for the reason that they are constantly revising their first impressions after a little experience. Some either like one, or they do not. There is no middle course. Their close friends are great people; all others are scoundrels or fools. To be raised or lowered in estimation is to be reclassified in one or the other of these categories.

Such easy classifications, particularly when founded on nothing more than "looks" or similar surface considerations, point to a tendency which needs to be corrected. In advanced stages, it manifests itself in an obsession that certain people are involved in dark intrigue to destroy us. We feel comfortable and safe only with the few people we like; and even their number may dwindle down to a point where the whole world is against us. It is only natural that we should prefer the company of those who are more of our particular type, but at the same time it is of the utmost importance that we develop a tolerance for others, who may not be pleasing to our temperament and ego.

These observations are applicable also to our outlook and dealings with other nationalities and races. I recall riding in a compartment for four persons in a French railroad coach, some years ago, together with an Englishman and a Frenchman. The Englishman, like myself, was interested in fresh air. The Frenchman, who wished to go to sleep in his seat, was definitely opposed to opening the window. Each time he dozed off, the Englishman reached for the window to open it, whereupon the Frenchman, aroused by the air, would wake up and close it.

After several of these movements, I remarked to the English-man that there appeared to be a difference among nationalities on the virtue of fresh air.

"Yes, but this isn't all," replied the Englishman with a broad cockney accent. "The Frenchman 'ates the Germans and Hitalians. The German 'ates the Frenchmen and Hitalians. The Hitalians 'ates them. But we 'ates them all."

There was a good-humored twinkle in his eye; but it carried a profound note all the same, as anyone acquainted with the history of European conflicts and efforts at co-operation is aware. Even in America, which is made up in large part of immigrants from Europe, the same tendencies to maintain national prej-udices are obvious. Those who do not belong to our group are often looked upon as foreigners, or at least not as 100 per cent Americans, as we are. It is easy to bunch national groups together and label individuals with names which indicate a deep contempt, distrust, or humorous dismissal, such as *dagos, hunkies, polacks, irishers, kikes, krautheads,* and the like. It is true that these epithets are often used in fun, but they also carry the implication, sometimes with less polite expressions, that people of a particular national origin or background possess special criminal tendencies which render them undesirable as citizens, untrustworthy as friends, and unthinkable as members of the family circle.

The fact is that we are all molded from the same clay. The European nationalities, while distinguished from one another by language, boundaries, history, and literature, are generally mixed in blood over the course of centuries and possess a com-munity of culture. The melting pot of America is simply carrying on, perhaps in accelerated form, a process that has been going on in Europe for centuries. Special characteristics, of course, are developed regionally in the passage of time, which serve to create what is called a national type. But personal experience bears witness that individuals are much the same in their human qualities, frailties, and reactions, regardless of which side of the border they happen to come from. There are good persons and bad, among all nationalities. The good have less desirable qualities at times; and the bad ones occasionally show the same fine characteristics that we possess.

The problem of tolerance becomes more acute in the case of difference of races. For some persons discussion of this question is dangerous for the reason that it may induce apoplexy. The mere thought of racial equality is regarded as preposterous. For many of the white race a program to extend equal educational and economic opportunities to Negroes is utterly repulsive, and is pictured almost as handing over one's daughters into black slavery. While the Negroes, generally speaking, have been admirably patient and reasonable in their upward push for education and full rights as citizens, some of their spokesmen unfortunately have fallen into dreams of disorder and communism as the solution of their problem.

A considerable element of jingoism has characterized the relationship of the white and the yellow races, often with the easy assumption of superiority on the part of the former, who have felt the pressure of what Kipling referred to as "the white man's burden," and of resentment on the part of the latter, who can trace their cultural origins back beyond the Greeks and who resent their classification as colonials.

The development of friendlier relations, greater co-operation, and a fuller measure of justice for all races and continents is a matter that calls for the most profound thinking of our best minds and the greatest measure of good will on the part of national and international bodies. After-dinner discussions which end in upset stomachs and cracker-barrel arguments, sometimes terminating in broken noses and the loss of friendships, are not going to settle the matter. From the standpoint of mental poise, constructive thinking and influence, the individual can do much good by maintaining an open mind on these questions and an attitude of charity to all in conformity with the principles taught by Christ.

5

These principles should find practical application also in the problems of mental health as dealing with religious prejudice and intolerance. Prejudice signifies judgment, before or without reference to the facts. Intolerance refers to inability or refusal to allow a faith or an opinion to exist with which we are in disagreement. Religious prejudice signifies an attitude of hostility toward the religious faith and practices of others, without any genuine understanding of what is involved or any sincere attempt to learn. Religious intolerance is based on the belief that other religions than the one which I profess are false and harmful and therefore have no right to exist.

To a large extent, religious prejudice is inherited or engendered in the child mind by parents, teachers, and associates. It differs from religious faith, with which it is frequently confused and for which it is often substituted. Faith is directed to a positive creed of religious doctrine, whereas prejudice is simply a form of opposition and hate for that of others, built up on rumors, hearsay, and possibly even malicious misrepresentation. The enemies of the early Christians circulated the report that commemoration of the Last Supper consisted in killing and eating children. Persons who accepted this report without careful investigation became righteously indignant; and in this way persecutions were launched to free the community, so it was thought, from such a criminal sect. In modern times, the manufacture and propagation of falsehood have reached fantastic proportions, to accuse religious persons of idolatry and lechery, and to associate various churches with carrying out the work of the devil, in league against civil authority, conspiring to enslave the minds of the people, and generally acting as a cancer in society. Whipped up into a frenzy by such propaganda, persons who should be more intelligent and more considerate of their neighbors often join in various movements of sabotage and destruction. Jews, Christians, and persons of all faiths suffer from whispering campaigns of a malicious character, some of which come out into open violence; and, sad to say, they sometimes nourish similar prejudices themselves and launch countercampaigns with the same objectives.

As a matter of fact, a prejudice may be either true or false. That is not the point. There is, however, an obligation upon responsible persons to verify their facts before they assume attitudes or take action against others. A prejudice may be mental poison, deadly in its nature and effects. Before we sit in judgment upon others and circulate accusations against other religions, we should ask what it is that others really believe, what it is they really practice, and why they do it. The mind that is nourished on falsehoods and makes no endeavor to come out into the atmosphere of truth is mentally sick and potentially dangerous.

Intolerance which is fed upon religious prejudices or antireligious prejudice is the evidence of a fanatical and narrow mind. There is, of course, such a thing as "the intolerance of truth"; and men have been known to give up their lives in defense of the truth. A man who is convinced from rational evidence that two and two equal four or that China exists or that he is the legitimate son of his parents certainly cannot — in the interests of tolerance — agree that perhaps his arithmetic is wrong, that China is only a figment of the imagination, or that he is some other person. Similarly, a person who believes that God exists, that Christ is a divine Person, that His Church is true can hardly be expected, under any claim of intellectual honesty or social refinement, to admit that the contrary propositions are equally true. But what he is required to do — by the laws of social charity and justice — is to acknowledge the inherent right of every person to worship God according to the dictates of his conscience, the same right he demands for himself. Nor can he rightfully demand that others be deprived of the exercise of their religious faith and morals, unless it can be truly demonstrated that such exercise is basically wrong in itself and conflicts with the natural law and the common good.

A healthy mind is a friendly mind, open to association with men of good will, whoever they may be or whatever they may be as to their religious faiths. It is objective in its outlook, thriving on the truth, and never battening on unverified rumors or gossip of an unfavorable character which might do harm to others. Maintaining its own integrity of principle, it is tolerant of the weakness, the errors, the delusions of others, respectful of their good intentions, and considerate of their search for the truth. "For this is good and acceptable in the sight of God our Saviour, who will have all men to be saved and to come to the knowledge of the truth."[7]

Mental peace does not come from strife, from settling grudges, or from the righteous indignation of an ill-conceived crusade against those who believe differently on the matter of salvation; but rather from the practice of those virtues of kindness and restraint that make one worthy of friendship, and from the pursuit of truth in patience and charity.

---

[7] 1 Tim. 2:4.

CHAPTER IX

A Clean Mind

I

ACCORDING to the Freudian theory of psychology, which has exercised a profound influence on the development of psycho-analysis and treatment for mental health within recent years, all impulses which come to the surface of consciousness some-how originate in the instinct of sex. Mental disorders, in this school of thought, are to be traced back to a derangement of what is referred to as the *libido,* or instinctive sexual drives within the individual; and the correction of these conditions, if possible, is to be effected first by an analysis of the train of experiences so that the original sexual origin can be discovered and then neutralized.

This theory is subject to serious criticism on several counts. There are numerous elemental instincts which account for the actions of men, even on a sheerly physical basis; and in the spiritual order, there are vast fields of activity which are not even remotely begun or even influenced by sexual considerations or by physical concupiscence in any form.

Nevertheless, it is obvious that many human actions, including various mental and emotional reactions, do arise from the instinct of sex and are affected, directly or indirectly, by this force. Perhaps to a larger extent than is ordinarily realized, the attitudes of the mind, its interests, its powers, and its inhibitions are related to sexual powers and directions. The emotional pressure of sexual passion may reach great intensity and place a severe strain on the entire bodily system. This same activity exercises a profound effect upon the imagination; and, in turn, the imagination affects the rational faculties.

It has been demonstrated that sexual impulses can be sublimated or converted into other energies leading to the most exalted spiritual aspirations. History is full of Magdalens and Augustines, who have conquered their flesh with the love of God and converted their passions into a source of strength for a more spiritual life. It gives witness also to many sad examples of men and women of great ability and virtue who have been dragged down from the heights of success to wallow in sexual dissipation and scandal. Whether in the immediate direction of an activity or in an indirect and remote way, the sexual instincts play an important part in shaping human affairs and influencing mental health and productivity.

The significance of sex in the great plan of life is evident from a study of living things, beginning with one-celled, microscopic creatures. After the instinct to hold on to life, that of procreation, or continuance of the species, comes next in the natural order of vital existence. With the one-celled plants and animals this process is effected simply, by division of the nucleus and further multiplication. With the higher organisms it takes on a more elaborate development, as in flowers and seeds for plants. It is exemplified in a more pronounced division of male and female elements in the animal kingdom, united by various methods of insemination for the creation of an egg in one form or another, from which a new individual life is developed. Some idea of the strength of this instinct may be formed when one contemplates the fact that life has survived on the earth for millions of years, by a process of parental transmission, and has steadily evolved and become more complicated despite the rigors of the elements and the constant warfare among living things.

With many, if not all, of the animals, where a family unit is formed, there is an evidence of affection and a definite instinct of protection. In the human race, which represents the highest expression of the Creator's handiwork on this earth, procreation is normally tied in with some mating preliminaries, a ceremony of marriage, and the establishment of a family unit. In the case of mated men and women, at least where there is any developed culture and civilization, this blossoms into a union of minds, hearts, and bodies, designated as marital love. Under ideal conditions, this union, culminating in the physical act of sexual intercourse, is an expression of the highest natural ecstasy known to man and woman.

Like most human instincts, however, that of sexual development and reproduction with its many complex phases seldom proceeds with mechanical perfection or functions with complete psychological satisfaction. The development of the reproductive glands during the period of puberty, roughly between the ages of eleven and fifteen, is often a disturbing process. At a time when the outside world is difficult to understand, the average boy and girl, throughout adolescence, is confused by strange new internal emotions and elements of physical excitement. The matter of sex, which during childhood carried no special significance or interest, suddenly becomes a subject of mysterious fascination and strange embarrassment. Within the body itself, strange movements begin to stir in an atmosphere of wonderment and secrecy. Often, curiosity about these developments leads to self-stimulation, with solitary sexual excitement and gratification and possibly the formation of habits of sexual self-abuse.

During the mating period, mental and moral balances are

easily upset. The awakening of love between young men and women is a beautiful thing, but usually follows an uncharted course. Love has its pangs of uncertainty and anguish, of jealousy, desire, and disappointment, under which the mind and the will do not always function at their best. Impetuous persons are often under temptation to anticipate the sexual rights of marriage. Passionate lovers frequently live in a world of distortion, disturbance, and sometimes of tragedy. Disappointment in love leaves deep and often permanent wounds. Illicit love frequently leads to blackmail, revenge, and crimes of passion.

The problem of sexual mastery and mental serenity assumes a different character for different ages in life as well as for different states in life. For the child who has not yet reached the age of puberty, there is practically no problem, although even during these years a certain vigilance is advisable to prevent injurious mental shocks and the formation of harmful physical habits. The age of greatest intensity generally comes during the passage from adolescence to maturity, particularly during the experience of making love, when mental patterns are formed and adjustments are made, in the pursuit of a happy and settled life. This instability may recur during the forties or even early fifties, particularly for those involved in the meshes of an infatuation. For people who have passed the crest of life, the physical element diminishes or extinguishes itself; but the problem of mental control may still remain. There is a saying that "there is no fool like an old fool."

2

For all persons who have become aware of the instinct of sex, regardless of age or state in life, there are certain common principles which must be observed, so far as mental health is concerned. These may be summarized, at the risk of some repetition, as follows: (1) a correct knowledge and understanding of the facts of life; (2) a recognition that the natural func-

tions of sex are serious and good, an important part of the
divine plan; (3) an understanding and acceptance of ethical
principles and practice, as a matter of personal responsibility;
and (4) practice of self-control, in conformity with these principles and the needs of one's particular state in life.

A correct knowledge and understanding of the facts of life
in matters of sex is basic to mental health. There has been a
great deal of discussion on this score by churchmen and educa-
tors, some advocating a frank, graphic exposition of the subject
in the schools, and others leaning toward a more cautious
view of the matter. In my humble opinion, instruction should
be gradual according to the age of the person and considerate
of previous preparation and experience; but it should be factual,
true, and scientific, not a process of evasion, fiction, and postponement. This is a responsibility which should be shared by
parents, teachers, and spiritual counselors; but it should be
shared, not passed around. It should also be adequate and pointed
to the personal problems which may be expected at the age level
involved. Adults who are uncertain as to pertinent facts and
problems will do well to consult a reliable physician for instruction and guidance.

As a matter of fact, all the essentials of sex from a physical
or physiological standpoint can be explained in less than one half
hour. The evidences of reproduction in nature are so abundant
and clear that parents and authorized teachers should have no
real difficulty in explaining the matter gradually and according
to the age and development of the child or youth, and in such
a way as to reveal the beauty and logic of the separation and
union of the sexes, in the nature of God's plan.

Instruction in the meaning of these developments and in the
proper conduct of self during periods of sexual excitement is,
unfortunately, a rather desultory matter in most cases or is left
to the child or the youth to provide for himself. At a time
when arithmetic, history, the languages, and the marvels of the
physical universe are all explained in the classroom, and Holy

Scripture is revealed in the Sunday school or religious class, the adolescent is usually left to himself to work out the highly important and extremely explosive mysteries of sex. Sometimes this takes place in the alleys and toilets, with the aid of primitive wall drawings and murals, poems, and jargon not to be found in respectable dictionaries. Older boys and girls pass along bits of information, with sly winks and laughs, which help to explain and confuse at the same time. More daring youth, boys and girls, are admitted into clubs, often of a homosexual character, to be initiated into "the facts of life." More often than is suspected in respectable society, boys are ushered into the knowledge of "what it is all about" through a circus side show or a paid-for adventure; girls are instructed in menstrual hygiene by their mothers and often learn the rest from the advances of impetuous lovers whose ethical standards may be urgently in need of adjustment and control.

For too many boys and girls adolescence brings with it much needless mental and moral anguish, because of the mystery of these problems, which they try to solve by secret recourse to medical books, while hoping for honest instruction on the subject from their parents, teachers, or spiritual guides.

A surprising number of persons develop a prurient curiosity about sex which they try to satisfy by subscribing to sex and physical health magazines or by secretly ordering books which are advertised as lifting the veil of mystery on the subject. It seems incredible, but it is a fact that many young men and women enter marriage with only the most rudimentary ideas of what will happen thereafter and how they should conduct themselves as man and wife. Many married people continue to entertain strange ideas on the subject. Neither for the married nor the unmarried, is there anything particularly holy about ignorance. On the contrary, it may be moral dynamite, through the formation of distorted notions, the development of unfortunate habits, a false conception of, and nameless hunger for, forbidden pleasures, and a conscience racked with uncertainty and half guilts.

It is important, then, that the matter of sex be regarded neither as a hush-hush object of shame nor as a laughing matter and source of lubricous thrills, but as it really is in the plan of God — serious, sensible, good, and holy.

Not only has the division of sexes been ordained by the Creator as the means of continuing human life on the earth, but the union of man and wife for the purpose of begetting children has been singled out for special blessing. As leading up to marriage, love in courtship should be regarded as a beautiful thing. Within marriage, after the vows of possession and exchange have been made, the complete union of bodies follows as the natural expression of a great mutual confidence and love, under the impulse of the natural laws of God and with His divine aid and approval. Marriage, which is a natural contract in itself, was raised to the status of a sacrament by Christ.

If this is properly understood, there is no reason why anyone should be shocked by the corporal aspects of love or be deprived of the joys of love, marriage, and parenthood by a false sense of modesty, shame, or superiority. There may be reasons why one cannot marry, because of circumstances, lack of opportunity, family obligation, poor health, the requirements of a career, or dedication to a life of religious celibacy. Under various conditions, there may be ample reason for one's drawing the line on friendships this side of courtship or love of a connubial direction. But to regard human love or courtship simply as a powder keg of sin, and the full familiarity and union of marriage as unholy and revolting, is to miss the significance of life itself.

3

The expressions "a clean mind" and "purity," of course, must be realized as related to one's state of life, if they are to have any real meaning. There is such a thing as a dirty and diseased mind on the subject of sex. This is exemplified in the attitudes of those who regard the other sex simply as animals and as objects of carnal passions and whose sense of humor is stirred only by what is called the "dirty joke." But the matter extends far beyond this scope. It enters the realm of rights, of justice, and of obligations. The unmarried person is limited in rights. The married person is restricted by the claims of justice. A person who has undertaken the vows of religion or who is otherwise bound to complete continence or chastity has certain obligations. These various limitations, rights, and duties also set up certain danger zones and signals, each in its own category.

For some people, the preservation of a clean mind and ethical standards involves practically no problem at all; for others, it means a constant struggle. Undoubtedly, the physical constitution of the individual has much to do with the character of the activity of the mind. It seems clear that certain glandular movements have a powerful influence upon the imagination. During the periods of menstruation in women and seminal accumulation in men, the nervous system is likely to be agitated or depressed, and the imagination is stirred with exciting images, which are called "bad thoughts." Some persons of the highest ideals and most blameless lives are tormented by this kind of activity, at the most unusual times, even on their knees at prayer.

As a general rule, a person who is trying to lead a clean life need not be concerned with these temptations. Such thoughts and images are not "bad" in themselves, since they arise from a subconscious or physical impulse. They assume an immoral character only when they are deliberately detained and encouraged for the purpose of giving pleasure. Sometimes the trouble is due to insufficient exercise in the fresh air, to general inactivity, or to a failure to develop interests which are sufficiently vigorous to keep the mind active and to drive out distorted images. The practice of prayer, turning the mind into other fields, and directing one's activities into something external are recommended as usually effective for dealing with this problem. In extreme cases there may be a functional or organic disorder, which indicates the need of medical treatment.

One cannot excuse himself from such disturbances, however, if he or she stimulates the cause. The reading of lewd and suggestive literature, listening to and retelling smutty stories, contemplating pictures which stimulate sexual desires, frequenting sexy shows and exhibitions — these practices can have only the effect of producing reflexes and later images of a sensual character, from which the guilty person cannot well exonerate himself. Some people eat, sleep, and drink sex; and they serve as a contamination of the society in which they move. Dirty minds are suspicious of everyone else. They are quick to see evil where none has been committed or intended; and they often impute their own evil deeds to others. The healthy mind will avoid this atmosphere as it would a plague.

Because ethical standards and conceptions differ so widely, however, the problem of adjustment to the psychological problems of sex is not always easy. Some persons are reared in a completely puritanical atmosphere and acquire the idea that sex is a bad and sordid thing to deal with. As children, they were led to believe that babies are delivered by a mysterious bird called the stork or produced from the suitcase of the doctor. Then, when the facts of the matter finally dawn on them, they are shocked.

Some people never recover from that shock. They never learn to distinguish a natural concern or legitimate interest from a brooding on sexual matters for moronic pleasure. Hence they regard themselves as guilty of bad thoughts every time the subject of sex comes up.

Others are reared in circumstances of vulgarity, neglect, and low standards. For them there are no inhibitions. Sensuality seems to be natural; and they regard those who maintain a sense of moral responsibility or a code of honor as lacking in sanity and good red blood.

How to modify these views, bringing the one into line with reality and the other to a comprehension of what is decent, moral, and considerate, is often a serious problem in mental health. The matter of personal adjustment may become acute during the period of courtship. When two persons of widely different standards enter marriage, without having reached a satisfactory meeting of minds, their troubles begin. Many divorces in the mad society in which we live can be traced to an irreconcilable divergency in this important field of human relations. Mutual attraction and pledges of love soon grow stale when people cannot agree on the fundamental principles of the sexual union for which marriage was first designed.

4

Under these circumstances, the development of a clean mind must begin with the establishment of a code of ethics. We cannot speak of self-discipline and control unless there is some standard or norm by which right is distinguished from wrong. We cannot exercise caution unless danger is recognized in its relationship to some standard of conduct which must be preserved. We cannot enjoy the mental health that comes from a clean mind unless we are willing to recognize dirt as such, no matter what its form, and to sweep it out of our lives.

The same principles apply to discipline of the emotional life. We all find ourselves attracted to persons of the opposite sex. There is certainly no evil in this. Some of the grandest friendships and associations have existed between men and women, whose qualities and abilities have complemented each other in the performance of useful and noble tasks, quite apart from any contemplation of marriage or any yielding to carnal desires. Many of the saints have thus been associated in the foundation of religious orders. Many good women were associated in the life of Christ Himself, and remained with Him up to His death. In the business of the modern world, it would be impossible for most organized and productive activities to continue without this association, co-operation, and even inspiration. The fact that small and evil minds take a pharisaical scandal from this and impute evil motives and immoral relationships is no reason why serious people should be frightened or accuse themselves of wrongdoing.

What is necessary, however, is an alertness to the ever present danger of confusing friendship with emotional interest, of letting business fade out into an informal atmosphere of personal fascination, of taking advantage of a social situation to start a clandestine courtship — when such developments cannot be reconciled with existing obligations. The casual freedom and social ease of men and women today, in offices, clubs, organizations, and homes is a wonderful thing and a sign of a great civilization. Unfortunately, it is also a dangerous thing, of which too many people take unfair advantage. Loneliness and attraction have broken too many homes and brought the marriage contract and the perpetuity of the marital bond to a very low estate. The harsh words "fornication" and "adultery," which once designated serious moral lapses and merited severe social penalties, have fallen into disrepute in many circles of polite society, for the reason that what they designate has come to be regarded in these groups as normal and justifiable.

Whether from yielding to flattery, desiring to recover one's faded youth, or struggling against the complacency of established society, men, who have led exemplary married lives and reared splendid families with a faithful and loving wife, sometimes face the problem of infatuation for a young and attractive woman; and in this strange fascination, they appear to lose all control of their judgment and free will. Lusty passion and the temporary feeling of being a spring colt again, however, cannot justify the continuance of such an adventure, nor save it from disaster. Under these circumstances, the greatest personal vigilance must be exercised, and one must be willing to accept the protective conspiracy of one's friends, to solve a compromising and difficult problem.

From a sexual standpoint, personal temperaments differ greatly. Some people are highly sexed, in imagination or physical impulse. Those of this temperament are affectionate and demonstrative, as a rule, often enthusiastic in nature and artistic in appreciation. Others are of more serene disposition, hardly aware of their sexual life, and not particularly moved or disturbed by it. For them sex presents no special problems, matters of special interest, or persuasive motives of action. Still others are of frigid nature, and for them sex is a kind of necessary evil. They may appreciate the company of the opposite sex, for various reasons; but the conception of sexual union or even of affectionate embrace is distasteful and often revolting to them.

In many instances, persons who shrink in embarrassment or fear from the opposite sex are secretly highly sexed themselves. Men of this type, in particular, think of women in highly disturbing, lurid, and distorted sexual patterns. Usually introverts by nature, they may tend toward a secret sex life with themselves, by developing the habit of masturbation and trying to solve the riddle of sex by reading exotic or semiscientific literature on the subject. Men and women of this temperament find it difficult to dance or to be in the close company of the other sex, without experiencing physical tensions and disturbances of a sexual nature. Occasionally, they break out in some moronic demonstration or perversion.

Persons of this temperament need help and should not hesitate to ask for it from those who possess social poise and are willing to be helpful. Young men and women, whether bashful or not, should learn to dance and to feel comfortable in mixed groups. Living in a paper-doll world of "pin-up" pictures and retreating from the reality and the facts of life, through a highly colored imagination, work havoc to one's mental health. Persons who are afflicted with such tendencies should make a special effort to lead a normal social existence, to overcome their embarrassment, and broaden their outlook on life. Continued determination and effort are bound to succeed.

Note may be made also of another distinct type, the person who is attracted sexually to his or her own sex, the homosexual. This tendency may be psychological or temperamental, or it may be the result of a physical tendency. In some instances it is due to glandular and organic abnormalities. There are, moreover, wide variations in temperament within this type, ranging from the effeminate man to the manly woman. These characteristics are not *necessarily* a matter of sexual or moral concern, but they may create social problems for the individual to cope with.

Proper and effective treatment of this problem differs with the specific nature of the case, and is beyond the scope of this work. The question of personality traits and mannerisms out of harmony with one's sex should be submitted, if they are a cause of embarrassment, to a prudent counselor or spiritual guide capable of offering sympathetic, constructive criticism and positive assistance.

The idea that homosexual tendencies and perversions are always physical in character is not true. Habits of sexual perversion may originate in various backgrounds of confusion, suppression, or unfortunate experience. Nor is there any validity in the conception that persons with this tendency cannot help themselves. The solving of this problem is partly spiritual, and it may also call for treatment by a competent and ethical psychiatrist. What is required toward stabilization of character and ethical living, in all cases, is a recognition of the problem, a correct analysis of the backgrounds or causes of the problem, and a determined effort at self-discipline and control.

This is true in practically all tendencies to sexual perversion. There are many instances of persons excellent in other respects who have lapsed or have a tendency to lapse into sexual abnormalities. Unless one is mentally defective, however, there is no reason why such tendencies cannot be corrected by proper instruction, vigilance, useful activity, and prayer.

In very rare cases, known as hermaphroditism, the individual may be physically abnormal, possessing rudimentary organs of both sexes. There are cases on record in which the sex of an individual has gradually been modified and even changed by medical treatment, surgical operation, and the processes of nature. Such exceptional cases call for expert consideration in the field of abnormal physiology and psychology. The problems of mental health which may be involved in such abnormality are usually quite distinct from those of the person who is physiologically normal.

5

Some psychologists and not a few writers have endeavored to portray sex, in its various manifestations, as an irresistible force. When it strikes, there is no holding back. Even the perversions of sex, they regard as something for which a person is not responsible. Others are of the opinion that, while one may be free and responsible for one's acts, love has a way of purifying everything. These views come as an easy and attractive rationalization to everyone faced with a serious temptation to overstep the bounds of social ethics and sexual propriety in extramarital love. Both theories, separately or in combination, pave the way for a complete junking of morals in courtship and for the elimination of law or fair play in marriage. According to these notions, which are widely prevalent in this mad world, when lust or love strike, there is nothing to do but surrender. If society, church, state, family, or friends disapprove, the problem may be complicated; but we must not be swerved, it is said, from following the clear call of sexual impulse and of emotional love, no matter where it may lead.

Like most false theories which have a wide appeal, these have an element of truth which cannot be ignored. Sexual excitement, having gained a certain momentum, is very difficult to stop, and, after a certain point, moves on almost irresistibly to completion, as if by mechanical action. Similarly, emotional love, allowed to grow to a point of possessiveness, takes command and makes it extremely difficult for either the mind or the will to function freely. The impulses and emotions do not possess in themselves any power of judgment or freedom. They are like the fire which is started from a match thrown carelessly in the wastebasket. Unless quenched in the beginning, this may increase in intensity until the blaze is beyond control. Beyond a certain point, sexual excitement no longer obeys the will. If allowed to develop, emotional love defies the conventions, and reduces all ethical considerations to a vanishing point. Illicit passion acts in just the same way as honest love, so that those who are embroiled in a divorce scandal may find themselves pleading all kinds of plausible reasons for a bad case.

In the action of sexual impulse and the development of emotional love, one must keep in mind the fact that we have been entrusted with a force which may be as gentle as a lamb or as explosive as an atom bomb. It may be beautiful to behold or it may be something hideous. To a large extent, the individual is responsible before God and men for the guardianship and conduct of this impulse and emotion.

A common error, shared by puritans and libertines alike, although for different reasons, is that the whole question of sex will take care of itself if left alone. Unfortunately the matter is not this simple. Human nature and temperament need vigilance and control, both personal and social, in the operation and behavior of this great instinct. For persons who must live in the world, and even for those who embrace the religious life with a vow of perpetual chastity, a sound, objective view of the sexual factor in human personality is essential, both for personal mental health and guidance and for the guidance of others, when this is indicated.

For the irrational animals, sexual activity is governed entirely by instinct, although, as in the case of certain birds and animals, the mating process is rather involved and a family unit is maintained, at least on a temporary basis. Even where sexual violence is involved, the animals are not to be held responsible for their acts, since they respond solely to the physical laws of their natures and do not possess freedom of will or choice.

This is not true of human nature. Here the problem is complicated by the fact that the sexual impulse is largely controllable by a rational mind and a free will. The question of sex does not take care of itself, nor does free rein to one's temperament answer the question. Morality is involved because of personal responsibility for the use of the faculties with which nature has endowed us. There is a right use and a wrong use. The sexual faculties are designed to serve certain natural ends. To contrive or to allow their use simply for the nervous excitement or pleasure they give, while deliberately preventing the fulfillment of their natural function, or to use them for any perverted purpose, is unnatural and immoral.

To bring these faculties under control and retain mastery over them for moral and orderly living, the imagination, the mind, and the will must all work together as a team, to hold the emotions in check and to make the body behave. What needs to be watched is a tendency toward deliberate stimulation of the imagination, the retention and entertainment of dirty thoughts and immoral purposes in the mind, and the planning or encouragement of situations and acts which cannot be justified.

The answer to this challenge is self-discipline and the practice of self-control from the beginning. Inasmuch as sexual impulses and emotions strongly affect the nervous system and the imagination, it is obvious that this control must begin with a discipline of the external senses and of the imagination itself. From this point, the emotions must be subjected to critical examination, to determine whether they are licit or not, and be trimmed or suppressed accordingly. As the result of failure to exercise self-discipline and control, we can point to numerous divorces and broken homes, abandonment of religious faith, immorality before marriage, irresponsible use of marital rights, a wide breakdown in ethical proprieties, confusion, disillusion-

ment, and tragedy. Once we surrender our most precious
human possessions — the intelligence of the mind, the integrity
and freedom of the will — we fall to depths far lower than the
animals. Any appraisal of pleasure which is predicated on the
abandonment of moral standards and personal responsibility
must be prepared for unhappy consequences.

What may be proper for the birds and the bees in their
annual cycle of mating, nesting, and dispatch at the end of
the season will not do for men and women. Mental health as
related to one's sexual life — clear thinking, a clean imagination, and a determination to live up to good moral principles
— is an instrument of the greatest value. Its care will save one
from many a mistake, and may well be the key to a life of happiness and contentment.

6

The maintenance of a clean mind, as already indicated,
requires, not only good basic principles, but also a constant
vigilance over one's activities. In these times, moreover, there
is need for a sensible but firm and high conception of decency
and propriety on a social level.

Within recent years, there has been a notable increase of
literature, ranging from obscene illustrated magazines of a low
character, to novels by so-called best writers dealing with lurid
sexual situations and expounding personal and social doctrines
in sex, courtship, marriage, and divorce at complete variance
with Christian morality. On the stage, the claims of realism
and entertainment have been perverted to portray a cynical and
often brutal view of sex. While the Legion of Decency and
responsible motion picture producers have done much to maintain vigilance against immorality on the screen, there is a constant effort on the part of unscrupulous elements to break down
all standards, in the name of "art" and the "facts of life."

Arguments against censorship usually boil down to the principles that "to the pure all things are pure" and that mature people
can read anything and look at anything and make up their own

minds with confidence. Both of these principles are false. A pure mind cannot purify what is impure or make right what is wrong. It can, however, become the depositary of mental sludge. There is no satisfactory protection of the human imagination, mind, or body against certain sexual representations, except that of avoidance. The same is true, at least as a general rule, against obscenity in literature.

It is sometimes alleged that, while children and youth should be protected, adults may freely indulge without harm in what is called sexual "sophistication." The fact is, however, that the human mind and physical system of the adult remain susceptible to evil influences, and the moral law applies to adults as well as to children. It is true that adults should not be limited in their appreciation of art and literature to what is accommodated properly to the mind of a child or adolescent. But there is a radical difference between what is suitable for adults and what is suitable for no one.

These observations are applicable also to the communication of doctrines which are incompatible with sound morality and the truly Christian way of life. In subtle ways, not only individual lives are swerved from the path of virtue and duty, but nations are led to corruption and decay. Cleanness of mind calls for a sense of social responsibility; and mature people will not be misled by the sweet voices of false prophets.

A clean people are a strong people. Like the meek, they shall possess the land. And in the words of Christ, "Blessed are the clean of heart: for they shall see God."[1]

---

[1] Mt. 5:8.

CHAPTER X

The Endurance of Suffering

I

ONE of the great mysteries in life is the existence of suffering, physical and mental. For the reason, perhaps, that some form of suffering is inflicted by human justice as a penalty for misconduct, and the threat of suffering is held out as punishment for sin in the next life, many persons have the idea that somewhere along the line the sufferer has done wrong and is paying his debt. What makes suffering so hard to accept, in this theory, is the unevenness of its distribution. The connection between health and virtue on the one hand, and misfortune and personal misdeeds, on the other, is not always apparent or logical.

Some people walk through life with roses all the way, or so it seems. Others have to pluck the thorns. Poor health, a succession of accidents, and tragedy of one kind or the other seems to be their regular lot.

I recall, as a youngster, playing ball with another boy who had the reputation of being a target for misfortune. We were warned to be very careful when playing with him, so as not to invite further disaster. During the second inning of the game, he walked too close to the batter and was hit in the head. A short time later, as he was recovering from a sickness, he happened to pick up a dynamite cap. This stirred his curiosity. As a result of his probing, he lost two fingers in the explosion.

Some persons manage to avoid sickness and serious trouble for a long time and come to regard themselves as exempt from the ills that beset the rest of mankind. When the lightning strikes, they are not only surprised but often indignant that they should be singled out for such treatment.

The fact is there is very little in this life that is perfect. The human body is a wonderful thing, but like the most carefully built piece of machinery, it can break down or wear out. We may plan our lives to the last detail, only to be frustrated by the stupidity or ill will of others, or by some sport of nature which we had not thought of or which is beyond our control.

Suffering or pain is part of this imperfection. But it is also part of an elaborate system of signals and warnings provided by nature to let us know that something is in dangerous condition or has already gone wrong. Physical sickness and pains are a message from the senses, through the nervous system, to the brain, that an injury has taken place. Without this information we might not be able to take corrective measures and profit by the experience. A stomach-ache indicates that we have eaten too much or have taken something poisonous or that the organ itself is in need of repair. A sensation of pain is enough to inform us that an object is too hot to be touched with safety. A friend of mine burned his hand severely while holding a cigar, for the reason that the nerves in his fingers had been cut and he could not feel the burning end of the cigar pressed against the flesh. Without the terrible pain of appendicitis as a warning, a ruptured appendix would soon develop into peritonitis. After peritonitis has become general, there is no pain; there is also little hope for recovery. As the result of a permanent injury, suffering may be prolonged and will continue as long as the nervous system is functioning normally. These facts, of course, are well known, but it is important to keep them in mind when dealing with the meaning and usefulness of pain.

Mental suffering, apart from physical pain and without any necessary relationship to insanity or cerebral disorder, is also a perfectly natural reaction. It likewise may be the warning or signal that something has gone wrong in one's personal affairs, or in one's relationships with others or with God, which should be corrected if possible. There is considerable pain involved in the realization that one has bungled a golden opportunity. Disappointment and discouragement can make people mentally ill. Strained relationships with family and friends or with superiors, or the weight of a responsibility for which one feels unequal, may not only produce a sensation of mental nausea, but react in a similar fashion on the body, to affect one's digestive processes and upset the nervous system. The burden of a guilty conscience and the awareness of need for reconciliation with almighty God can weigh on one's mind night and day, as a genuine torture, right to the deathbed. The pangs of unrequited love, and the grief of being subjected to ingratitude and scandal are indeed heavy crosses to bear. The sorrow of seeing loved ones in suffering and being taken by death is shared by all and is sometimes a shock, from which people never fully recover.

2

There is an old saying to the effect that if one cannot do what he likes to do, he will end up by liking what he has to do. This is sound philosophy so far as suffering is concerned. No one likes to suffer, but most of us must endure it. The problem is one of acceptance and reconciliation. In some instances, we are inclined to view the matter very much like the mischievous boy who has been summoned by his father for the application of a hickory stick or similar sturdy instrument on his nether regions. There is nothing to do but to accept the ordeal and get it over with. In other instances, it may require a continuous resignation and adjustment. A person with heart trouble or arthritis must face the unpleasant situation and learn to live with it. It is remarkable what we can put up with when we have to.

There are other cases when suffering may be a blessing in disguise. Many an irresponsible life has been made over into something admirable because of the shock of a painful experience. Many a splendid character has been forged on the anvil of suffering. Many a saint has been drawn to God by turning his or her suffering into an act of love. Christ has pointed out the way, in His words, "If any man will come after Me, let him deny himself and take up his cross and follow Me."[1]

Many people regard any form of pain or suffering as an experience to be avoided at all costs. Some are distressed even by reference to it. I have known persons to go blocks out of their way to avoid the sight of a funeral procession. Many people refuse to permit any medical examination, for fear that something wrong may be discovered. Some women so dread the thought of pain in childbirth that they refuse to have children. Some persons are supersensitive on the subject of their health. The first cough sends them to bed. It is said that men are more apprehensive of illness than women, more inclined to regard their sickness or pain as the beginning of the end. Women, as a rule, can tolerate suffering better, even though they may be more demanding under the strain.

Much suffering is more imaginary than real. Children suffer and cry if they are not given money for candy or permission to go to the motion pictures with the neighborhood children. Spoiled youth suffer from the boredom of an easy existence and complain if their free time is curtailed by the assignment of

---

[1] Mt. 16:24.

special tasks. Most of us suffer every morning when the alarm clock sounds to remind us that we must arise and go to work. Doctor's offices are filled with people who have imaginary ailments that are best treated by pink sugar pills and a sympathetic bedside manner. Some people develop strange symptoms and disabilities whenever they are called upon to assume responsibilities they would like to avoid. And undoubtedly many people remain healthy, survive their aches and pains, overcome their griefs and disappointments, and live to reach success, happiness, and old age, for the simple reason that they cannot afford to get sick and do not have the time to nurse and encourage their troubles.

Certain types of suffering are self-inflicted. Many a problem arises from stupidity, or from lack of instruction or experience. There are persons who insist upon doing things "the hard way," when new and improved methods and safeguards are easily available. Stinginess and laziness account for much suffering. Many persons suffer from the heat or the cold because they are unwilling to spend money or effort to dress properly and to provide their homes or offices with the necessary fuel and insulation. Suffering, self-inflicted, is sometimes used as a dramatic way of calling attention to oneself or to a cause. The famous Indian leader Mahatma Gandhi resorted to hunger strikes on several occasions to emphasize a political principle or to strengthen popular resistance. Men have died because of self-imposed rigors for similar motives. Whether from stubbornness or a desire to attract attention, many persons in daily life inflict injuries upon themselves and make themselves miserable until they have gained their objective or their case seems hopeless.

Self-inflicted suffering is exemplified also in various forms of self-denial and self-discipline. Dieting to reduce one's weight or to safeguard a faulty metabolism, as in the case of diabetes, may be indicated by physician's orders and involve considerable anguish, particularly for those who love rich eating. With the purpose of improving their figures, women sometimes undertake reducing diets and medicines, even without medical advice, and with more zeal than prudence. There are cases on record in which permanent injury to health and even death have resulted from such procedure.

Fasting and abstinence have been prescribed from motives of religious observance, as an evidence of religious self-sacrifice and in penance for sin. Many religious persons practice their own private forms of self-denial, self-sacrifice, and penance, with a spiritual motive. This practice, it may be noted, has ample approval and even command in Holy Scripture. Christ repeatedly uttered the injunction, "Unless you shall do penance, you shall all likewise perish."[2]

In ancient times, through the Middle Ages, and to some extent even today religious zeal and penance for sins have stimulated some to severe corporal restrictions and punishment, such as self-lashing, the use of hair shirts, chains, sackcloth, and ashes. In India today, a class of religious devotees, known as *fakirs*, resort to weird practices such as sitting on nails, starving themselves, burial alive, and the like.

While it is not possible to read into all the motives of men or to make rules from the practices of extraordinary individuals, one may venture the opinion that voluntary penance and self-denial serve a useful purpose only to the extent that they are used in moderation and do not injure one's health. The purity of one's spiritual motives may also be judged by whether the penance is done quietly as a personal offering to God or whether it is done as a matter of public display and comment. One should also ask himself whether such penance and self-denial are supplementing positive virtue and the fulfillment of one's daily duties, or are falsely substituting for them or even going contrary to common sense and good living.

Some forms of physical pain and mental anguish are necessary to prevent or heal others. It may be necessary to apply a

[2] Lk. 13:3.

painful antiseptic or to cauterize a wound to prevent infection and blood poisoning. A major operation may be necessary to remove a defective organism or malignant growth. We are all required to say *no* to forbidden objects we should very much like to possess and to inadvisable actions we should like to perform; and we are frequently called upon to say *yes* to things that displease and hurt us. The other alternative is to pay the penalty. Hospitals, cemeteries, and jails are full of people who failed to govern their impulses in accordance with good reason. And the world is full of the failures and tragedies of those who have taken what appeared to be the easiest way out of difficult situations.

All of this indicates the importance of self-discipline, both as a watchdog against those indiscretions which are responsible for much of our sufferings and as a strong arm to sustain us when we have been actually overtaken by pain or grief. A strong sense of principle, the application of will power on behalf of what we believe to be right, and a willingness to endure suffering in a cheerful spirit — these are the marks of a sterling character, to which we should all aspire. We must all live with suffering. It is the way we cope with it that counts.

An acquaintance of mine, whose theological convictions are not entirely clear to me, offers this bit of homely wisdom, which seems to square with good natural philosophy:

> We are born in this world
> All naked and bare.
> We go through this world
> With sorrow and care.
> When we die, we go only God knows where
> But if we are thoroughbreds here,
> We'll be thoroughbreds there.

The verse of this jingle limps somewhat, and the comparison with "thoroughbreds" may need further clarification; but the general idea is good. In final values, the important thing is how we behave under stress and strain.

3

There are a number of short cuts to relief which are available and frequently used by those who regard pain as the worst, and possibly the only, evil in life. The most familiar is the pillbox. Upon the slightest indication of a headache, many people reach for a painkiller. With the first flurry of nerves, from an argument or unpleasant experience, others begin a routine of sedatives. If natural sleep does not come soon enough to wipe the slate clean, sleeping tablets are always at hand.

There can be no doubt that these and other sedatives are helpful in relieving tension; and there is no point of enduring continued pain when simple remedies are available. There is danger, however, in the use of drugs without the direction or advice of a physician. Many minor ailments pass away by themselves. Many drugs have to be eliminated from the system after the pain has gone; and in some cases, a reliance is developed upon habit-forming drugs, which undermines self-confidence and produces stupefying aftereffects. It may be noted also that some doctors are inclined to be overindulgent in prescribing painkillers to persons of a nervous temperament, with the result that habits are formed which weaken moral fiber as well as physical resistance. It is often better to suffer a little and let nature take its course, than to develop a dependence upon sedatives which develop their own pain or tension as an aftereffect.

Refuge in drink is a form of escape taken by many persons, some for physical pain, others for mental or emotional disturbance. It is a fact that alcohol tends to dilate the blood vessels, and is sometimes indicated as a relief for high blood pressure. As a stimulant, with narcotic aftereffects, it helps to relax tense and jagged nerves and may reduce pain temporarily.

Despite the religious scruples of some people, it cannot be demonstrated that there is anything evil in alcoholic beverages as such. The ancient observance of the Jewish Passover involved the use of wine, and it was this that Christ took and shared with His Apostles at the Last Supper, together with bread, when He pronounced the immortal words, "This is My body. . . . Take ye and eat. This is My blood. . . . Do ye this for a commemoration of Me."[3] His first public miracle was to convert water into wine at the marriage feast of Cana. St. Paul, who was a rigorist in many ways, prescribed a little wine for the "stomach's sake."[4] If a drink helps to calm one's nerves or to induce a brighter view on life, it may be considered one of God's good gifts, not a poisonous draft of the devil.

What is one man's meat, however, may be another man's poison; and drink is no exception. There are some people who cannot drink without going to excess. For them, one drink is enough, two are too much, and three are not half enough. It is easy to regard drink as a panacea for all ills and as an antidote to prevent many. The first sign of a cold is the signal for a little "snifter." A heavy pain calls for repeated libations. If one is feeling "low," a drink may be indicated as a morale booster. Great sorrow may be drowned out or be more easily endured with a generous dosage from the bottle. Almost any excuse becomes plausible, as the habit develops, from a drop to tone up the appetite to something by way of protection against nonexistent snake bite.

Suffering, both physical and mental, has produced more alcoholics than the records show. Arthritis, rheumatism, and nerve injuries where great pain is involved may be relieved by an occasional drink, and some physicians prescribe this with caution. But where there is a tendency to excess, to dependence upon drink, or to the growth of alcoholism, the greatest care and self-discipline must be exercised. Even greater vigilance is necessary when drink is taken to relieve the suffering of grief, of strained relations within the family, of a broken love affair,

---

[3] Mt. 26:26–29; Lk. 22:19, 20.
[4] 1 Tim. 5:28.

of disappointment in business, of maladjustment in one's work or career, of loneliness, of tedium and boredom.

Men engaged in physical labor are very susceptible to the evils of drink, particularly if their home ties are weak or unpleasant or if they have few interests to hold their attention when the working day or week is ended and the pay check is in hand. But intellectuals and others engaged in mental tasks are also subject to the weakness, when they begin to take to drink as a surcease for their woes or as a "letdown" from too much activity. Many a fine mind has been wasted away in the multiplication of many cups, beginning in the morning hours. This may not be enough to make a man actually drunk, but sufficient to keep his mind in a fuzzy condition, often producing the illusion that he is important after all. In this condition, some persons are always preparing to do something great which never gets done. Nor are women exempt from the habit. If one has plenty of time on one's hands, and one's nerves become "jumpy" or life becomes weary and confused, a simple way to remedy the situation is to drink, innocently, of course, first with one's friends and later secretly with oneself. In too many cases, this form of escape from suffering or boredom leads to personal disaster. No one can say that he is completely immune to this danger.

If pain or suffering becomes extremely acute or prolonged and appears to have no hope of relief or termination, there may be a temptation to suicide. Shock and the mental derangement, under these circumstances, can radically alter one's sense of values and even suppress a moral sense which would normally revolt against the suggestion. Within recent years, attempts have been made by certain social reformers and members of the medical profession to legalize the administration of death to persons in extreme suffering from apparently hopeless diseases, under conditions known as euthanasia. Under this proposal, hopeless cripples, the aged, and others in hopeless physical or mental condition may be put to death by painless methods, at their own request, or in some cases at the request of their relatives, or even upon certification of the state. Such practice, which is murder or suicide under another name, must be unreservedly condemned as immoral and unjustified under any circumstances. In itself, it represents an unwarranted usurpation of the right over human life which belongs to the Creator; and it can lead to horrible abuses, as it did in Germany under the Nazi regime.

For ailments of a less intense character, many people find relief in complaining or in describing their symptoms and troubles to others who are willing to listen. Misery loves company. There is comparatively little harm in this activity; but one runs the risk of developing an invalid complex, or what is sometimes call "hospitalitis." It is remarkable how soon others become tired of listening to our tales of woe or even the descriptions of our operations.

4

There are a great many forms of annoyance, discomfort, and suffering over which we have little or no control, and which we may as well make up our minds to endure cheerfully. The weather, for example, is hardly ever perfect. Most people have run the gauntlet of children's diseases, from measles to whooping cough, and now and then something more serious. Fortunate is the adult who escapes without a major illness or operation. With the approach of old age, which no one likes to think of, the body is certain to develop aches and pains; and sorrows and regrets accumulate. This is part of life, and we may as well face it.

Comparison of our sufferings with what others have to endure is sometimes a constructive way of helping us feel better about life and more grateful for the many benefits we still possess. From time to time, I remind myself of this bit of wisdom: "I felt badly because I had no shoes, until I saw a man who had no feet." No day should pass without a prayer of thanksgiving to God, who has given us so many things to be grateful for. Everyone should visit a hospital occasionally, to remind himself of the suffering, pain, and misfortune which many others must endure. One will find there much agony, but he will also find a lesson of great resignation and cheer.

We may resent the idea of having to wear glasses. Many people are blind, but find it possible to lead happy and useful lives. When I am tempted to feel sorry for myself, because of a cold or a hurt, I think of a number of friends who must go through life with crippling, painful arthritis or who are confined to a wheel chair because of polio or a physical defect from which they can never expect deliverance. These people manage to do their daily work, with a smile on their faces and an example of inspiration and encouragement for all around them. They are not looking for sympathy, and they are the first to appreciate their opportunities and to place themselves at the service of others. From these people we learn that suffering is not incompatible with happiness, which is interior and rises above the considerations of bodily pain.

When I am disappointed in not receiving some desired object or feel that my life is too confined, I can think of a number of friends and acquaintances who for years have been obliged to give up practically all social activity because of necessary attention to a child, defective in mind or body, or both. This must be a terrible disappointment, not merely in foregoing the pleasures of life but in seeing the daily frustration of one's hopes and plans for the child who can never fulfill these ambitions. But I have seldom heard any expression from them except of affection and devotion to carrying the cross which God has asked them to bear.

5

In the course of human events, suffering, although unevenly distributed, serves a number of useful purposes. For one thing, it gives us a deeper comprehension of life. We become more understanding of others, more sympathetic of their problems, and more helpful in their distress. Persons who have never known sickness or sorrow are likely to be intolerant of others who slow down or fall by the wayside. Personal experience teaches us to be patient with others as well as with ourselves. As a matter of fact, we never know what others have to put up with until we ourselves are stricken.

I happen to be one of those with a broken vertebral disk. Until the accident occurred, I had never heard of the thing or at least never averted to it. In the beginning the pain was almost unbearable, and I wondered how long I could endure it. The bottom had dropped out of my life, so it seemed. Then I learned that the experience is rather common. A number of my friends had gone through the same agony, but I did not know of it. Apparently, they must have suffered in silence. They survived, and so did I.

Suffering has the effect also of making one more reflective about matters of importance and often opens the way to good resolutions and even to a personal reformation. It has often been said that if one wishes to live a long life, he should develop heart trouble or a similar chronic ailment early in life and take good care of it. An accident or serious illness, at any time, may have the effect of sobering one to the realities of existence, of taking a more serious view of one's responsibilities, or of slowing one down to a more deliberate pace. Most people refuse to recognize that they are getting older. A little reminder in the form of a setback may serve to make them act their age, in more ways than one.

History is full of interesting cases of men and women who first found the meaning of life on a sickbed and began upon a useful career as the result of reverses. Everyone knows the story of St. Francis of Assisi, who was a gay and aimless young blade, interested principally in swaggering and brawling, until he was captured in an attack upon the neighboring town of Perugia. While he lay on the straw pallet of his cell, he began to see a spiritual light which was to transform his character and give rise to the great Franciscan Order. Nearly four centuries later, a similar experience came to Ignatius of Loyola, a battered soldier of Spain, who began to realize that life meant more than drawing blood on a battlefield. He arose from the hospital where he was confined and became the founder of the great missionary and teaching order of the Society of Jesus. Real suffering has caused many a man and woman to think. Sometimes, it takes a heavy blow to bring us to our senses.

These examples might be multiplied many times over to illustrate the point that suffering, no matter of what character, should never lead to despair. We can do much to help ourselves, even in effecting and hastening recovery and readjustment, by a mental attitude of acceptance and hope. There should be no indulgence in self-pity, no matter how strong the temptation may be, and no slipping into a mental case for others to pity. The decision, whether to make this trial a miserable episode of wasted time or an opportunity of rich experience and spiritual gain, depends upon the individual.

If one cannot find instruction in adversity, or if the outlook for recovery or improvement is dim, there is still a treasure of great value in suffering which no man should overlook or neglect. It is well to remember that the great redemptive act of Christ was His suffering and death upon the cross, to save all mankind, Jew and Gentile alike. Both the Old and the New Testament bear plentiful witness to the value of suffering, as united spiritually with the merits of the Saviour's sufferings, in penance and reparation for sin. It is part of the Christian faith, moreover, that by our prayers and sufferings we can gain spiritual benefits for others.

There is no more dramatic or convincing example of the difference between suffering which is sterile and that which is fruitful than the story of the two thieves who were crucified with Christ. One of the two blasphemed the Saviour as they cried out in agony. The other rebuked his companion and said,

"Neither dost thou fear God, seeing thou art under the same condemnation? And we indeed justly: for we receive the due reward of our deeds. But this man hath done no evil." Then he said to Jesus, "Lord, remember me when Thou shalt come into Thy Kingdom." Jesus replied, "Amen I say to thee: This day thou shalt be with Me in Paradise."[5]

---

[5] Lk. 23:40–43.

CHAPTER XI

A Saving Sense of Humor

WITHOUT a doubt, the most effective form of mental relaxation is humor. So long as one can laugh, things are not too bad. One sees the relationship between incongruous things and takes that larger view of life upon which good judgment is founded. The tension is broken. No matter how desperate a situation may appear, if one retains a saving sense of humor, something can be salvaged.

I recall a rather awkward situation in connection with a public lecture series for which I was the presiding officer. An important speaker had been billed for a particular date and had been widely announced, when on the morning of the great day I received a telephone call from his manager in New York.

"I have some rather bad news for you," he began. "Mr. X has been taken down with a bad case of virus influenza and will be unable to keep his engagement for your audience this evening."

Stunned by this sudden revelation, all I could manage to say was, "Is that so?" There was a pause.

After a half minute of silence, the man at the other end of the telephone asked, "What is the matter? Aren't you feeling well?"

"Yes," I stammered. "I feel as well as the circumstances permit. Why do you ask?"

"Why?" he replied. "With news of this kind, most people would become furious."

"Well," said I, recovering from the shock, "if you will please tell me what good it would do for me to become furious, I shall promptly become furious."

That broke the ice. The gentleman at the other end began to laugh. The humor of the unhappy situation struck me; and within an hour we had arranged for a substitute speaker, who incidentally pleased our audience immensely.

The marvelous quality of humor is that its effect is automatic and instantaneous. The great Roman orator Cicero advised public speakers to begin by rendering their audiences "well disposed, attentive, and willing to learn." The easiest and surest way, generally used by speakers and toastmasters, to render an audience well disposed is to begin by telling a witty story. A helpful device in stirring an audience from its tendency to go to sleep or in breaking the tension in the course of an address is to insert a humorous episode at a strategic place. A good laugh has a refreshing effect and makes people willing to devote their attention again to the weightier matters at hand.

It has always been a matter of interest for me to observe the reaction of motion picture audiences. Very often the principal feature is followed by a comical cartoon of the kind with which most people have become acquainted, such as Mickey Mouse, Donald Duck, Popeye the Sailor, and other international characters of the same category. After the heavy emotional pressure and frequently depressing effect of the main drama, the audience breathes a vast sigh of relief and sometimes shrieks with delight as soon as the comedy is announced on the screen.

The employment of a humorous anecdote is often used to lighten the emotional atmosphere in real life. When a meeting or discussion or argument begins to enter a dangerous phase and teeth are put on edge, a touch of humor may sweeten sour dispositions, soften bristling tempers, and save the day. An acquaintance of mine, whose occupation frequently puts him in the midst of contentious situations, is famous for dodging apparently head-on collisions, by remarking at the strategic moment, "You know, this reminds me of a story —" By the time he has come to the "punch line" of his story, the contenders are in a better mood in which to come back to the problem.

In fact, the possession of a small collection of humorous anecdotes, drawn from real life or culled from others and written down in one's own little black book for use at an appropriate time, is an excellent investment, sometimes worth more than gold. And the ability to laugh at the jokes of others, even though we may have heard them many times before, pays rich dividends in convincing others that, after all, we are human beings.

A sense of humor and dependence upon it in the more difficult moments of life is by no means inconsistent with seriousness of purpose, nor is it simply an escape from the harsh realities of life. After discoursing on the importance of gravity in looking at the problems of existence, Phillips Brooks remarks, "The gravity of which I speak is not inconsistent with the keenest perception of the ludicrous side of things. It is more than consistent with — it is even necessary to — humor. Humor involves the perception of the true proportions of life. . . . It has softened the bitterness of controversy a thousand times. You cannot encourage it too much. You cannot grow too familiar with the books of all ages which have in them the truest humor, for the truest humor is the bloom of the highest life. Read George Eliot and Thackeray, and, above all, Shakespeare. They will help you to keep from extravagances without fading into insipidity. They will preserve your gravity while they save you from pompous solemnity."[1]

---

[1] Phillips Brooks, *Lectures on Preaching* (New York: E. P. Dutton Co., 1878), pp. 56, 57.

With some persons, a sense of humor is native, spontaneous, and naturally brilliant. It shows itself as the evidence of a delightful personality, and functions without effort even under dismal and trying circumstances. As Addison wrote of Thomas More, describing him in the last days preceding his execution: "That innocent mirth which had been so conspicuous in his life, did not forsake him to the last . . . his death was a piece of his life. There was nothing in it new, forced or affected. He did not look upon the severing of his head from his body as a circumstance that ought to produce any change in the disposition of his mind."[2]

With others, humor comes only after special effort and by special concession, as it were, to the whims of frivolous and empty-headed people. In particular, creative humor which arises from the natural, ordinary situations of daily life calls for special alertness and sensitivity to human nature and its amiable weaknesses and inconsistencies.

I recall a hot Saturday afternoon in late August many years ago, when I decided to inform my mother that I felt a call to the priesthood. She had just finished cleaning the linoleum floor in the kitchen and was baking bread in the coal-burning Majestic range. My baby nephew was playing on the floor. Meanwhile, she listened patiently and sympathetically as I discoursed on the spiritual life and the lofty motives which I believed were urging me on to this noble vocation. Suddenly, the telephone rang in the next room. The bread began to burn, and smoke poured out of the oven. The baby on the floor performed one of those involuntary functions characteristic of the age of "three-quartered pants" and began to cry.

Half in desperation but with a twinkle of humorous comprehension in her eye, my mother looked at me and said: "James, I think you have chosen the better part."

Another person might have resorted to violence. But I shall

---

[2] *Spectator*, No. 349.

never forget that masterful bit of maternal humor. Even under circumstances which might provoke a feeling of frustration and anger, the person of humorous insight retains self-mastery and derives a sense of fun in the annoyances and incongruities of life.

A sense of humor is something which should be cultivated both as a matter of policy and in a practice of mental hygiene. One can determine to look for the laughable side of situations, as well as for their grim and dismal aspects. We must learn to make a distinction between what is comical and what is merely crude, what is fun and legitimate sport and what is cruelty and perilous adventure. Within recent years, there has been a decided trend among cartoonists specializing in so-called "comic" strips to get away from the fun of normal life and to depict sordid crime or endless adventures of a fantastic type. With the advent of cowboy adventures on television and radio, children are reared almost from infancy on a recreational diet of violence and murder. Even death has become stereotyped as the product of some kind of gun-play, so that the first question of the small boy upon hearing of the death of a friend, "Who killed him?" seems a normal reaction.

From this narrow and bitter, artificially exciting view of life, the mind aspiring for health must rise to see the fullness of human nature and pause to enjoy some of its incongruities and inconsistencies, its merriment, and even its nonsense. There is wisdom in laughter as well as in tears. A sense of humor can save many a tear and heal many a heartache and headache.

2

What is wit and what is humor, what is funny and what is not are matters that depend much upon age, nation, temperament, and point of view. According to *Crabb's English Synonymes*, which, despite its title, is a most informative and entertaining volume, "*Humor* literally signifies moisture of fluid, in which sense it is used for the fluids of the human body; and as far as these *humors* or their particular state is connected with, or has its influence on, the animal spirits and the moral feelings, so far is *humor* applicable to moral agents." Humor, it is indicated, is variable, so that one can be in good humor one moment or in a bad one at another time. Taking words in their basic meaning, Crabb indicates that humor differs from temper, as a variable element in one's personality differs from what is habitual or regularly characteristic of one's normal disposition. He attempts to make a further distinction between humor and mood, attributing the former to "the physical state of the body, and the latter to the moral frame of the mind."[3]

Turning to the subject of wit, the same author notes that, according to its original meaning, the word signifies *wisdom,* "but it has so extended its meaning so to signify that faculty of the mind by which knowledge of truth is perceived, and in a more limited sense the faculty of discovering the agreements or disagreements of different ideas. . . . Reflection and experience supply us with wisdom; study and labor supply us with learning; but *wit* seizes with an eagle eye that which escapes the notice of the deep thinker and elicits truths which are in vain sought for with any severe effort." *Humor,* he adds, is a species of wit which flows out of the *humor* of a person. *Wit,* as distinguished from *humor,* may consist of a single brilliant thought; but humor runs in a vein; it is not a striking but an equable and pleasing flow of *wit.*[4]

Prescinding from the theory to which Crabb alludes, namely, that humor is connected with a fluid in the body, there is much truth in his conception of the word as a state of feeling with a physical foundation, and in his joining wit to humor as a keen faculty of relating apparently unrelated ideas, the former in a flash of insight, and humor in a sustained attitude of sympathetic alertness and pleasure. A person who is sick or in a sour mood

---

[3] George Crabb, *loc. cit.* (New York: Harper and Brothers, 1917), pp. 424–425.

[4] *Loc. cit.,* p. 711.

is not physically or mentally disposed to good humor in general. Nor is he disposed to the entertainment of what we call, perhaps rather loosely, a "sense of humor." On the other hand, a person of dull comprehension is likely to be limited, in his appreciation of wit or comical situations, to the more elemental and obvious forms of incongruity that form the basis of humorous appreciation. In irrational animals, there may be a playful disposition, as is evident in puppies, and a tendency to mischief, which may be laughable in itself. But no irrational animal ever really laughs, for the simple reason that genuine laughter signifies a grasp of the relationship or disrelationship of ideas.

A circus clown is funny for the reason that his distorted features and exaggerated costumes strain at the limits of reality, while his silly antics are reminiscent of the frustrations which everyone faces in daily life. Slapstick comedy is easy to grasp, with its broad situations of mistaken identity and its total disregard for dignity, as in the throwing of pies and falling into water.

These things are funny when they happen to others, for the incongruity is immediately evident to the side-line observer who himself suffers no pain. But in real life, particularly when we ourselves are the victims of such minor disasters, they are not likely to appear so comical. Only in retrospect, when the pain has passed and we can view our embarrassment in clearer relationship to the circumstances, can we laugh at ourselves and dismiss the event as a humorous experience.

The anecdote with its "punch line," regularly used by after-dinner speakers and toastmasters, is one of the most characteristic forms of American wit, so much so that books are compiled for the ready use of amateur orators on all occasions. With the British, an elaborate form of circumlocution, to describe something rather insignificant or familiar, with words and definitions out of all relation to its importance, often serves the same purpose. The French are particularly keen in detecting human frailties and local inconsistencies and in relating them, not only in mimicry but also in song. German humor often takes lusty forms, in exaggeration and grotesque conceptions of actions and objects. Needless to say, these and other forms of wit and humor run the gamut from crassness and crudity to great refinement. What may seem uproariously funny to one person may be nauseating and offensive to another. What strikes one person as rich humor may go completely "over the head" of another. Children often wonder why their elders laugh at a particular story or description.

Wit and humor take a wide variety of types, which may be more or less accurately classified and recognized in operation. The joke is an endeavor to stimulate good humor in others or an indulgence of one's own good spirits. It may take the form of making light of serious things or assuming a heavy attitude toward inconsequential matters, in a spirit of fun; or it may take the form of the so-called funny story. On the other hand, there are bitter and biting forms of wit, such as the jest, which is directed at a particular person or object to make it laughable or ridiculous. Satire openly makes fun of an object. Irony is an indirect form of ridicule or derision, which condemns someone or something in terms which, if taken literally, would seem to praise it. The man who sees his wife with her face in a mud pack is indulging in irony when he says, "How beautiful you look today, my dear." Sarcasm is a form of wit which holds up a person or object to ridicule, to give vent to personal resentment, and to humiliate the other. Irony can be used either good-humoredly or to express indignation. Sarcasm always has the calculated effect of hurting others.

3

From these observations, it is clear that not all forms of wit and humor serve the purposes of mental health. The ability to jest about people and things must be closely guarded lest it lead to the ridicule of sacred things or encourage a type of cynicism which is bitter and corrosive in nature. In this category may be mentioned that kind of smutty wit and dirty joke which, although clever, takes a low and cynical view of sex, of love, of marriage, and of motherhood. When this kind of wit takes possession of the mind, clean humor begins to appear insipid and silly. The mind itself becomes stimulated, as with a poisonous drug, to a prurient interest and view of the physiology of sex; and the imagination concocts distorted situations which can lead to considerable mischief.

Some people acquire a reputation for having a repertory of dirty stories and of being able, by a quick twist of wit, to turn almost any situation into a spicy and comical resemblance to the private aspects of sex. The immediate response to their endeavors may be a laugh; but such a talent has serious drawbacks. The prudent person will think twice before cultivating this form of wit or of allowing his mind to become a depository for the sensual offscourings of others.

Some forms of wit tend to develop a crabbed mentality and to irritate others rather than to render them well disposed. Such is the facility of ridicule and sarcasm. It is frequently employed, somewhat in the manner of rapier, by people who wish to paralyze or prostrate others, politely and deftly, without shedding blood or being arraigned for murder. The sharp tongue, as it is sometimes called, reveals a nimble wit and can be cultivated almost to the point of a fine art. But it leaves a trail of enemies and draws a circle of fear and animosity around the person who becomes expert in it. Sarcasm and ridicule may become positively cruel. Many a promising career has been nipped in the bud because of a frosty, biting remark. In this way, many a happy friendship has been lost, and much potential influence for good has been dissipated. Some literary sarcasm makes enjoyable reading; but the person who develops the habit of sarcasm, either to be smart or to gain his point, is usually making a serious mistake.

Of a different character, but almost equally deserving of special caution, is burlesque and what is called the "practical joke." Burlesque, as we understand it here, consists in making a person or situation appear funny by exaggerating or distorting certain features, so as to reveal weakness or abnormality. The humor of a clown is burlesque. Cartoonists often burlesque their subjects by enlarging prominent noses or teeth or seizing upon some feature of sensitivity for special emphasis. Mimics heighten the humor of their imitation of persons or situations by playing up some eccentricity of dress, manner, or characteristic of their subject. There is such a thing as good-humored burlesque, and there are many mean, vulgar, and even cruel varieties. There is also good, bad, and questionable taste in its use. "Anything for a laugh" is not a good policy, particularly when the laughter is at the expense of another who may be offended or injured. Weaknesses and foibles which we can safely laugh at in general may not be safe material for derision in a particular case. Before one undertakes to play the part of the clown or to imitate others in a way calculated to draw a laugh, it may be advisable to ask oneself whether this performance will serve to prejudice others or whether it will be related back to the person re-enacted, with possible misunderstandings and other unfortunate repercussions.

The practical joke shares the nature of heavy-footed burlesque, inasmuch as it may serve to gratify a sense of humor on the part of the perpetrator rather than on the part of the object or butt of the joke. The practical joker depends upon tricks and pranks which tend to confuse, annoy, or embarrass someone else; and he draws heavily upon the good humor and sufferance of the person or persons at whose expense the alleged joke or prank is performed. Most practical jokes are juvenile in character, ranging from Halloween escapades to college capers and various forms of shocks and surprises. In many cases the humor is difficult to detect, particularly where physical loss or injury is involved; and sometimes the author of the joke preserves his immunity by remaining anonymous, as in the case of comic valentines or in letters of the "poison pen" variety.

Children who develop these tendencies should receive elementary instruction on the ethics of inflicting pain or loss and of making restitution where necessary; and adults who are addicted to the practical joke should think twice as to the possible effect of their fun. Once, as a small boy, I thought it funny to place a discarded snake skin, which I had picked up in the woods, on the dining-room table. A case of mild hysterics developed in the guests, which might have turned into something serious; and I learned a lesson which I have never forgotten.

Humor which causes pain, costs others money or serious loss of time, or results in the alienation of friends is not good humor. The idea of some people as to what constitutes a joke is indeed weird and leaves room to question not only their good judgment but their sanity as well.

A form of wit which is harmless enough in itself but may become a nuisance is the pun. Now and then a play on words may be clever, but the constant twisting of words or of verbal sounds to give them a double meaning can become extremely tiresome. Punning may become a habit; and it is one which should not be encouraged.

4

With some people, wit and humor are forms of self-defense. Unwilling to show their true selves or to express an honest opinion on anything, they resort to the strategy of constantly joking, laughing, slapping others on the back, and behaving as if everything were excruciatingly funny. When one comes upon a group of adults whose normal method of social intercourse takes this turn, one may be sure that they are uncomfortable in each other's company and are trying to cover up their mutual boredom or suspicion.

Others are in a constant mood of laughing, joking, and "kidding," for the reason that they fail to take themselves seriously. Their presence in a group is enough to set a comic tone of conversation, so that nothing serious is ever brought up. Some regard themselves as funny men, as the only way of gaining attention; and as a result, they come to be looked upon as buffoons by their acquaintances. While we should be on guard against taking ourselves too seriously, we can commit the opposite error of taking ourselves too lightly. There must be a balance; and it is not until one looks seriously upon life and regards himself or herself as occupying a position of some importance and responsibility, that one can have a true perspective on humor.

There are many things which some persons suppose to be funny but which the serious-minded and considerate person does not laugh at. There are times for fun and humor, and there are times which call for the putting aside of jokes.

Some persons develop a habit of nervous laughter or giggle, which signifies nothing except perhaps an overflow of animal spirits or a kind of emotional immaturity. It may be important for us to reflect on our tendencies in this regard, if for no other reason than to make a correct social impression. A silly laugh or a readiness to laugh on all occasions, regardless of the provocation, should not be confused with a sense of humor. It may rather indicate the need for self-control and for a more reflective spirit.

5

Some people have a natural talent for wit, for the telling of anecdotes, and for mimicry which is genuine entertainment. Others cannot tell a joke without forgetting the point before they come to it. Some can play pranks and practical jokes in a way which gives no offense. Others succeed only in making themselves awkward and in stirring resentment or contempt in the effort. In the matter of taste, some speakers are beyond reproach in selecting a humorous anecdote which is appropriate and effective to the occasion. Others must be held strictly in line, lest their selection be off-color and completely irrelevant. There is an art in correct and effective funny-story telling, just as there is an art in the development of musical expression. Not everyone has the requisite talent or experience, or even the courage, to be a success in this field.

In the development of a sense of humor on the receiving end, however, everyone has at least an elemental capacity, which should be recognized and encouraged. The first requisite is a willingness and disposition to enjoy the fun in life, even when it is directed against oneself. There is a comical as well as a tragic side of every situation. One can be serious in things that matter and carry a full load of responsibility, yet enter into a lighter vein and learn to laugh with good nature at the weaknesses, the foibles, and the inconsistencies that are part of the human burden. There is such a thing as being a good sport and of learning to take the quips when they come our way.

From a practical standpoint, there is much difference between the making and the taking of humor. Some people are at their best when they are concocting a joke at the expense of someone else; but when the shoe is put on their foot they become extremely sensitive and sore. A genuine sense of humor implies the ability to receive as well as to give. The question often comes down to this: "Shall I become angry, or shall I choose to laugh it off?" Much depends upon the issue; but more often than not, the saner way lies with laughter.

A sense of humor grows with a comprehension of life and often serves as a profound guide in our dealing with others. As Oliver Wendell Holmes remarks in *Autocrat of the Breakfast Table,* "Be very careful how you tell an author he is *droll.* Ten to one he will hate you; and if he does, be sure he can do you a mischief, and very probably will. Say you *cried* over his romance or his verses, and he will love you and send you a copy. You can laugh over that as much as you like — in private."[5] A person with a good sense of humor does not need an audience. He can laugh at himself or chuckle over the oddities of others, quite in secret, without giving any offense.

It was with a comprehension of this power of humor that Robert Burns wrote his famous lines:

---

[5] *Op. cit.,* from Part III.

> O wad some Power the giftie gie us
> To see oursels as ithers see us!
> It wad frae mony a blunder free us,
> An' foolish notion:
> What airs in dress an' gait wad lea'e us,
> An' ev'n devotion![6]

Humor has a great therapeutic quality, in helping one regain composure after a disagreeable incident and in helping to whittle imaginary ills down to their actual size and residual reality. There are many things that we can laugh at when our blood pressure has subsided, but which were highly annoying at the time they happened. In retrospect, many a tense and serious moment becomes comical. Many an experience can be told and draw a gale of understanding laughter years after the actuality. But most helpful is the sense of humor which can come to the rescue on the spot and save what might become a catastrophe from developing into such.

The story is told of a gentleman who owned a large grandfather's clock which had stopped running. Eager to have it repaired, he decided to take it directly to the jeweler's himself. As he was struggling down the street, his vision obstructed by the long cabinet, he ran into an old lady who was carrying a basket of groceries. In the collision, she was knocked to the pavement, and her groceries were scattered on the ground. This might have been cause for lawsuit. He deposited the clock on the ground and rushed to pick her up and to gather the groceries. "I'm so sorry," he cried. "What can I do to help you?"

"Nothing," she replied. "But I would suggest that you get up to date. Why don't you throw away that antique instrument and buy yourself a wrist watch?"

A sense of humor which can rise to the occasion so quickly is an asset far more precious than wealth. It serves the mind as health serves the body, and carries a person through many an obstacle right to death's door.

---

[6] *To a Louse.*

CHAPTER XII

Intellectual Honesty

I

ONE of the surest tests of mental health is a devotion to and keenness for truth. The reason for this is that the mind, by its nature, searches for truth; and speech, as a servant of the mind, utters what the mind commands. Truth is the conformity of an object with the mind, or of the mind with an object, depending on how one approaches the matter. Philosophers tell us that the final intrinsic truth of an object or of an idea depends upon its conformity with the mind of God. To the extent that a human mind grasps this relationship as it exists between the mind of God and these external objects or ideas, which are reflections of the divine mind, it apprehends truth.

This is a rather abstract way of approaching the question of truth, but it is basic for a clear understanding of the subject. In other words, there is such a thing as absolute truth, for the simple reason that the mind of God is absolute. The final validity of impressions, sensations, imaginary pictures, and ideas or judgments depends upon whether they fit into this pattern.

If they do, there are no two ways about it. As an absolute truth, two and two make four. This is not relative to any particular situation or circumstance. This truth stands absolutely, because it is in the nature of things as ordained by the eternal mind of God; and there is nothing that I or anyone else can do to change it. The same observation can be made of facts, which may be described as things which are done or which have existence of some kind. It is a fact that you are reading this book. To recognize this as a fact is to recognize the truth. To read this book and at the same time to fail to recognize the fact indicates that there is something wrong with one's mental processes. To deny it is an evidence of intellectual dishonesty.

The ethics of truth is derived from the fact that we are morally responsible for the right or natural use of those faculties over which we exercise control. Therefore, the person who willfully distorts his mind to confuse truth with falsehood or uses his speech to utter seriously for the truth that he knows to be false commits an immoral act. If he calls upon God to witness as truth what he knows to be false, he tries to make a liar of God; in the civil courts, this is known as perjury — a crime to which the most severe penalties are attached.

2

In normal social intercourse truth is taken as a matter of course. Only with this assumption can we live with one another and do business. While we make allowance for a margin of error because of insufficient evidence or possibly mistaken judgment on the part of individuals, we believe most of what others tell us. We read the newspapers and listen to radio news reports in the spirit in which they are delivered. If something is fictional, sheerly imaginary, simply a possibility, only probable, or a joke, we expect this qualification to be attached to it. To a large extent, our position in society is shaped by the confidence which others place in our word, in the reliability of our reports, and in the honesty of our minds.

Some people have a scrupulous regard for the truth, so that, as we say, their word is as good as their bond. This standard is absolutely necessary in the case of scientific development. In the science of chemistry, for example, where one may be working with high explosives, one cannot guess at the combination of elements or play around loosely with acids or radioactive matter. The recognition of truth here and exact respect for the known powers of nature may be the difference between life and death. In engineering, the tensile strength of steel and of structural design can be reduced to mathematical equations. To tinker with these facts, particularly when applied to the construction of bridges, ships, automobiles, or utensils where weight, speed, tension, and impact are involved in human safety, may be criminal.

Careful regard for the truth is requisite also in the representation of products which are designed for public use and consumption. The manufacturer, retailer, or salesman with a conscience or even a reputation to sustain makes sure that his representation squares with the facts, that he is not calling veneer a solid wood, that he is not selling cotton material for woolen goods or that his tonic is not colored water. Fraud and deceit sooner or later become known and contribute to put the guilty parties out of business. Most governments take more immediate precautionary measures by setting up standards of weights and measures, materials and specifications, and by enacting laws to protect health by pure food and drug regulations.

In the matter of personal statements and representations, likewise, respect for the truth is an asset of the greatest value, not only for reasons of individual protection and integrity, but also in establishing and maintaining the confidence of others. When we find ourselves doubting the observations of a certain person, or taking what he has to say "with a grain of salt," or not regarding as serious his various reports and proposals, we naturally shy away from that person. When we find that a certain person cannot be relied upon to tell the truth, particularly when his own interests are involved, we lose interest in what he has to say. If he or she is inclined to deal in gossip, to play loosely with the reputation of others, to be inaccurate, or to exaggerate where truth is important, we recognize that we are dealing with a dangerous person. Even one breath of evidence of a lie or deliberate misrepresentation is to put us forever on our guard.

3

Some people have no scruples whatsoever about the truth. They will lie or cheat without hesitation or qualms if they feel that it serves their purpose and that they can avoid detection. With many others, however, the difficulty seems to be rather a looseness with the truth, an unawareness of responsibility in dealing with facts, a disorderly and uncontrolled imagination, or the emergence of self-interest which makes some cowards and others braggarts.

Some of the most remarkable cases of mischievous imagination occur in children. Whether to gain attention and acquire a feeling of importance or to secure revenge for real or fancied wrongs, some children have a remarkable facility for creating imaginary situations and reporting fantastic tales in and out of home. Strange feuds have been started in this manner, as a result of credence on the part of adults who should have suspected a hoax or at least investigated the facts and made some inquiries before accepting the stories.

We are all aware of the force of imagination in dreams. The most fantastic objects and situations appear before us with the illusion of full reality; and sequences pass before us that we could never conjure up during our hours of awakened consciousness. To a certain extent, the same process takes place in what are called daydreams. It would appear that in some people the "make-believe" world of children passes over into adult life, and the phenomenon of daydreams enters into their mental processes to such an extent that they are unable to distinguish fantasy and reality.

I recall an individual who appeared to be perfectly sane in all respects except when relating personal experiences from his past life. Once launched on the story of his career, he proceeded to tell the most fantastic and impossible episodes, hour after hour, in a completely matter-of-fact manner. His friends dared not take exception to these weird tales, as he would become insulted. Many others, while not reaching this extreme, have a tendency to embellish personal experiences or the relating of facts with dramatic additions, which make the story more worth the telling and the individual more important. The most familiar example of this is the story of the fish that got away and that grows in size each time the story is retold; but there are many variations of this situation which enable the teller to command attention and to become more heroic in his or her own eyes.

This tendency has its amusing aspects; but it is sufficiently dangerous to bear careful watching. Unless curbed, it can grow into a mental habit, which disqualifies one from clear thinking for himself and from confidence on the part of others. Before sizing up a situation, one should ask himself very carefully whether he is interested in facts or whether he is letting his imagination and his emotions run away with his judgment. Before reporting to others, one should make reasonably certain that he is telling facts and not simply building up a case from conjectures, desires, and dramatic fancy.

The element of personal interest often has a way of distorting the truth or of giving it a special slant, even when the inventive genius of the imagination is held in check. When one is placed in an embarrassing position, there is often a temptation to squirm out of it by passing the blame on to others or by finding extenuating circumstances that diminish or eliminate personal responsibility. At this point, one's memory may become defective, and only those details which are favorable seem to stand out. If the situation is really bad, then a general mental fuzziness may result which blots out all possibility of an honest analysis. On second thought, a new sequence of events develops, and the mind rehearses the event, dropping out important items or reducing them to a position of secondary importance. With this rearrangement made plausible, we endeavor to regain our self-respect and composure and decide to stick to the revised story, for ourselves as well as for others.

Sometimes, although far more seldom, the individual decides to take all the blame. If there are any mental short cuts, they are in the way of assuming full responsibility, as a measure of safety or as a gesture of generosity. This is calculated to simplify all problems and to disarm others who might be inclined to take a vindictive attitude. In extreme cases, people plead guilty to faults or crimes which they had nothing to do with. Many unsolved crimes are cluttered with unsolicited confessions of persons who, for one reason or the other, declare themselves to be the guilty parties.

With many persons, one or the other of these reactions or forms of rationalizations comes spontaneously and almost by instinct. Having determined upon a line of thought and action, they have no further qualms on the matter. With others, however, this is just the beginning of a long series of rationalizations and of a state of mental restlessness and dissatisfaction. Counselors and spiritual guides are acquainted with the tender or "scrupulous" conscience, which is always at sixes-and-sevens with itself and never quite certain that its judgment has been correct or honest. Behind this indecision is a combination of cowardice and pride, which makes it difficult for one to recognize and admit to the truth as it is, without extenuation — courageously, humbly, and honestly. Unless this is done, as a matter of habit, there is no such thing as mental peace. There is an old saying to the effect that honest confession is good for the soul. Before there can be an honest confession, there must be honest acknowledgment to oneself.

4

One of the most familiar forms of mental derangement is

that of mistaken personal identity. A case in point is that of demented persons who imagine that they are Napoleon. I once encountered an individual who was convinced that he was a pure spirit without a body. Others imagine that they are the reincarnation of some ancient personage, such as an Egyptian Pharaoh. These are extreme cases. But there are numerous others who, without mistaking their identity, entertain certain illusions about themselves which seriously interfere with their good judgment and social behavior. An exaggerated opinion of one's intellectual superiority, personal talents, or social position gives rise to attitudes of snobbishness or habits of bluff, bragging, and pretense. To keep up the sham calls for considerable ingeniousness. Liars of all kinds have to continue inventing stories and situations to make their position plausible; but in the long run they fool nobody but themselves. Such activity becomes ludicrous after a while; and a false pose, like a false story, strips one of all claim to the confidence of others. Far better to be what one is, to act one's age, to live in the world of reality, and to take the consequences than to create an artificial atmosphere which deceives no one whose opinion is worth cultivating.

The same observation may be made regarding one's personal qualifications and preparedness to assume a position of knowledge or guidance, particularly where valuable considerations may be involved so far as others are concerned. There are many people who are quick to give an opinion or offer advice whether they know what they are talking about or not. Financial advice, medical advice, and legal advice proceed freely from many who are not in the least qualified to speak on these subjects. There are some people who have no hesitancy in giving directions to passing motorists, although they themselves are totally ignorant of the correct route. Others are ready to pass out confidential information or circulate stories and rumors without having made any effort to verify their statements, regardless of whether harm may be done.

Counselors and spiritual guides should ask themselves whether they are qualified to direct others or to give correct answers on subjects of vital importance. The person who sets out to solve specific personal problems and to guide the lives of others should be reasonably sure of his competence in the particular matter or field involved. Intellectual dishonesty and pretense can be just as reprehensible as quackery in medicine. If one does not know the answers, it is far better to say "I don't know" than to misdirect and confuse others. It is a wise man who knows his own limitations and is not afraid to acknowledge his own weakness.

Among authors who are overambitious to break into print, there is frequently the temptation to commit what is called plagiarism — that is, to steal the work of another and pass it off as one's own. This often happens among students; and from time to time otherwise reputable and established writers dip into the published work of others, without acknowledgment, when their own stock of ideas runs low. Even preachers have been known to deliver as their own, word for word, sermons which they have memorized from their more celebrated peers and predecessors.

I recall, as a teacher, assigning a subject to my class for composition, with the solemn injunction that this was to be strictly original and kept short. One of the papers submitted was beautifully written in twelve pages. My suspicion was aroused by the graceful flow of the first few sentences, quite unlike the ordinary style of this student.

"Is this your own composition?" I asked. "Have you consulted any book on the matter or engaged anyone to help you write this?"

"I wrote it all myself," came the answer; and, in view of what followed, I became convinced that the young man really believed that he had. Skipping the intermediate pages, I turned to his last sentence, which read, "For further information, see page 298."

Composers of music are exposed to the same danger of copying, although here there is more possibility of innocently picking up a musical theme from another work without realizing that it has been heard before and is not original. Of course, there is such a thing as a legitimate development in variations of standard works, providing proper credit is given to the author or composer or the requisite permission has been secured. Imitation, it is said, is the sincerest form of flattery; but when it is offered as an original or steals the credit that belongs to another, it is nothing short of being dishonest.

5

Intellectual dishonesty takes another form, of saying what one does not really think or believe. In familiar social exchange we all offer little compliments to make others feel happy, even though the accuracy of our observations may not meet exact scientific standards. The gallant gentleman who assures a venerable lady that she does not look one day over twenty-one is evidently taking liberties with the truth, which may be excused on the understanding that a pleasant illusion is created without intention to deceive. Various forms of what the Irish call "blarney" are permissible to render others well disposed and to stimulate a more rosy outlook on one's self and the world in general. But even this practice can be carried to extremes and, when combined with malice, may give rise to mischief and injury.

Nearly everyone appreciates a compliment and a friendly word of praise, even though it may be recognized as slightly undeserved or exaggerated. But when it comes from a source which we know is insincere, we become suspicious; and if it is laid on too thick, it may become embarrassing and offensive. Compliments and kind words offered ironically simply build up walls of animosity. Many apparent compliments are hurled with barbed hooks to dig into the skin of their victims.

But there are other forms of insincerity and double talk

which are even more confusing and subject to wonderment. Some people never say what they honestly think. When pressed for an opinion, they succeed in giving out generalities which can be interpreted in almost any direction. Or they will say one thing to one person, another thing to another, depending upon the reaction expected or upon considerations of self-defense. Such is sometimes called "talking out of both corners of the mouth." Perhaps it may seem strange, but there are persons whose real opinions and convictions are the opposite of what they express. They say "yes" when they mean "no" and "no" when they mean "yes." If they praise a thing, it is because they regard it as inferior; if they blame or condemn, it is because they recognize real merit.

Some people adopt these tactics as a humorous device to trap others who are unacquainted with the procedure and sufficiently gullible to take it seriously. They tell the most fantastic stories, utter scandalous opinions, or express ridiculous views, to startle or horrify others, or to provoke a silly argument. There can be no reasonable objection to an occasional harmless prank. The difficulty with this, however, is that the technique of good-natured deception can develop into a habit. Many jokers of this kind have only themselves to laugh with and at. We never know when to take them seriously, and consequently we come to pay little attention to anything they say. We become on our guard against such individuals, because we never know when, for a practical joke, they may ascribe to us remarks and actions for which we were not responsible.

6

Intellectual honesty, of course, does not require that we open our bosoms and pour out the secrets of our hearts to everyone who evinces interest or asks questions. There are a great many busybodies who would like to add to their store of information about matters that are none of their concern. Many would like to know just what we know and just what we think on matters of a delicate or confidential character, so that they can pass this along to others, possibly with embellishments. We do not have to confess our faults in public, or give an account of all of our movements to everyone who would like to know. We do not have to tell just what we paid for things, simply to satisfy the curiosity of others. At times, discretion may indicate an evasive answer. If this does not satisfy an insistent inquisition, we may be required to remind others, politely but firmly, that this is "none of their business."

This brings up the question of just how much truth one should tell. How frank should one be as a general rule? The answer to these questions is largely a matter of justice and good judgment. If one goes to a doctor for medical consultation or treatment, it is folly to withhold essential information or to attempt to deceive him with a recital of false symptoms. If one make a sacramental confession, unburdening one's soul to God, nothing can be achieved by telling an untrue story or interjecting circumstances which change the facts of the matter. If one consults a lawyer about a case, no good purpose is served by misleading him as to the elements involved. And if one expects a square deal from one's associates, nothing less than frankness and honesty are indicated to them. Withholding of basic facts and issues or twisting issues so as to avoid personal embarrassment is simply to postpone the day of reckoning. Far better to face a situation straight on and, if necessary, to throw oneself on the mercy of God or man in the beginning, than to follow a tortuous path of deceit, half-truths, and double-dealing, which lead to eventual disaster. In the long run, tactics of intellectual dishonesty fool only oneself and harm one's own case. Justice is never served by injustice.

On the other hand, one must be considerate and prudent when dealing with facts or alleged facts which may hurt others. Confidential information about oneself is best kept confidential except from those who have a right to know. Even more, confidential information about others must be respected. Much harm can be done by spreading stories about one's family or circle of friends. Many matters of domestic concern had best remain there. There is no point in hanging one's dirty linen out on the line for all the neighbors to see.

Petty quarrels with friends need not disrupt true friendship. These incidents can be patched up in the course of human events. But when circulated to eager ears, to gain comfort or small revenge, they are almost sure to be reported back. Very few secrets remain secrets once they are told. People will promise secrecy, but in a short time they forget what they promised secrecy to. As someone has said, "I can keep secrets, but the persons I tell them to cannot."

As a general rule, when dealing with gossip, rumors, and the reputations of others, it is far better to err on the side of silence than on the side of talk. So much harm is done by wagging tongues and over-the-fence chatter. The person who can keep a confidence and who can be trusted to maintain a discrete silence is a jewel. Many people love intrigue, conspiracy, and trouble. They feel that their position is strengthened if they can "get something on others." There is no one so perfect in this life that a plausible case cannot be cleverly maneuvered to discredit him, on faith, morals, or good judgment.

The most dangerous form of intellectual dishonesty is that of the hypocrite. Hypocrisy eats into mental health, for the reason that the individual leading a double life is in a constant turmoil trying to justify his conduct and unify the irreconcilables of right and wrong. Failing in this attempt he or she is always on the lookout for evidence of weakness in others which might appear to drag everyone down into the category of secret sin and thus justify wrongdoing as a rather normal procedure. If hypocrites cannot find what they are looking for as a matter of fact, they proceed to smear others with scandal or innuendoes, even in the most innocent circumstances. The philosophy of the scandalmonger and liar is that if you throw enough mud, some will stick.

These are strong words but true. No human mind can maintain its health unless it can live in peace with itself. And no mind can live in peace with itself unless it dwells in the interior assurance of truthfulness and fair dealing. The deliberate propagation of error and falsehood leaves a deepening scar upon the mind until the wrong has been righted. And self-deceit simply adds to the disquiet of one's soul.

CHAPTER XIII

Self - Confidence

I

A BASIC need for mental health is that of self-confidence. This means essentially a conviction of one's personal worth and ability, together with the interior assurance that one has a definite place of honor in this life and an important purpose within God's providence. Unless one starts with this conviction, life is hardly more than a complex maze of uncertainties, fears, and frustrations. One must be convinced of his or her personal worth and equipment to meet the challenges of life, if life itself is to have any real dignity or if any progress is to be made in solving its problems.

To understand the meaning of self-confidence in a constructive sense, it is important to make several distinctions. Self-confidence must not be confused with brass or brashness or silly pride. It is not the same thing as stubbornness or cocksureness of opinion. It is not manifested in a determination to have one's own way at all costs. It is not the pose of a false front or an endeavor to convince others of one's importance.

Self-confidence exists side by side with a full awareness of one's personal shortcomings. It admits of respect and deference for others in higher positions and of more developed talents. It observes all the rules of courtesy and kindness. It recognizes one's obligations toward others. It maintains at all times a prayerful spirit and submissive attitude toward God. In short, having a sense of right proportions, it is a feeling of being comfortable with oneself, without being smug about it.

The development of a well-modulated self-confidence presents vastly different problems for different temperaments and for persons in various circumstances. Some persons are born with an easy assumption of their place in life; and their education proceeds in such a way as never to develop any serious doubts as to their own qualities or their place in society. With others, life is a struggle from the outset. Perhaps some physical handicap holds them back and makes them the object of ridicule or pity on the part of playmates and associates. Within their family circle they may experience a leveling process, which begins with the admonition that little children "are to be seen and not heard," and proceeds with jerks and bumps through an awkward adolescence to a point of finally being taken seriously by others and being allowed to express an opinion with some degree of assurance. Lack of education, poverty, physical hardship, origin in an obscure community, a foreign accent, remembrance of public embarrassment, or general dissatisfaction with one's work may contribute toward personal diffidence and timidity.

On the other hand, one who possesses exceptional talents may be singled out for the envy and petty intrigues of others and find it difficult to make a satisfactory social and personal adjustment. A woman of exceptional beauty or a man of striking appearance may possibly find that these gifts are really liabilities rather than assets, subjecting one to the crosscurrents of envy, flattery, conceit, and self-consciousness.

For self-confidence to operate as a source of mental health

and strength, it must be definitely attuned to humility. The word "confidence" means "with faith or trust." The word "humility" comes remotely from a Latin word *humus* which means "earth." The combination of the two signifies a realistic view of life, in all of its material, passing, and corruptible aspects, with a spiritual outlook of faith and trust in the abiding qualities of human nature and in the goodness of God.

From these observations, it is clear that the development and maintenance of self-confidence depend upon the acceptance of certain principles, not only as regard one's own dignity and responsibility, but in relation to the character of others as well. Mere external acting or pretense must not be mistaken for interior strength and composure. What is called an "inferiority complex" often manifests itself in noisy argumentation or demands. A "superiority complex" often betrays itself in great condescension and excessive deference. The man who bows and scrapes too low often entertains a profound contempt for those in whose presence he makes these gestures; and he sneers or snickers after they have departed.

2

The first principle upon which rational self-confidence is developed is that of self-respect, regardless of one's station in life, talents, or achievements. Every individual represents the creative act of God and is made to the "image and likeness of God," with special reference to his faculties of soul. Every individual is made to know, love, and serve God in this life and to be happy with Him forever in the next. This applies to all persons, regardless of rank and personal condition. One must not think less of himself than does the God who made him.

Every individual, likewise, regardless of race, color, national origin, or creed, possesses the same basic universal rights and duties, which are correctly described in the American Declaration of Independence, as "life, liberty, and the pursuit of happiness." Everyone, conscious of his inherent dignity, should hold his head high. It is only when we begin to indulge in self-pity, to compromise with moral standards that we know are low, and to behave like irrational animals or worse, by disregarding the rules of temperance and clean living, that we lose our grasp upon the most precious of human possessions — self-respect.

The second principle is a willingness to stand upon one's personal merits and honest efforts. There is no point in exaggerating what one is and what he has. To go through life with a puffed-up idea of one's abilities or personal importance is to invite derision and disappointment all along the line. On the other hand, there is no sense in underestimating what one is and is worth, as if the struggle for life and success were lost at the outset for lack of the necessary qualifications and tools, or from the competition and opposition of stronger rivals. Even in the mystery of the supernatural life there is assurance of strength and assistance sufficient for one's needs. St. Paul, describing his own struggles, writes: "And lest the greatness of the revelations should exalt me, there was given me a sting of my flesh, an angel of Satan, to buffet me. For which thing thrice I besought the Lord that it might depart from me. And He said to me: My grace is sufficient for thee: for power is made perfect in infirmity. Gladly therefore will I glory in my infirmities, that the power of Christ may dwell in me."[1]

The conviction that a person is doing the best he can, and that his conscience is clear so far as honest effort is concerned, is the greatest of all rewards and an assurance of mental peace. For one thing it means that one does not depend in his standards of success upon personal triumphs over others or the achievement of any particular competitive goal. Success comes in the joy of doing things which are worth while in themselves, whether they win first prize or the plaudits of others or pass unnoticed. Composure arises from the conviction that what is

---

[1] 2 Cor. 12:7–9.

right and true and of value exists independently of any particular decision, argument, or award. And if one needs consolation to live with an apparent failure or disappointment, he can say to himself and to God, "I have done the best I could." No one can ask for more.

The functioning of these principles is of the utmost importance for civilized living and for adaptability to the changing circumstances of life. The idea that the only thing that counts is *winning* has proved disastrous in more ways than we can illustrate here.

There is nothing wrong with the principle of competition, as such. It is used in educational processes and as a method of selection among various candidates for a position or prize. It stimulates progress and helps to maintain desirable levels and controls. It provides the basis of legitimate interest and excitement in all kinds of games and serves a recreational function.

But when the purpose and spirit of competition narrow down to the one grim business of *winning,* people begin to use the principle of "the end justifies the means," and all kinds of abuses creep in. College and professional sports have been corrupted through this. Political positions, elections, private and public honors, and prizes of various kinds have been bought and sold. Cases in court have been won through the introduction of false evidence and perjury. In these ways, the public sense of fairness and confidence is outraged; democratic processes are thwarted and held up to ridicule and cynicism; force and violence take the place of co-operation and peaceful adaptation to social needs and changes.

For persons who tie their ideas of success and their sense of values to victory, as if nothing else counted, defeat, failure, and disappointment come hard, sometimes too hard; and the bottom drops out of their existence. For many students, the experience of losing a school game, a debating contest, or an essay competition remains as a bitter sorrow and void for months and years. It may even affect their whole outlook on life. Failure to be elected to a coveted class or fraternity office sometimes results in a determination never to aspire again to a position of responsibility. Some people cannot play a game of cards without winning or becoming furious. There are some who should never play any kind of competitive game because of the injury to their blood pressure induced by failure or defeat. I have known of golfers who break their sticks and walk off the course, swearing that they will never play again, because of a bad stroke or a high score.

Some people are never content to discuss a question. They must argue it to prove their point and to triumph over an adversary. They cannot tolerate a difference of opinion, as this seems to reflect on their sense of rightness and security. If they lose an argument, because their position is weak or their contender is better informed, their day is ruined and their spirits become profoundly agitated or dejected.

One must learn to live quietly with others who differ in matters of religion, politics, current events, family evaluations, and personal reactions. If one thinks that one is right, he or she can always cherish the interior comfort of being on the side of the angels, no matter what others may think. If one thinks the others are wrong, there is no point in trying to convince them against their will. If discussion is going to lead to a heated argument or injured feelings, without settling anything that really matters, prudence would suggest that we remain satisfied with the serene assurance of our own thoughts.

I recall some years ago listening to a lecturer relating his experiences in a foreign country and violating, as I thought, most standards of gentlemanly courtesy, truth, and sensibility. As my discomfort grew, I must have become audible in my mutterings, and I prepared to rise and challenge the speaker. A lady at my side in the audience, noting my disturbance, turned and whispered, "I quite agree with you that this man is very unfair. I am sure that many in the audience disagree heartily with him. I don't think a demonstration of any kind would do any good or is really necessary." Her remarks have stayed with me through the years and have taught me a lesson in urbanity and maturity that have helped me, on many an occasion, to preserve my integrity of faith, knowledge, and opinion, without having to battle for it.

3

There are many people who are never content with an absolute sense of their importance. It must be *relative* to others. They must be more important than someone else. So they use the device of belittling others who seem to challenge their preeminence. If they praise others, it is but faintly in such a way as to point up limitations and to highlight other defects. If they think in terms of money, beauty, strength, social position, honor, intelligence, personality, or any qualities, possessions, or achievements, it is always in reference to someone else. They must have more than others. If such is not the case, then they think others have gained the advantage through unfair or foul means, or that their apparently more favorable position is a fraud. Since no one likes to admit being envious, such people try to whittle others down in size and to keep them there.

One of the most interesting, but least convincing, methods of impressing one's importance upon others is to assume an attitude of great strength and assertiveness. The bully on the schoolyard, the loud voice in the parlor, the "he-man" who pretends to be tough and contemptful of gentle manners and cultured living, the mother who insists upon dominating her children and "taking the words right out of their mouths," and the individual who must have the last word in every argument or discussion — all are examples of strong exterior and a profound sense of inner void and insecurity. It is difficult to break down this defense. Some people can put on what is called "a very good act." But the artificiality of the situation is obvious to all others concerned.

I once attended a dinner given for a distinguished visitor,

whose views on certain current matters were regarded as of considerable importance. Every time the host attempted to draw him out and he began to speak, another member of the party was inspired to break in and tell just what his ideas were on the matter. This performance, which amounted almost to a duet, continued until the honored guest stopped short and remarked politely, "Perhaps our friend at the other end of the table would like to comment." The latter, who had already begun his comment, floundered around, while growing more red in the face, and finally ended in the middle of a sentence which was obviously headed nowhere. After this, the dinner continued easily and without uncalled-for interruptions.

People who feel insecure in their position or possessions very often become, not only insistent, but extremely jealous of their right and priorities. Children of this disposition are reluctant to let their playmates use their toys, lest a block or a stick might disappear. Adults of the same mentality are unwilling to share or delegate authority, or to appoint strong committees of an advisory character which might offer opposition on occasion to their pet schemes or share in the credit for success. Jealous lovers, husbands, and wives make nuisances of themselves by watching every movement, demanding explanations, occupying full attention, and applying various tests and proofs of the other's fidelity and submission. Rights and affections which are held secure by these techniques are never very happy; and sooner or later they are certain to explode.

4

This suggests a third basic principle in the development of self-confidence, which is a willingness to work with others. It is sometimes said that people who are "cocksure" of themselves are likely to have little confidence in others. The fact of the matter is that one never achieves genuine self-confidence until he has learned to trust others and to have at least a reasonable confidence in their ability and good will. It is impossible to face the world alone. One must learn to co-operate with others and to depend upon their co-operation in return. For almost any enterprise, teamwork is necessary.

People who are unable to co-operate with others can never be sure of themselves. One cannot say that he has acquired self-confidence until he has learned to be comfortable in the company of others, to behave normally like others and join in the fun and struggle of existence. The child who is bashful, the man or woman who feels ill at ease, except when alone, develops eccentricities and mental quirks. We are social beings and must learn to face the world and to deal with our fellows on equal terms, even when we should much prefer to be alone.

As a small boy, I remember being urged to take off my shoes and stockings and go barefoot for the summer. I do not recall the exact circumstances, but I balked at the proposal, alleging a sense of shame lest people should see my feet. This silly reason was just enough to stiffen my father's suggestion into a command. Many people go through life offering similar reasons for not facing up to the social realities of existence, and then crying in secret because the world has passed them by.

Children who show a tendency to remain by themselves should be required, gently but firmly, to go out and learn to play with others. Growing boys and girls should be encouraged to join their school clubs and participate in various activities that call for teamwork, co-operation, and good sportsmanship. Bashful young men and women should make a special effort, even though it hurts, to move into social circles, to get away from the status of a "wallflower," to learn to dance, and to enjoy doing things with other people. Men and women of all ages and conditions should make it part of their regular program to invite guests into the home, to accept social invitations, and to join some social, civic, cultural, or philanthropic groups — if for no other reason than to rub elbows with people, to remain human, to develop their self-confidence, and to stay sane.

This means, of course, that one is going to run up against

disagreeable people. One is certain to meet opposition. In almost any social setting, one's sense of self-confidence and comfortable self-assurance is going to be challenged and perhaps sorely bruised from time to time. Anyone who deals with others must be prepared for this and learn to accept the shocks. It is impossible to join even in a conversation without experiencing a difference of opinions. We have to learn not to insist on having our way all of the time. No one is perfect. Others have to endure our shortcomings as we do theirs. Such is life.

Rebuffs, rudeness, lack of consideration, and unfair dealing may all be expected in the course of a day's work. One must consider the source in some cases and make allowance for unknown factors in others. Persons in positions of responsibility must develop a hide as thick as a rhinoceros and perhaps wear armor plate as well, if they are to survive the scorn and criticism of those whom they direct and serve. To some extent everyone must learn to ignore petty jibes and to "laugh things off." In a spirit of understanding and charity, we recognize that much peevishness is simply the result of a migraine headache or sluggish metabolism, a sleepless night, or a family disagreement.

Particularly for persons who are inclined to be sensitive and retiring, it is important to guard against discouragement or a feeling of failure. Before melting into tears of anger or frustration, one should carefully study the situation and even take advice. If one has made a mistake, the honest and sensible thing to do is to acknowledge it, make amends if necessary, and profit by the experience. If the failure has resulted from attempting something beyond one's powers or for which one was not prepared, there is no good reason for being permanently disabled. The proper course of action may be to resume one's work of preparation and try again or to attempt something for which one is better adapted and qualified.

Not everyone is qualified to become a concert pianist; but there is room for good teachers of music. Not everyone is cut out to be a great orator; there is need also for good counselors, businessmen, and men in the various professions. Not everyone can make the grade for a certified public accountant; but many have other abilities which make them equally, if not more, valuable in commerce or administration. Not everyone can master the typewriter and stenography, but there are other positions of equal importance for which one may be superlative.

What if one's early dreams of becoming president of the United States or leading lady on Broadway do not come true? How seldom they do! There is still much merit and much happiness in remaining an unsung hero, an honest breadwinner, and a good homemaker. Such shall possess the earth, and of such is the Kingdom of Heaven.

5

Like every other quality or virtue worth having, self-confidence must be put to work and practiced if it is to become effective. The mere *feeling* of self-confidence is nothing in itself. This can be shaken at any time by the appearance of a problem, a burden, or a challenge. Self-confidence is only a form of self-delusion unless it operates as a productive and constructive principle. We must learn to do things on our own initiative, to assume responsibility, and to be prepared to assume the consequences. If one does only the things that come instinctively, the things which are easy, or the things to which one is accustomed, it is impossible to make progress.

It seems to me that I learned a great deal on that spring morning when I was told to take off my shoes and stockings and to walk in my bare feet. For one thing, I learned how good the green, wet grass feels on one's toes. I learned that people did not laugh at me; in fact, they paid no attention to my bare legs and feet. From tender soles, my feet became tough as leather, able to walk over the sand and pebbles as easily as over grass. In the course of time, my feet were cut with sharp stones and glass and nails; but I learned how to endure pain and to take care of the lesions.

To learn, one must try. Many people never learn to drive an automobile because they think they are too nervous. Many never learn to swim because they are afraid they may drown. Many never travel because they are not sure that they would like new places or because they are afraid that the rest of the family at home could not get along without them. Some will not ride in an airplane because they think they may become dizzy or the ship may fall. Some will not try a new dish or eat anything beyond their home fare because they may not like it. Many people will not try anything alone. Others will try nothing new.

Self-confidence should not excite one to wild or reckless deeds; but it should stimulate one to keep growing in knowledge and experience. It should inspire us to share our energies, talents, and time in the service of others as well as of ourselves. It should enable us to recognize when we are wrong.

That these considerations enter into the saving of one's soul and apply also to spiritual development is apparent from Christ's parable of the talents. Of the three servants who received money from their lord for investment during his absence, two traded with it in productive enterprise and made a substantial gain upon his return. The third had this to say, "Being afraid, I went and hid thy talent in the earth. Behold here is that which is thine."

To the first two, the lord replied, "Well done, good and faithful servant. Because thou has been faithful over a few things, I will place thee over many things. Enter thou into the joy of thy lord." As concerns the third, he gave this order: "And the unprofitable servant, cast ye out into the exterior darkness. There shall be weeping and gnashing of teeth."[2] This may seem like rather harsh treatment for cautious people; but it illustrates the principle that the Creator expects us to put what we have to productive use and not to allow ourselves to rust and stagnate from fear of making a mistake.

---

[2] Mt. 25:14–30.

6

Sometimes our self-confidence fails to operate for the reason that we give up too easily or that we like to be petted and pampered. After a period of illness, comes a period of convalescence. There is a certain delightful sensation in feeling weak, in requiring the special attention and assistance of others, and in enjoying what are called a sick man's privileges. This kind of thing can be prolonged beyond reasonable measure and be turned into a permanent condition of convalescence, in which the patient becomes a mental invalid. The time comes when one must exert some energy to recover the use of his limbs, to eat something more than milk and toast, to get out of bed and help himself.

There are people who pamper themselves even before there is any real sickness or need; and they expect others to feel compassionate for them, provide extra service, and assume the extra burden of duties at home or office which their disability entails. A slight headache, the first sniffles of a cold, a temperamental disturbance, or a tired feeling serves as an easy excuse for remaining in bed. This works an imposition on others; but the real loser is the person who effects the excuse. Such behavior, if pursued as a regular policy, disqualifies one from serious consideration; and it may indicate a mental condition in need of correction.

Nearly everyone experiences pain, discomfort, and fatigue in one form or the other. There is nothing extraordinary about this. One must learn to endure these things, quietly and patiently, and not allow them to change the pattern of our existence or to interfere with our normal duties and enjoyment of life. Many people have no one to fall back upon or to rely on except themselves. Nevertheless, they manage to keep going and to remain cheerful through it all.

In some cases, lack of self-confidence comes as the result of being protected and pampered too much by others. A relationship of affection between mother and son or between father and daughter, likewise, may have the effect of retarding development toward maturity and self-confidence. Parental affection, however beautiful, should never permit itself to monopolize the attention and love of the children. Life moves on; and one of the greatest gifts that can be passed on to those under our care is the feeling of security in life with the ability to cope with its problems on an equal basis.

CHAPTER XIV

Keeping Up Appearances

1

To a large extent, the maintenance of mental health depends upon the importance which one attaches to the business of keeping up personal appearance. When the flame of interest in life burns high, life's details come into better focus, new aspects appear, and more things seem worthy of consideration. Life becomes richer, and the beauty and joy of existence become more keen. From a symptomatic point of view, we may draw some pertinent observations on the state of our mental health from the degree of interest and awareness that we exhibit in the things that extend beyond the essentials of bare existence. When one's interest in personal appearance, order, and external impressions burns low, there may be reason for serious concern.

The healthy mind is interested, not merely in things, but also in appearances. It cannot be satisfied with knowing that a friend is alive or dead. It wishes to know where he is, what he is doing, whether he is in good health, and how he is looking. A good cook and a lover of good food are not content merely with a bowl of proteins and starches slapped on the table. Food to be edible must have what is called "eye appeal." It must be served in such form and fashion as will bring pleasure and art to eating. A precious stone may be of great value in itself; but, except to the expert, it means little until it has been shaped and polished. A good picture is, of course, a good picture; but it is much improved and ready for display after it has been properly framed. The same is true of one's personal appearance. A robust mind and a strong body may, absolutely speaking, require nothing further in the way of adornment than the sunshine and breezes; but clothes help to improve the situation. There can be no doubt that a healthy, vital outlook on life itself is manifested in an attractive exterior, so far as a reasonable combination of nature and art will allow.

We must admit that clothes do not make the man or woman, despite a popular saying to the contrary. We are not literally what we wear any more than we are literally what we eat. There is more to the human personality than skin, bones, and clothes. A window dummy can be dressed like a fashion plate. Beauty and fine dresses do not necessarily indicate virtue or keen mentality in a woman. The expression "beautiful but dumb" often summarizes a reality. There are men, known as "stuffed shirts," whose air of importance and whose elegant wardrobes are but a thin veneer over incompetence and laziness. But even here there is a strong element of compensation. Good grooming and good taste in the selection of clothes indicate that effort and thought have been exerted. A clean, neat, and attractive exterior is an evidence of interest and pride in oneself and of concern and compliment for the discerning eye of others.

It has been observed, of course, that many geniuses, careless of material things, retain their extraordinary powers of mind nevertheless. A well-known writer was once described as a "one-man slum." But for most of us, the attention given to external order and appearance — to our visible and extended personality, so to speak — is something which we cannot afford to neglect, without the loss of important stabilizing values.

2

In the selection of proper apparel, one's financial means, the occasion involved, the purpose of the garment, and one's age and station in life must all be taken into consideration. If one does not know what to wear, one can always inquire and find out. There is no point in assuming a lack of concern or a superior, independent attitude in this matter or of risking the embarrassment of unfavorable comment. To ignore the appropriate use of clothing, or to scorn the etiquette of clothes in various places and on different occasions, is to brand oneself as boorish and inconsiderate or as lacking in common sense.

In recent years a casual note has been introduced into the wardrobe of both men and women. No one can question the desirability of being comfortable. But there is such a thing as propriety among civilized people. Sports clothes, sweat shirts, overalls, slacks, and hanging shirttails may be acceptable for an informal outing or among people lounging in their rooms or engaged in the field, garden, or workshop. But a total lack of concern for appearance or an assumption that one may saunter into any place or gathering without regard to one's dress or undress is to give evidence of poor breeding and mental derangement. It has been said that some people would smoke in church unless informed in advance that this is prohibited.

On a tour of Rome a few years ago, I happened to be thrown in with a group of students from different countries and in different states of attire. Several girls of college age were traveling in slacks and bras. This went along without much comment, as we visited the Roman Forum and various public monuments, until we came to the church of St. Paul-outside-the Walls. After passing through the beautiful courtyard, on the threshold of entering the church, the guide found himself obliged to ask the young women to don jackets and to cover their heads in deference for the shrine. "What?" they shrieked. "How silly! If we thought we had to do that, we would not have come on this trip."

A reaction of this kind indicates a lack of appreciation, discipline, and training. A happy mind is one which has learned to conform with certain conventions, to see the meaning and purpose of rules and regulations, and to take a certain pride in following the proprieties. Deference and consideration as expressed in proper attire is but one manifestation of a mind at ease with itself and adaptable to the requirements of the world about it.

From time to time crusades are inaugurated against immodesty in the dress of women. Just what constitutes immodesty is not always easy to say. Some authorities on this subject indicate that it means indecent or excessive exposure, and go so far as to indicate the number of inches that stand between decency and indecency, the color of garments and stockings, the quality of the cloth, and so forth. Others take a less moralizing view of the subject and make objection to excessive display or unusual combinations which serve to attract curious attention and excite ridicule. Almost any sudden change in women's styles is likely to appear daring and possibly scandalous. The hats and clothes of a decade ago always look funny. What is acceptable in one place may be regarded as shocking in another. What would be entirely acceptable beach garments in the United States or France might land one in jail in Spain or Portugal. I happened to be in Peru one Sunday morning when a number of lady tourists were turned away from the church because they were wearing hats instead of veils on their heads.

While there is a wide difference in the connotation of immodesty and eccentricity in dress, the two come close together inasmuch as both indicate a lack of good taste and social sense. The woman who arouses the prurient leers or sneers of men by suggestive or indecent exposure is guilty of one type of offense. But the woman who gets herself up in peculiar attire, or in clothes which are out of keeping with the occasion, may be equally unacceptable from a social point of view and develop an unfortunate reputation. One may argue that it is nobody's business except one's own what one shall wear or how one shall look. But we cannot ignore these considerations without giving rise to derision, exciting scandal, or being regarded as queer. This applies to men as well as to women. Clothes are a badge of mental health or of mental disorder. They can help us or harm us. Personal appearance is the outward expression of the inner personality.

3

With many people, clothes and general appearance serve as a barometer of current mental condition and personal fortune. When things go well with them, they show it. As soon as things go wrong, at home or at work, they become "seedy." Others appreciate good appearance in the members of their family or their associates, but have to be prodded to keep themselves looking neat and presentable. Many a charming bride dresses herself in the home after marriage like a sack of potatoes. Men whose positions and opportunities call for a well-groomed appearance often become careless of their clothes and for the details of personal attention which sometimes mean the difference between advancement and stagnation.

Besides the social effects of good appearance, there is a notable morale-raising power in the consciousness of being well dressed. When in low spirits, women gain a new lease on life by purchasing a new hat or dress. Notwithstanding the romantic claims of many advertisements, they use perfumes — so I am informed — not to snare men, but to give themselves a "lift." Undoubtedly, the fresh odor of soap and shaving lotions produces the same effects in men.

I have been asked by women whether it is sinful for them to use lipstick and rouge to heighten their charms. Upon reflection and some observation, it has been humorously suggested that it might be a sin not to do so. Certainly the best rule is common sense.

With men, especially young men merging from adolescence, there is a kind of timidity and a sense of shame in giving to their grooming more than what is required by absolute necessity. But they leap this hurdle as soon as it becomes clear that romance and slovenliness do not go hand in hand.

Many men have to be taught that dirty fingernails are unsanitary and that biting one's nails is a sign, not of masculinity, but of unsteady nerves. There comes a time in the career of youth when the care of one's hands, as well as the washing of one's ears, marks the transition from the sand lot to maturity. Attention to these details, combing his hair, shining his shoes, the maintenance of a clean, pressed suit, frequent changing of his shirts and socks, and the presentation of a clean-shaven face are all evidence that a boy is coming of age and is beginning to realize that it takes more than muscular prowess to make one's way in the world.

In this respect, men need more help and encouragement than women. Left to themselves, men often remain in the culture of the stable or the alley. A good wife or an observant mother or sister can do much to keep a man presentable and proud of his appearance.

4

On this entire subject, one thing is basic, prior to the selection of attire, personal adornment, or any other form of beautification. From the standpoint of health and social acceptability, nothing can take the place of cleanliness. No accumulation of grease, perfumes, beauty lotions, or fancy clothes can substitute for a well-washed body, a complexion cleaned with soap and water, and fresh, laundered clothes, be they ever so humble. Some people have a clean look and, if we may say so, a clean odor. They have learned the art of regular bathing and washing and of regular, frequent changes of garments. Others have a murky, cloudy, grayish appearance. Their clothes do not bear close inspection, and the exuberance of nature lingers unpleasantly in garments which have been made to serve for too long a period without change. Their teeth reveal a lack of attention, through need of brushing and repair. If they suffer from an intestinal disorder, they communicate the fact through a bad breath from which others must back away.

It is difficult to call these defects of personal hygiene to the attention of offenders. A healthy mind should be aware of the processes of nature and take the necessary precautions in advance, to avoid rancid developments. With the abundance of soap and water available in most communities, there is no excuse for neglect. Frequent and even daily bathing, in the tub or shower, is within the grasp of nearly everyone. Daily brushing of the teeth, a routine washing of hands before meals, the cleaning of fingernails, and general vigilance over body odors should become matters of regular habit. Socks and stockings should be changed daily, and such other renewals should take place as may be indicated to keep onself clean and approachable.

Some people develop phobias on this subject and go to needless extremes. They will not shake hands for fear of picking up germs. They dust off their dinner plates and wipe knives and forks with their napkins before using them. I have known persons to use their handkerchief over a doorknob to avoid contamination. Such fastidiousness, of course, is to be avoided. One must live in a world of reality. We must deal with the good earth. Even dirt and grime have their place in honest toil. All that is required is a reasonable standard of cleanliness and a decent respect for the processes of nature.

5

Improved standards of sanitation and hygiene, together with advances in nutritional habits and medication, have done much in recent years to extend the span of life. Not only has the rate of infant mortality been reduced, with the effect of raising the average life expectancy, but the symptoms of old age have been pushed back, so that people are living longer and retaining their vigor for active work far beyond what was once regarded as normal. People are staying young longer. Whereas men and women once regarded themselves as getting old after the age of forty, they now remain in their prime through the sixties. Many are active in business and travel through their seventies, and in appearance definitely belie their age.

This raises the question as to how far one should go and what measures one should take in retaining the habits and the appearance of youth. For many people, the question may be of considerable practical importance, particularly where business and even social interests are involved. After the forties and possibly the middle thirties, certain changes take place in the physical system, which render it inadvisable for many people to continue in athletic games or sports of a strenuous character. Tennis is a young man's game, like boxing and handball. The businessman looking for outdoor recreation after forty will do well to turn to golf or walking. Men and women who are not used to strenuous physical labor may be advised against taking up heavy loads after this age. It is dangerous folly for one to continue acting like a child or to carry on the activities of youth in middle age. Many people learn this through sorrowful experience.

With respect to attire and general appearance, the same observations are applicable. There is nothing more ridiculous than the sight of an aging woman who continues to dress like a sixteen-year-old girl. Time marches on, and each period of life receives what is appropriate to it. Nevertheless, it may be remarked as both legitimate and proper for people, without infringing upon either their dignity or the claims of time, to keep themselves looking younger, by artificial means if necessary. A woman in business may have to decide whether it is to her advantage to conceal the fact that her hair is graying. The modern age is far more tolerant in this respect than former times. Women today, with strokes of color in their hair, brighter dresses, and sprightlier attention to themselves, need not descend into the little black caps and heavy rustling robes of their mothers and grandmothers. They have learned the art of retaining their youth and their interest in looking young long after the age which marked the declining years and the backward glances of previous generations. This is all to the good. Men likewise have learned that art can sometimes improve nature and that one need not give the impression that one is becoming old or decrepit. The worldly advice "keep your hair on and your stomach off" has much merit. It is probable that more men tint their hair than is commonly realized. If this helps them to keep their positions and to inspire confidence in their business or social relations, who can take reasonable exception to the practice? All that is required in keeping up the appearance of youth and vitality is the exercise of good taste and the practice of sensible habits of living.

6

What applies in the realm of one's personal appearance is true also in the disposition of the environment over which one has control. I am acquainted with students, scholars, writers, and editors whose desks are piled with papers and whose floors are covered with books, so as to constitute a fire hazard and defy the comprehension of anyone except themselves. From such piles of apparent debris, they seem to be able to extract the desired materials at a moment's notice. Any attempt on the part of wife, secretary, or housekeeper to clean up or create a better order would result in a major disaster. For most people, however, more definite procedures are necessary to produce order and to find things when they are desired. In other words, mental health should manifest itself in a home, a study, or a place of business which is clean, orderly, and attractive.

In the training of children, constant emphasis should be placed upon the importance of hanging coats and hats where they can be located and of cleaning up after the game or the party is over. System and order are the first laws in the keeping of business and accounting records and files. The orderly maintenance of one's personal effects pays rich dividends in saving time and money. Cleanliness and order are essential to health and peace of mind. All of this takes effort, but the effort is definitely worth while.

The maintenance of attractive living and working quarters should be one of the joys of existence. Granted that this is not always easy, particularly where there are small children or where the dirt and the smoke of the large city create special problems, we can still manage to keep things in proper place, to keep a clean house, and to give some evidences of cultural appreciation in the selection of decorations, pictures, and furniture. If one's means are modest, he can still live in decency and comfort by the principle of careful selection and care in the upkeep of what he has.

Nothing gives a more distressing impression than a run-down house, where the bathroom is littered with dirty towels, the kitchen with dirty dishes, the bedrooms with shoes and clothes scattered on the floor, and the parlor strewn with the odds and ends of toys, half-read magazines, broken furniture, and torn curtains. From time to time, we all have the experience of going into a place whose heavy odor of antiquity fills us with a strong desire to throw open the windows and to marshal a battery of brooms and mops with plenty of good soap and water, and then perhaps a supply of plaster and paint.

Some people can be given the best of everything in living quarters; and within a short time they manage to turn it into a shambles. Others can turn the humblest of dwellings into clean and delightful places in which to live and work, and they keep them that way. The difference is not necessarily one of money. It is rather one of interest, of pride in one's surroundings, and of the expenditure of effort. I have visited fishing villages in Holland where one could eat on the floors of the little homes, with perfect security in their immaculate cleanliness, and where the few household decorations were a joy to behold. We can all name other places where to eat on the tables would be to take one's life in one's hands.

7

The principles which apply to personal appearance and to the upkeep of premises are equally pertinent to manners and etiquette. Mental health shows itself in a spirit of friendliness, of deference and courtesy, and in a desire to please, even under the most difficult of circumstances. Some people let themselves become shabby and run down in appearance when they feel poor, sick, discouraged, old, and sorry for themselves. Others betray their unhappy moods and tenses in their social behavior. The crude greeting, expressed in grunts, and the reluctance to accommodate others are indications that not all is well under one's skull. Under these circumstances, friends and associates, or the public in general, are required to adjust themselves and comply meekly with commands issued in the form of a bark, blast, or whimper. People are willing to make allowances up to a point. Beyond that, our attitude changes in the problem of coping with a person who is mentally ill.

To a large extent, the way we deal with people, the manners we exhibit, and the appearance we present to others create the world in which we live. If we produce an atmosphere of urbanity, others are likely to follow the example, to take pleasure in keeping clean, in dressing well, in maintaining a pleasant home, and in observing the amenities of existence. Everyone likes to "keep up with the Joneses." When our manners begin to slip, when any old thing will do, when we begin to scorn the formalities of gracious living and to take others for granted, then we can expect casual treatment from others and may look forward only to the leftovers of life.

Keeping up appearance is more than simply maintaining a front. It means the expression of a vital and progressive mind and the burning of a bright beacon light of encouragement and inspiration to others who need our help, perhaps more than we know.

CHAPTER XV

The Uses of Money

I

NEARLY everyone is acquainted with the story of King Midas, whose love for gold was such that he persuaded the gods to grant him the power of turning everything he touched into the precious metal. His delight knew no bounds, until one day he accidentally touched his favorite daughter, who was promptly turned into a golden statue. To undo the harm and have her restored to life, he found himself gladly agreeing to relinquish his golden touch. At the same time, all the other objects which he had turned into gold and hoarded in his royal treasury were converted to their original state. Midas learned, through sorrow, that there are other values in life worth treasuring more than gold and that there are some things that gold cannot buy.

The problem of money is one which plagues most people. In our economic system, as the normal medium of exchange, money serves to purchase the necessities and luxuries of life. It enables us to travel. It provides the sinews of industry and development. It offers not only the means of meeting current needs and obligations, but, wisely accumulated, gives assurance of future security. It often serves as a badge of social prestige. It wields power. It promotes the causes of charity. But it can also harden hearts, lead to corruption, and destroy character. St. Paul refers to the desire of money as "the root of all evils." Christ asserted that it is harder for a rich man to enter heaven than for a camel to pass through the eye of a needle.[1]

There can be no doubt that money in one form or other — including securities, credits, and real estate — enters vitally into the problems of mental health which face the average individual. Few people seem to get enough of money. Complaint about the high cost of living forms the substance of much daily conversation. The struggle to "make ends meet" is a common preoccupation. There are some persons who never seem able to pay their bills and achieve the peace of mind that comes with a comfortable bank account. The more they make, the more they spend, so that they always appear to be treading a water mill in a desperate effort that never ends. At $10,000 a year, they are as financially flat as at $2,000. Even those who have the golden touch, or a facility for making and saving money, are never entirely satisfied. The more they get, the more they want. They raise their voices against exorbitant taxes and bad government, the demands of capital or labor, and high prices. They see themselves as "bled white" by appeals for their contributions to various causes. Some people have what is called the "poor mouth," that is to say, they specialize in telling others how little they make or how little they are able to save, precisely so that they will not be called upon to make a contribution or to pay their share in a common cause.

In formulating a philosophy of life on this subject, it is important for us to regard money for what it is — a medium of exchange. It should not be regarded as a commodity, like food, or clothing, or furniture, or houses. Its value consists in the

---

[1] 1 Tim. 6:10; Mt. 19:24.

fact that it can purchase these things; and in the capitalist system in which we live, it can be invested in productive enterprise from which dividends or interest are paid back. There is nothing magical about it, nor is it a god. The purchasing power of money can go up or down; and if the assets behind it are lost or foreclosed, it becomes worth no more than the paper or the metal on which the money denomination is printed or stamped. Such was the fate of Confederate money, and such has been the destiny of many stocks and bonds during the period of depression, notwithstanding all their fine engraving and promises to pay.

To the extent that money is necessary or helpful, there is certainly nothing bad in it, no matter what the amount may be. For one to assume an airy attitude, as if money were beneath one's dignity or attention, is simply to transfer to someone else the obligation of providing it. Even those who take the vow of poverty need money to keep going. The same may be observed of those who regard money as filthy or somehow associated with the devil. There is no particular virtue in poverty as such, any more than there is anything inherently wrong in possessing riches. Nor should one assume that rich men have made their fortunes dishonestly, while the poor are always the victims of injustice.

One cannot reasonably gather from the words of Christ "What doth it profit a man if he gain the whole world and suffer the loss of his own soul," that the accumulation of money and wealth is necessarily immoral.[2] What He meant was that no amount of worldly goods in this life can compensate for the loss of one's soul in the next life. At no time did He state that making money or accumulating wealth is immoral; but He repeatedly warned against the dangers of dishonesty, covetousness, and hardness of heart that often accompany money-making and the amassing of a fortune. And in particular He described the growth of a ma-

---

[2] Mt. 16:26.

terialistic spirit that places the possession of wealth above all other considerations, resulting in an obsession for gold to the exclusion of spiritual values.

Many people are victims of this obsession, which colors all their thinking, warps the mind, and directs all activities into channels of materialistic calculation. They see nothing of value except in terms of money. Their friends, their social life, and their interest all revolve around this subject. They make friends only because of business considerations, or to secure further contacts which will pay off later on. If they entertain, it is to discharge business debts or to solicit new business. If they give to charity, it is to advertise themselves in the expectancy of financial returns. For them, nothing has value unless it can be expressed in terms of dollars and cents. If they look at a beautiful picture, their interest is in its appraised value. Clothes are worn for what they cost. "What did you pay for it?" is their first question as to things, and "How much money do they have?" is their way of judging personal worth and importance.

2

In order to make money, to save and invest it, and put it to the best advantage, of course, one must take a realistic view. Businessmen have to consider effective measures of solicitation and advertising, and there must be some reciprocity in human relations if we are to gain good will. There can be no doubt that there are prestige values in expense. Where a woman buys a dress and what she paid for it may sometimes be as important as what it looks like. Anyone who takes the business of making a living seriously must watch the dollars and cents with an eagle eye; but to allow these considerations to become an obsession and to dominate one's life to the exclusion of everything else is to develop a warped mentality, to make a god of material gain, and to take the joy out of existence.

This obsession can take hold of persons in poor or modest straits as well as those who have extensive financial interests and holdings. Many wealthy persons are extremely generous and considerate of human needs, while others suffer pain whenever they miss an opportunity to add to their pile or they are asked to contribute to a cause from which no pecuniary return is in sight. Many persons of limited means enjoy life with what they have, far more than the rich, and they are always ready to share with others; but there are some whose pinchpenny policy actually prevents them from getting ahead, and whose nose is never lifted from the grindstone of life for any other purpose than to take in more money.

When I was a student, the annual oratorical contest always brought out at least one portrayal of a miser, whose solitary pleasure consisted in letting the gold and silver coins slip through his fingers and who finally went crazy when a thief robbed him of his hoard. George Eliot's famous novel *Silas Marner* drew a similar picture, with the difference that the golden hair of a child came to replace the lost gold of the miser, whose life was redeemed by a human love. In present-day life, however, miserliness seldom takes these cruder forms. But it still corrodes the minds and shrivels the lives of people in all walks of life, for whom the only thing that counts is money.

With an increasing number of people, this is manifested in their attitude toward their work or profession. Their only reason for working is to make money. They are not interested in what they are doing. They refuse to take a professional attitude toward their work or profession. They have no desire to improve themselves in their skill or career. They take no pleasure in their occupation. It never occurs to them that they can make a social contribution by a task well done. They have no desire to assume responsibility. They are interested in only one thing — the pay check. In their minds, overtime to finish a job or to do it better is unthinkable except in terms of "time and one half." If they are offered another job which pays more, they have no hesitancy in leaving what they have. Conditions in which one is working, the cause which one is serving, the various human values involved appear to have no weight in making a decision. "How much money is there in it?" is the one question upon which the answer depends.

3

The problem of what to do with the precious stuff receives different solutions for different temperaments and various circumstances. With many, it soon vanishes in the struggle of daily existence after payment of the many bills that eat up their substance. Under these circumstances, there is practically no fun in living, since work itself is regarded as a drudge. With some, the surplus is quickly drained off in pleasure and distractions or forms of display — movies, liquor, fancy clothes — usually with little to show in the end and always the same complaint, "I don't know where the money goes." With others, money is something to cling to as to life. Such people are always complaining about being "broke" even though they may have substantial savings stored away. They suffer when called upon to give anything away; and they begrudge even themselves the things that they need, such as clothing, or the things they could enjoy, such as travel or any form of diversion that costs money.

Some people regard money as a kind of magic talisman which can purchase anything. They feel that its possession puts them in a position to make any kind of demand. They buy their way, or attempt to do so, to honors, social position, influence, power, public office, and arrogance. From certain classes of individuals, money can obtain almost anything, including sexual surrender, the breakup of homes and divorce, the spreading of falsehood, the ruination of reputations, and even murder. Unscrupulous persons, with plenty of money at their disposal, sometimes develop the easy assumption that money can buy anyone. When they meet with resistance or indignant refusal, they are bewildered, furious, and dangerous. When money takes the place of ethics or cancels out the principles of morality, it destroys the individual and society.

The effects of money differ with persons of various temperaments and are often difficult to predict or foresee. Many people who are charming, cordial friends in moderate circumstances become hard, cold, and grasping when prosperity comes their way. Just as many change into petty tyrants when given a little authority, so, under the influence of money, others change their whole attitude toward life, toward their friends, and toward human and spiritual values. Undoubtedly many people who are leading happy lives and performing unselfish services, under pressure of having to make their way in low or medium brackets of income, would be altogether different if they were financially independent.

The effects of quick and easy money are often very dramatic. Those persons who are not prepared to handle large incomes or fortunes easily go to pieces. Drink, dissipation, sexual looseness, and all the confusion that money can buy tell the familiar story of scandal, divorce, personal disintegration, and suicide. One might think that material prosperity would bring about a sense of deeper appreciation and gratitude to God for these liberal favors. Unfortunately, it frequently produces exactly the opposite. Prosperity often brings about a loss of religious faith and a rejection of God as the leading force in life.

In the words of Oliver Goldsmith:

> Ill fares the land, to hastening ills a prey,
> Where wealth accumulates and men decay.[3]

In this sense, Christ laid down the perennial principle, "You cannot serve God and Mammon."[4] For the sake of mental health, happiness in life, and the salvation of one's soul, it is far better to forego many of the pleasures and conveniences of life which only money can buy. In the pursuit of wealth, one must be prepared to assume its great responsibilities and to cope humbly with its dangers. Otherwise, it may turn out to be a bitter fruit indeed.

---

[3] *The Deserted Village.*   [4] Mt. 6:24.

4

The observance of two great virtues is essential, if one is to cope successfully with this problem and to live in peace with one's conscience and with society. One of these virtues is justice. The other is charity. Both must work together, and one must temper the other. Justice needs the softening hand of mercy and of human understanding. Charity needs the guidance of intelligence and prudent consideration. And both need divine assistance.

Justice involves the whole world of human relationships. Economic justice, in its full implications, includes a far wider and deeper range of considerations than are contemplated in this present study. Larger forces are at work than we can fully grasp, such as the laws of supply and demand. There are natural inequities over which we have no direct control. The rival interests of individuals, groups, and nations give rise to problems for which there is often no easy answer. Nevertheless, the peace of individuals, like the peace of nations, requires earnest and sustained effort in fair dealing to secure what is right and just. The accumulation of money or of wealth in any form, by unjust means, may produce a temporary illusion of success and power. But ill-gotten gains gnaw away at peace of mind, at the same time as they upset the equilibrium of peace in society. Mental health cannot be sustained so long as the scales of justice are out of balance.

The lure of quick and easy money has been one of the greatest temptations of the mad world in which we live; and has probably done more than anything else to leech the land, uproot populations, and dissipate our national resources. The publicity given to the fabulous salaries of the movie stars, news of sudden fortunes in oil, the sudden emergence of "new rich," and the constant prodding of advertisements of expensive conveniences and gadgets of various kinds, all contribute to arouse dissatisfaction with the ordinary processes of making a living and to stimulate a search for the bonanza.

No one can deny the desirability of improving one's fortunes by all legitimate means. But when the rush for money means the abandoning of all ethical standards and the reduction of human relationships to the laws of the jungle, we have reached a condition which is pathological and deadly. Cheating, stealing, defrauding, underpaying, overcharging, misrepresentation, adulteration, issuing shoddy goods, absconding funds — the newspapers carry these stories every day, together with the gruesome stories of the long arm of the law, wrecked homes, and ruined reputations. The acceptance of graft and "hush money" assumes tremendous proportions in many communities, reaching up from the underworld into the businesses and homes of apparently respectable citizens and often corrupting the whole fabric of public administration.

To be on one's guard against the temptation of easy money calls for a high and unshakable sense of principle and often for extraordinary vigilance. Under the seemingly innocent guise of a gift of appreciation, many a good man has been sucked into the whirlpool of corruption and been blackmailed into silence and inactivity.

Within recent years, the appeal of quick and easy money has led to a spiral of inflation, which in some countries has wiped out the entire middle class and in others has reduced the purchasing value of money to a fraction of what it once was. Excessive profits, quick turnovers through speculation in real estate, ever mounting taxes, and similar devices have had the effect of increasing costs and in some cases of making rapid fortunes. But the over-all result has been to diminish the value of savings, sometimes to the vanishing point, and to increase the cost of living to a point where the advantages of more money are illusory rather than real.

In an endeavor to reach "Easy Street" in a hurry, some people resort to gambling in one form or the other. There is nothing inherently wrong in gambling. We all take risks and chances in various forms. Many people play the horses for recreation. Some gamble with cards, raffles, and various games of chance, for charitable causes, excitement, and the possibility of gain. To the extent that one can afford to take a loss, there can be no reasonable objection to this in itself. The same is true of speculation on the stock market, even as a livelihood. But when one's interest in this becomes a preoccupation to the neglect of regular business, the endangering of one's funds, temptation of dipping into the funds of others, or the fraying of nerves — the time has come to call a halt. Some people are driven crazy through tension of this kind. No amount of money or prospect of making money is worth this risk.

Before participating in gambling, the good citizen should also ask himself or herself whether it is legal or not and make some inquiries into the background of the scheme. Illegal gambling has developed into a tremendous business, involving the corruption of public officials and crime of every kind, including murder. The little clerk or innocent housewife may be unaware of this while joining with thousands of others through small contributions, to make it possible for criminals to undermine good government and encourage men of the lowest caliber to dominate public power. The people who are shocked by the exposures of public investigations are often the ones who have made big crime possible by investing their dimes and dollars in underground games of chance.

This would be a far better world if people concentrated on their work, fulfilled their obligations, and took their joy in producing and serving well in their respective avocations instead of concentrating simply on money and the things that money can buy. Joy in living and the accumulation of material goods go hand in hand only when one's conscience is clear, when gain is the fruit of service, and peace of mind is the product of honest endeavor.

5

One of the most frequent causes of dishonesty and of mental unrest relative to use of money is the tendency to live above one's means. It has been said that most people are honest until they feel a desperate need for cash. This need may be real, in view of a pressing obligation, or it may arise mentally from a pressing desire to purchase a better car, a new home, a radio, a television, a refrigerator, fancier clothes, and in general to keep up with associates who may have more means at their disposal. In some cases, the wife, as well as the husband, may have to work to supplement the meager earnings. In other cases, she may have to work to keep up a more expensive establishment than a normal income can produce. In such cases, the question may resolve itself to an alternative between a home and children and a house with all the latest equipment and luxuries and no children.

Very often, the cause of mental unrest and complaint is a lack of system in handling one's business affairs. Everyone should maintain at least some kind of budget, so as to establish a relationship between income and expenses. Some people constantly find themselves in a position of having to ask for an advance on their salaries. With cash in hand, they proceed to spend everything they have on the first things they see. Then comes a period of distress. Under these circumstances, it is feast or famine, with famine predominating. Good management, economy, and a willingness to deny oneself and to be happy without some desirable objects are part of a solvent existence and a life of contentment and sufficiency.

Many people go through life with a constant, heavy mental baggage of unpaid bills. There is one important rule to follow: pay bills promptly. If there is a good reason why payment cannot be made as stipulated, then an explanation should be given as to when payment may be expected. If one takes exception to a bill, a protest should be made or an explanation be requested.

But it is inexcusable to allow bills to run on unpaid, month after month and perhaps year after year, with no word or response. These observations are valid whether the amount involved is large or small.

Quite apart from the ethical questions involved in the ignoring or nonpayment of bills, the reputation of being what is called a "dead beat" or a "cheap skate" is unenviable. There are numerous disadvantages in having one's credit impaired. There are some persons who apparently have no sense of obligation in contracting bills. Others have the sense of obligation but keep dodging the duty of payment. In either case, the public develops a case of resentment, and it becomes increasingly difficult for the offenders to do business on anything except a cash basis. The defense sometimes employed of looking upon creditors with contempt or of regarding business procedures as needless red tape is a poor substitute for paying one's debts.

There is no disgrace in buying on the installment plan or in borrowing money to launch a business venture or to meet current obligations. But such procedure should be carefully thought out in advance. One should determine whether the purchase or the loan is really necessary. If so, one should recognize the contractual nature of the commitment and be prepared to make payments punctually as agreed. The idea that things will somehow work out by themselves or that the burden of collection rests with the creditor is as shortsighted as it is dishonest. Similarly with borrowing objects, whether they be umbrellas, clothes, implements, or books. These things still belong to the original owner, and should be returned within a reasonable period of time without the owner's being put to the necessity of repeatedly asking for them.

I recall as a boy borrowing books from a public library and forgetting to return them on time. One Saturday afternoon, while rummaging in a closet, I discovered the books and suddenly realized that a fine would be due. I suddenly gathered them up and rushed to the home of the librarian, in the thought that this would be the way to avoid paying the fine.

"Young man," she said, "you borrowed these books from the library, not from me. On Monday morning, the library will be open. Bring them there, and at that time pay your fine."

It seems to me that I learned a good lesson from that experience. Since that time, I have had occasion to teach the same lesson to others whose tardy ideas of transacting business are always conceived to the inconvenience of others and at inappropriate times, in the expectancy of being relieved of an unpleasant and overdue obligation.

Anyone who is acquainted with human nature must realize the sensitive character of people when dealing with debits and credits. It has been said that, although we may forget what we have borrowed, we never forget what someone owes us. Acting on this principle, it is always prudent for us to keep our financial affairs in good order.

This applies also to the disposition of one's goods after death. Everyone should make a will, disposing of his estate as desired, and in such form as will be legal and binding. There is nothing more unpleasant or inevitable than the spectacle of a family torn apart because of an unsettled estate or a missing or defective will. The time to make a will is when one is alive, in good health, and in full possession of his mental powers. A will can be changed from time to time to meet changes in intentions. It is too late, after one is dead; and one never knows when death may come.

Much might be said on the subject of charity. There are too many people who make a great deal of noise about every penny that they give away. They do not realize that what they possess is only a loan from God; and counting up all that they give away to charitable, religious, and educational purposes, most persons still retain enough for themselves. We must learn to share what we have, and to pass some dividends back to society and to those who depend upon us. Bread cast upon the waters usually comes back buttered.

Of its own weight, money can be a millstone around our necks. Lightened with the gifts of generosity, consideration, kindness, and charity, it can give us what we need in this life and serve as a steppingstone to possess the infinite riches of God in eternity.

CHAPTER XVI

Enjoy Yourself

I

ONE of the basic rules of mental health is cultivation of the spirit of enjoyment. By its nature, the mind tends toward the true and the beautiful. All the faculties of the soul ardently desire happiness and strive for it under one form or the other. We are taught that the great reward of virtue in the next life is the perfect happiness that comes from contemplation of the beauty and perfection of God. If such is the culmination of mental health in eternity, does it not stand to reason that the enjoyment of life in this world is the natural and God-given evidence of mental health before the attainment of eternity?

Most plants and animals flourish in the sun and air. The higher forms of life in the water require freedom of motion and space in which to move about. The sensation of exhilaration and strength characterizes the physical health of all creatures which possess nervous energy and sensitivity. The human mind, as comprising both organic and spiritual faculties, is no exception. To compress it into an atmosphere of gloom and to deny it the pleasure that comes from the satisfaction of work well done or from legitimate recreation and experience is to deprive it of a basic expression and natural reward.

The gloom that enshrouds many lives is the result of an unwholesome fear of enjoyment as somehow sinful or associated with the work of the devil. The ancient sect of the Manichaeans, which arose in early competition with Christianity, had the idea that all material creation and all activity of the flesh were bad, including human love and marriage, and that any pleasure derived from these sources was to be avoided. This idea has reappeared in various forms through the centuries and even in modern times has set up a form of false rigorism under the guise of religion. Any form of card playing, dancing, smoking, drinking, or competitive gaming has been represented as shameful frivolity leading straight to damnation. Of this tendency, as exemplified by the Puritans of his day, Samuel Johnson remarked that its addicts objected to bearbaiting, not because it gave pain to the bear, but because it gave pleasure to the spectators. Under the pretense of destroying symbols of idolatry, even the joy and inspiration expressed in Christian art has been wiped out of religion by stern spirits for whom fear has replaced the love of God.

In some homes, the children are brought up in an atmosphere of repression and stern discipline, where any form of enjoyment is regarded with suspicion. Entertainment of any kind is regarded as needless frivolity. A chill is thrown upon any kind of social activities within the home; and extramural contacts of a recreational kind have to be carried on in secrecy. The parents engender a spirit of terror in the children, and everything is reduced to a dead level of silence and exclusion. In such a house and with such specifications, Elizabeth Barrett was brought up under an iron rule of a jealous father, and languished as an invalid, until Robert Browning braved the lion's den and delivered her from it with his love and courage. The story of the Barretts of Wimpole Street carries a strong object lesson for people who are striving for mental and physical health alike.

2

Some people deny themselves the joys of life because they are burdened with the idea that pleasure interferes with work. There is such a thing as taking pleasure in one's work; and this principle is basic to a happy and useful life. But there is such a thing also as becoming a drudge and slave to work, with no time out for play or rest. Everyone needs a refreshing pause from work, if only to regain his strength and to broaden his perspective on what he is doing. "All work and no play makes Jack a dull boy," according to an ancient adage. There is such a thing as keeping one's nose too close to the grindstone. Burned-out lives, nervous breakdowns, heart failure, and a record of mediocrity or disappointed hopes are often the fruit of overwork and drudgery, unillumined by the light of what comes from an occasional idle moment.

Sometimes, the deterrent to real enjoyment in life is the fear that recreation of any kind may cost too much money. It is folly, of course, to scatter one's means to the winds simply for the sake of a good time. On the other hand, it is well to remember that money is good only for what it will buy. Many people needlessly deprive themselves of entertainment, good food, proper clothing, travel, and social life, because they hate the idea of spending, on themselves or on others. As a result they live a cold, shriveled existence, and leave their savings to relatives who meant little to them in life and whose only prayer may have been for the early death of their benefactors and a generous place in their wills.

Some keep putting off the enjoyment of life to the age of retirement or until some definite date, when they can start drawing on a pension or from their accumulated savings, with the feeling of perfect security. No one can doubt the prudence of saving for a "rainy day," or of making provisions for one's old age. But even with these worthy objects in mind, there are many pleasures that come with each period of life and that can never be recaptured. The enjoyment of many plans, unfortunately, is never brought to fruition, for the reason that with old age one loses the physical energy, the interest, the taste, and the zest that make for enjoyment. Many a millionaire has moved into his dream house after arthritis and ulcers have made it impossible for him to enjoy expected pleasures. Indefinite postponement of a trip or a vacation often means that it will never be taken. The purchase of a helpful convenience or of a thing of beauty may come when it is too late. For people who live stingily, for themselves or their families, particularly when there is no real need to do so, in the expectancy of enjoying life at a later date, this adage is pertinent: "It is later than you think."

Some philosophers have spurned the joy of life in the thought that all joys are fleeting. For them, pleasure is a waste of time. But, as a matter of fact, all life is fleeting, so that the same argument might be used against the value of work. Time is the measure of motion; but the value of motion is not measured by whether it is long or short. A kind word takes but a moment; but it is certainly as valuable as a long speech which conveys only generalities and confusion. A moment of enjoyment may be just as valuable as a year or a lifetime of unwilling toil.

3

There is an art of enjoyment, just as there are rules and standards of guidance in the selection of legitimate pleasures. Some people fail to enjoy whatever they are doing or whatever they possess for the reason that they are unable to relax. Enjoyment is the product of recognition and appreciation. There is such a thing as pleasurable excitement. There is a pleasure in the glow of enthusiasm. But enjoyment, as such, arises from concentration on a particular object and a willingness to devote oneself to recognition and appreciation of the object or activity which produces a pleasurable reaction.

Many people are so preoccupied with the past or the future that they never live in the present. They never experience the joy of meeting people, for the reason that their minds are on other business. They cannot enjoy a social evening because they are wrapped up in the unfinished business of the day. They see nothing in a beautiful picture, because they are engrossed in a problem that needs to be solved. To overcome this absent-mindedness, a special effort may be necessary to force oneself to live in the present, to make a deliberate effort to participate in the here-and-now, and try to make the most of a moment or an hour of pause or recreation or beauty.

In some cases, the art of enjoyment may call for rigorous self-discipline. The trouble with many people who are under tension is that they do not give themselves sufficient time in which to get into the spirit of appreciation and enjoyment. They rush into a situation; and if the immediate results do not measure up to their expectations or challenge, they rush out again. If they start a detective story, and do not find three murders in the first chapter, they throw the book aside. If they go on a vacation and it rains the first day, they wish to return home immediately. If they take up a game or a sport and do not grasp the rules at once, they conclude that it must be very dull, and they drop it. If they go to a party and do not find themselves highly entertained within the first ten minutes, they leave in haste. Enjoyment takes time, patience, and willingness to learn and to share. Sometimes, it requires a willingness to be disappointed. One cannot expect the crisis of a drama to come in the first act, or a royal flush to appear with the first deal. Nor is there any good reason why, to provide for our pleasure, the rest of the world should always be moving on the double quick.

The same people rush through their meals, and they wonder why they have become dyspeptic, both in their alimentary tracts and in their dispositions. They rush through their work and wonder why it has become such a chore. The fact is that unless one takes time to enjoy the natural functions of life and the duties of one's calling, nature has a way of backing up in indignation and of punishing the offenders.

Others are prevented from enjoyment by mental disturbance over petty, incidental details. Every bowl of soup seems to have a fly in it; every pleasure seems to be marred by an unpleasant consideration. Every social gathering has something wrong with it; every friend has some defect of character. Every vacation trip has some drawback. Nothing seems to please, because of some shortcoming. One can concentrate on these imperfections, and remain in a perpetual state of disappointment. One can even anticipate them and take a dim outlook on all prospects of enjoyment. Or one can determine to see the brighter and more beautiful ensemble and overlook the little blemishes. Two persons with different points of view can look at the same scene and derive totally different impressions and reactions. One person can look at the Grand Canyon and marvel at the magnificent handiwork of God, counting it a tremendous privilege to view this marvel of nature. Another may be annoyed and distracted from the view because the grass along the rim is wet or dusty, or the day is warm, or there are a few flies buzzing around. I know a lady who disliked Rome because she was unable to buy peanuts there.

It may be necessary sometimes for one to ask himself whether the trouble lies outside or within oneself. It may be helpful to ask, "Why did I come here? Was it to allow myself to be annoyed by little things of no consequence, or by temperamental fits in myself and others, or to put my mind on the central object and enjoy it?" Few things in life are perfect. It is up to the individual to concentrate on the positive, beautiful, and pleasant aspects and to enjoy them, or to become engrossed in critical and complaining attitudes on details of secondary or quite incidental importance.

4

Some people are willing to enjoy life, but only in a cautious kind of way. They are on their guard against enthusiasm, lest there might be some snare or delusion under pleasant appearances. If they accept a gift or an invitation, it is always with a kind of mental reservation that there may be an evil purpose or ulterior motive lurking in the background. Some take their happier moments in a sad kind of way, in the thought that it may be unfair for them to enjoy themselves while someone is at home ill or there is so much suffering in the world. There may be merit in considerations under the heading of prudence or compassion; but it should be kept in mind that neither suspicion nor gloom have any real effect if something is really wrong.

A similar observation might be made on the subject of the worries about home or business which some persons carry with them on vacation. One of the prime purposes of a vacation is to leave these worries behind and to get a fresh start in life. To cut off from this mental baggage may require a special and continued effort. One should make the effort. It is amazing how many things manage to get done by themselves or with the assistance of others in our absence. The person who thinks that the world cannot get along without him would do well to meditate on the many centuries it existed before he came along and the many yet to come after he or she is dead.

With some, the problem is of an opposite character. Some people find it difficult to enjoy themselves without going to extremes. In a humorous or festive mood, they do not know when to stop. Their jokes become so pointed as to become offensive, and their playful tricks become obnoxious and end in the alienation of friends. Instead of leaving the party at a reasonable hour, they wear out their welcome. Instead of enjoying a convivial drink with friends, they proceed to empty the bottle or the barrel and have to be removed in an intoxicated condition. A friendly game of cards becomes a pitched battle, so that all the enjoyment is taken out of it. Almost everything that pleases them is a temptation to excess. Their early enthusiasm soon descends to crude levels, and they end in a surfeited and bestial condition, ashamed of themselves and shunned by others.

Referring to standards of urbanity and civilized enjoyment, the Roman poet Horace spoke of "the golden mean," or the spirit of restraint that must govern enjoyment if it is to serve a reasonable purpose and be self-contained. The ancient philosopher Epicurus has often been identified with the motto, "Let us eat and drink today, for tomorrow we die," and a host of so-called Epicureans have assimilated this motto as a way of life. Nevertheless, Epicurus, as a lover of the good things of this life, recognized that excessive indulgence defeats its own purpose. True enjoyment arises from the proper functioning of one's faculties. Overstimulation dulls the wits and sickens the body. Gluttony and excessive self-indulgence of any kind are contrary to the first principles of intelligent living and for the same reason are immoral as well as inadvisable.

In both the Old and the New Testaments, there is plenty of evidence to the effect that good eating and the enjoyment of wine, as well as of the other pleasures of life, are the gifts of God, when indulged in moderation and in accordance with the Commandments. Christ enjoyed the company of His friends, drank wine, even working a miracle at the wedding feast of Cana to refill the depleted wine reserves. He wore a seamless garment, and in general showed Himself deeply appreciative of the beauties of nature even to the lilies of the field. St. Paul explicitly recommended a little wine as good for the stomach, and all the Apostles showed themselves as men living close to the humble joys of the earth. But at the same time, they strenuously preached the doctrine of temperance in all things, and they urged the practice of self-discipline, self-denial, and even penance as the path to self-control, to expiation for sin, and to salvation.

This would seem to indicate that both enjoyment and self-denial have their appropriate places in life in the expression and perfection of virtue. Rational enjoyment gives glory to God, like the beauty of the lilies of the field, whom not even Solomon in all his glory could rival. But when enjoyment

threatens to run against the Commandments of God, it must
be disciplined; and when gratification means overindulgence, it
must give way to self-denial and penance. The person who cannot drink without going to excess should not drink. The person
who cannot gamble without squandering his resources or running
afoul of decent human considerations should not gamble. Considerations of moral standards, personal prudence, health, and
urbanity must always stand on guard to keep one within reasonable limitations. Everyone has his weakness; and everyone
must be vigilant in the practice of "the golden mean" or of
abstinence, when necessary, to maintain enjoyment on a rational
level, and to avoid the disgust and remorse that comes from
unbridled appetite.

5

The enjoyment of life does not always come spontaneously.
There is something deliberate and adventuresome in it. Apart
from the elemental gratification in sensory pleasure, such as
the feeling of a cool breeze on a hot day, or of satisfying one's
hunger, or of relief at the end of a busy day, there are many
pleasures which require some advertence and attention to the
subject. One can learn much from others who have learned to
discriminate and to pause in the presence of an object or
activity which is worthy of consideration.

I recall the first time I was privileged to visit the famous art
gallery of the Louvre in Paris. As I had but a limited time, I
asked my guide to select the outstanding masterpieces for my
attention. The first object he selected was Winged Victory of
Samothrace. "Now, stand here," he said in the manner of kinder-
garten teacher. "The thing to do is to pause and admire this
statue." My first reaction was resentment of this patronizing
attitude; but I soon recognized that he was quite correct. In my
rush, I should probably have passed by, thinking that there was
something more important ahead. His cold-blooded admonition
stopped me in my tracks and compelled me to focus my atten-

tion on what was immediately before me. I shall never forget the Winged Victory.

In conducting tours of my own since that time, I have repeatedly had occasion to remind the members of my group in similar terms. Often, in the presence of a magnificent mountain view, which people have come thousands of miles to see and for which they have laid out a substantial amount of money, they will rush to the curio booth on location and spend their precious time fingering cheap souvenirs or buying post cards of the beautiful scene to which they have given only a passing glance. In cathedral towns, tourists often prefer to haggle with street hawkers or spend their time in souvenir shops buying junk which they could easily get at home, until they are reminded that they are missing the things really worth seeing.

We do not have to go abroad to experience this tendency in ourselves or in others of overlooking the truly wonderful things in life. Nor does one have to expend large sums of money to derive deep enjoyment. It has been said that the best things in life are free. After health, the first essential ingredient for enjoyment is imagination. With a few sticks and a little yard to play in, children have the time of their lives playing games and living in an imaginary world far more wonderful than expensive reality. There are so many enjoyable things at our doorsteps and easily within our grasp that we need only open our eyes and make a little effort to take advantage of them. Of the millions of Americans who annually trail through the galleries, museums, and churches of Europe, how many take the pains of visiting the treasures in American museums and monuments of historical and aesthetic value? Very few people living in large cities are acquainted with more than their own neighborhood, and must wait for some country cousin of more curiosity and knowledge than they to take them around for a visit of the points of interest — the parks, beaches, theaters, museums, lectures, factories, schools. Countryfolk are usually better acquainted with their resources, but even they often squander their lives wishing for the "elsewhere" and the "otherwise," in oblivion of the beauty and interest around them, and living in squalor and needlessly cramped quarters.

We should not be afraid to use our imaginations in arranging our lives, our homes, and our program and way of doing things to bring into them the various notes of what is called gracious living. Nor should one scorn, in this process, the many and rich suggestions that are offered by others who know how to do things well. Many magazines are now available in the realms of house and garden. Such a small thing as the arrangement of flowers makes the difference between a "bunch" of posies and a thing of beauty. Likewise, the manner of setting a table and serving the meal makes the difference between feeding and dining. The formalities of cleanliness, a little prayer, and planned leisureliness, with perhaps some small surprise, can transform a dinner from a perfunctory satisfaction of hunger into a delightful social experience. The matter of careful selection and arrangement of home furnishings makes the difference between a house and a home in which one likes to live and to entertain friends. If one has a yard or garden, a little imagination, and perhaps a suggestion or two, can change it from a blank area into a delightful spot that one can use and enjoy.

Enjoyment in life usually requires advance planning. If things are done on the spur of the moment, there is no assurance of their success. And if one depends upon special inspiration, time will march on before we know it. Anniversaries, birthdays, social gatherings, picnics, and projects of any kind from which one hopes to derive recreation and enjoyment or to bring enjoyment to others, must be planned well in advance. So often, people say, "This year things are going to be different. We are going to take time out to enjoy ourselves. We must invite in some of our friends and fulfill our social obligations. Let us not forget our wedding anniversary, or let the children's birthdays go by without something special." Then they become so engrossed in daily drudgery or in various kinds of immediate demands, that another year rolls around with nothing to show for their good resolutions. One should keep a calendar or notebook, and definitely set aside important dates and things to do and then make provision for them well ahead of time. These matters are just as important as business or financial obligations, and the fact that they are calculated to bring pleasure and enjoyment into one's life or into the lives of others renders them no less important and imperative.

The fact that enjoyment takes effort and advance planning is precisely the reason why so many people lead drab and uninteresting lives. They see only the effort and regard it as a hurdle too strenuous to take for an unknown reward. Taking up a book, attending a series of lectures or concerts, learning to appreciate good music and fine art, going away for a trip — all these things seem to involve bother and a needless expenditure of time and energy. To many persons, the cultivation of a hobby appears to be the sign of a slightly queer mentality. But one must make the effort, or grow stale. Learning to enjoy life is like learning to eat. Most children have to be forced to eat a variety of foods; and those who resist often grow up unable to relish anything except one or two kinds of meat and unwilling to try anything else. The old saying "Variety delights" is effective only if one is willing to try variety. "I never knew what I was missing," can be said by many people whose distrust, prejudice, fear, or plain laziness keeps them from enjoyment of the worth-while things in life within their grasp, until it is, perhaps, too late.

6

For one's mental peace and equilibrium, it should be understood that enjoyment is but one facet of life. It is not an absolute, but is relative to many factors. The person who starts out with the idea that all of life is "a bowl of cherries," that there is a magic key to its fun, and that he is entitled to all and every pleasure that he can get, is doomed to disappointment. The fact is that life is full of sorrow, pain, disappointment, and unalloyed drudgery. We must recognize this and be prepared to accept our share and perhaps more than our share. As life shapes up, these things are unevenly divided, but no one can say in what proportions. Many individuals who seem to be riding the crest of life, and drinking its pleasures like the favorites of the gods, suffer deeply in one way or the other. Many who carry a heavy burden of sorrow or physical ailment often enjoy a profound inner peace, and love life even while they contemplate deliverance into the eternal presence of God.

There are conditions also under which the enjoyment of life is all but impossible. Under intense sickness and pain, we cannot speak of enjoyment. Under a profound sense of injustice, or with the mental nausea that comes from a sense of unfairness or of disappointment from which there is no apparent escape, joy goes out of life; and one must use special remedies and invoke special considerations to avoid the permanent injury of mental shock and despair.

Even within normal conditions of life, the average person has to face problems and obligations which are not exactly pleasant. The person who flees a situation because it is not pleasant will be kept in flight through a large part of his or her existence. Such people cannot possibly enjoy life. The capacity to enjoy is, indeed, the reverse side of the capacity to suffer, and can often be measured in the same proportion. The mature person must be prepared for both, to accept both in a spirit of understanding, to survive both in integrity of soul, and to give glory to God through a recognition that His power and beauty are manifested in the storm cloud as well as in sunshine.

Certain temperaments are confronted with the difficulty of being either in the heights or the depths. They find it difficult to live in the "golden mean." When things go well with them, their enthusiasm knows no bounds. With the first reverse, they are ready to quit this life. Insofar as these reactions are physical, there is no absolute solution or cure. Nevertheless, we can help ourselves considerably, particularly through a discipline of decisions. The panorama of personal experience is much like the weather. It changes. To act or to make decisions under the stress of a particular mood or moment is to be unrealistic. One can be reasonably certain that every pleasure will pass; but so will most pains, even those which lead to the grave. The sensible person will take both in stride and measure as part of the divine plan and part of the richness of life.

The basic element of human enjoyment is not physical or sensual pleasure, although this is not to be ruled out of legitimate consideration. Nor is it merely a matter of temperamental inclination or preference. It consists rather in an evaluation and appreciation of an intellectual and cultural character — a recognition of the truth, the goodness, and the beauty of things as the gifts of God. The enjoyment of a cup of cold water — which can be a matter of truly great enjoyment — has far deeper significance than merely quenching one's thirst. It partakes of the nature of gratitude. The enjoyment of a beautiful sunset comes not merely from the witnessing of many colors in afterglow, but in conveying an impression of eternity. The intimate relations of man and wife in the procreative act give rise to a pleasure which extends far beyond that of sensual pleasure and finds its meaning in the expression of a great mutual love. One suffers and sacrifices gladly, and even with pleasure, if the loss serves a good cause. And the greatest of all openhearted enjoyment is that which comes with the consciousness that one is sharing a gift and bringing a joy to another — be it man or God.

CHAPTER XVII

The Mature Mind

I

A CONSTANT objective in the development of mental health is mature action. Physically, a child advances from the infant stages of clinging to his mother's breast, then to creeping on hands and knees. When he has mastered the art of standing on his own two feet, he has achieved the first real triumph on the road to maturity. The expression "standing on one's own two feet" seems to be applicable to the entire range of human activity, intellectual and moral as well as physical. When one has cultivated confidence in his own judgment and learned to take deliberate, determined, and consistent action as his own responsibility, he has mastered the first and perhaps the most important secret of mental health and has become a mature person.

There are, of course, different kinds of maturity, some true and positive, others spurious and in the nature of a false front rather than of a sound and justified sense of security and independence. Genuine maturity may be described as a conviction of personal worth and dignity, together with a realistic appraisal of one's ability. Arrival at this conviction and appraisal is not always easy. For persons of different education, experience, and temperament, the problem of recognition may assume various characters; and personal adjustment to the desired standards and attitudes may call for special procedures.

The development of mental maturity begins with the understanding that everyone has a definite place in life and in the providence of the Creator. Everyone must take himself or herself seriously and require the same respect from others. Every individual is precious in the sight of God; and no one should regard himself in a less exalted position. This thought should be a guiding light in the conscious direction of personality. It should govern the thinking of everyone. It should serve as the keynote of personal responsibility and a constant source of strength and inspiration.

This appraisal of self is in complete harmony with the virtue of humility, for the reason that it starts with a recognition of one's relationship to almighty God. It is thoroughly consonant with the virtue of charity, for it recognizes the fundamental equality of all men and the bond of human unity in common origin and destiny. The person who is conscious of his spiritual dignity can never be guilty of false pride, on the one hand, or of hopeless pessimism, on the other. No matter how poor one may be in personal talents or in this world's goods, he still has the assurance of God's loving care and of sufficient strength to do his duty. A living awareness of Divine Providence is undoubtedly the most strengthening and sustaining of all factors in self-respect, self-confidence, and the assurance of a mature mind.

2

Whatever may be our background or experience, it is essential that we be willing to stand on our own merits and to develop our own abilities, be they great or small. A friendly pat on the shoulder can do much to assist one's morale. Honors and recognition are welcome to everyone who is trying to do a good job, even though he may not look for them. But the most positive form of assurance and the greatest human reward that can come to anyone is the satisfaction and self-respect inherent in honest effort itself. We may have to wait a long time for others to lay the laurel wreath upon our brow. But meanwhile we must live with ourselves and be convinced that what we are and what we are trying to do is of real importance. One must learn to be comfortable with himself before he can feel comfortable with others. One must recognize merit in his own efforts before he can accept honestly recognition from others.

This attitude of self-reliance and considered judgment within oneself is by no means to be confused with smugness or vanity. It is rather a positive and objective point of view. Many persons achieve a sense of importance only in negative ways by establishing forms of criticism and condemnation, or in relative fashion by making odious comparisons. If they cannot build up or depend upon themselves, they can tear others down and make it appear that the latter are worse than themselves. Some persons live in a world of envy and jealousy. Under one pretense or the other, they spend their best efforts in belittling others. They can never think of themselves or of others except in terms of comparisons which always show others in an unfavorable light. Maturity which is generated in this way is only sham and self-deceit.

The fact that one must make a show of temper, demand priority on all occasions, win every argument, assume an air of possessiveness, assert one's rights in a challenging manner, or look for notoriety, is no proof of maturity. On the contrary, it may indicate a profound sense of insecurity and self-distrust — a state of mind which easily turns into a sense of defeat. The spoiled child, who demands attention and insists upon having his own way, frequently develops into a frustrated adult.

The person of genuine maturity is willing to let truth and justice co-operate in his own defense. He realizes that there are times when he must act vigorously to maintain his position and other times when it is just as well to remain silent and let others make the noise or give the parting shot. Nothing is really changed by a difference of opinion or by shouting; and there is no good reason why we should become unhappy because others do not always agree with us or bow low to our desires.

3

In many cases, the difference between maturity and immaturity is a matter of temperament. Some persons are either riding high in the clouds or sinking to the depths of despair. One day they feel as if the world is theirs; the next day they are unable to come to grips with the simplest problem. They are overcome with melancholy, often for no apparent reason. They go to bed at night ready to quit their jobs, to abandon the projects which were conceived in an optimistic mood, and to regard themselves as total failures.

Nearly everyone goes through a cycle of this kind in some degree. The emotions may be stirred by a number of material factors which have very little to do with reason or with inherent values. Cloudy weather and low barometric pressure often produce a depressing effect on the nervous system, which in turn may induce one to take a dim view of life in general. Some women cry at times, with no explanation even to themselves. Men often feel sorry for themselves, for no other reason than nervous fatigue and tension. During periods of sexual disturbance or change, many persons of both sexes become irritable and take offense at the least provocation. In periods of menstruation women are likely to feel emotionally depressed. At the change of life, both men and women undergo physical changes which reveal themselves in unpredictable ways, causing the subject to think that life is about to end sadly.

It is important to recognize these symptoms and to analyze their causes; and one should avoid placing too much reliance on

personal views or decisions which are generated under the stress
of nervous emotion.

A very frequent and dangerous temptation, when one is
caught in a discouraging dilemma, is that of self-pity. This can
be completely demoralizing and lead to a chronic mental frustration, even in persons of great ability and apparent maturity.
When physicians encounter this in a patient, their problem of
effecting a cure is intensified and may become desperate. According to an old adage, "While there is life, there is hope." This
may be reversed to say, "While there is hope, there is life."
When a person becomes so afraid of his sickness or pain that
he abandons hope, he stands in the way of his own recovery.
Persons who feel sorry for themselves because of a failure or of
a formidable obstacle to success become incapable of any positive
action until they conquer this mentality and manage to start
afresh.

Nearly everyone has to face this temptation at one time or the
other. Even the greatest men and women have their moments
of mental depression — "the dark night of the soul" — either
from a temporary disappointment or from a permanent unhappy
situation. Poor health, loss of fortune, the experience of injustice, calumny, failure in a particular undertaking, unfair dis-
crimination, an unhappy home, disappointment in love, betrayal
by friends, or maladjustment in one's career — any one of these
experiences may rise to challenge personal faith and
steadfastness.

We never know what problems others have to face, until
we are brought within the intimate circle of their personal lives
and minds. The most attractive exteriors often conceal a heart-
breaking situation. Health, beauty, talent, and fame are but
bitter ashes to the person who has become dissatisfied or embit-
tered with his life.

Under such circumstances, many lives are wasted through
failure of those concerned to maintain their morale, to adapt
themselves and effect necessary adjustments, and to make the

most of what they have. They begin to neglect their appearance. Their habits become irregular. They avoid their friends. They neglect their duties and allow their talents to go to seed. Often, they take to drink and sometimes contemplate suicide.

There are cases of nervous tension or of high blood pressure in which physicians prescribe a moderate amount of alcohol for its therapeutic value. Indulgence in drink as an escape from reality, however, or as a substitute for the rational solution of one's problems is tragic and can never be justified. Personal vigilance becomes more and more necessary in these times, with the abundance of liquor and its liberal use as a form of entertainment. If the person involved has a physical tendency to alcoholism, the problem may call for strenuous action. In more advanced cases, where personal vigilance is insufficient to maintain control, the individual may have to rely upon the assistance of others to protect him from temptation or to effect a rehabilitation. The tendency to intemperance has become so widespread and so menacing in its many effects as to call for social alarm.

When self-mastery is lost through shock or some other unfortunate experience, the individual may become morose and inactive. After a physical accident or a harrowing incident, a period of rest may be indicated; but one should not allow this experience to create a permanent fright.

I am acquainted with a person who, as a child, was in an ocean storm while on a ship en route to Europe. The terror of that experience has never left him, and he has never been able to reconcile himself with the idea of going on the water again. This attitude is unfortunate. While there is no point in forcing oneself or others into a dangerous or repulsive position simply for disciplinary purposes, we should gradually accustom ourselves to resume normal activities after a reasonable period of recovery and relaxation. I have personally had several disagreeable experiences in connection with swimming; but while these have given me a wholesome sense of precaution, I have never allowed them to prevent me from continuing to enjoy the water.

4

The answer to rehabilitation, as well as to the strengthening of self-control and maturity of mind is honest effort. Instead of stressing the obstacles, we should concentrate on the objective. What others may think or say may be of secondary or of no importance. Whether we succeed or fail may be incidental. We demonstrate our ability only through trying. If we do not take the first step, we can never take the second. Everyone makes mistakes; but, if nothing is ventured, nothing is gained. Maturity develops with growth and experience. It cannot remain static and inactive. Either we go ahead or we go backward.

One of the most effective ways of developing maturity is to take action and to do things on our own initiative. Maturity grows with the satisfaction that comes from the testing of our powers. If we have talents, we should use them. If we have ideas, we should try them out. If we have energy, we should put it to work. If we have opportunities, we should seize them. There are many things that we should learn to do, by ourselves or with guidance, in the ordinary course of life. With an interest in life and a little determination, fear automatically drops away, and one learns to enjoy doing confidently and easily the things that formerly appeared beyond our powers and available only to others.

Lack of initiative is very often an evidence that one is afraid to assume responsibility. Many persons shrink from responsibility and pamper themselves in one way or another, pleading inadequacy, illness, or lack of preparation.

With the first sneeze, they feel the approach of pneumonia, and they must stay home from work. The slightest remnant of fatigue makes it impossible for them to arise on time in the morning. They are unable to undertake any task that calls for special thought or effort. If they are asked to sell tickets for a benefit or performance, they have no gift for salesmanship. If they are asked to introduce a speaker, they are terrified at the thought of standing before an audience. If they are asked to help to entertain at a reception, they have no talent for anything social. Apart from taking care of their own interests, their lives are spent in making excuses and in asking others to do the same for them. In some ways, this insures a very comfortable existence. But in most respects it amounts to a perpetual childhood which others resent and which deprives one of much of the joy of mature living. Persons whose principal activity consists in evasion tend to remain adolescent or to become eccentric.

Many early morning pains can be cured by arising and going to work. A little exercise and fresh air often does wonders in tuning up a sluggish system. It is not always the best thing to cling close to the bed or room or house. The stirring of one's bones out in the open, on the way to work, does much to build self-reliance and health. Only by making an effort, even with some pain and sacrifice, can one learn whether one is actually lacking in strength or is indulging in self-deceit. Personal vigor and self-respect can grow only upon an inner consciousness of responsibility and an honest evaluation of self.

5

From a practical standpoint, this inner consciousness and evaluation must be brought to the surface and be put to work socially as well as personally. The same principles which apply to the restoration or development of internal maturity apply also to one's dealing with others.

Many people can get along with themselves alone, and they have no difficulty in communing with God. But with their associates they experience a sense of inferiority and embarrassment. They shrink from any kind of competition as a challenge to their ego. Confronted with concrete alternatives in real life, they are torn with indecision. Any kind of social responsibility gives them a feeling of insecurity and discomforting childish weakness. They become limp and have to be prodded into trying anything that calls for new experience and special effort.

These reactions may be the result of several factors. They may be the product of insufficient or faulty social training and experience. They may arise from a false appraisal of self or of one's social position. Or they may come from temperamental sources which require special analysis and control. In some cases, embarrassment and social nervousness are physical in character. The face of the victim becomes red. One's laugh sounds nervous or silly. The voice trembles or loses itself. A kind of fright sets in. Even the digestive processes are thrown off balance.

Children reared in a repressive atmosphere often carry into later life unfortunate attitudes and reactions, which hamper or distort their sense of personal ease, their self-mastery, and social poise. In some homes, all activity is reduced to a dead level. Any kind of personal initiative or expression is discouraged, forbidden, or ridiculed. The members of the family group, instead of helping one another to develop into mature persons, maintain an attitude of envy, jealousy, and suspicion. The parents take the position that their children are infants, with no rights, no sense of judgment, and no power of expression or responsibility. This attitude is reflected from them to the older children and thence to the younger.

The effects of this influence on personal character depend largely upon the temperament of the individual. Some manage to survive and to emerge as mature persons with a profound sympathy and understanding for the problems of others as well as with mastery and discipline over themselves. Others develop an attitude of resentment and rebellion. They show their independence by a display of aggression. Their manners become belligerent and argumentative. They take strong stands or "make a case" on matters of small consequence. Others remain in a colorless, neutral state of emotional frustration and abandon what native ambitions they might have entertained.

In many instances, the problem of maturation develops, not from positive repression, but rather from excessive affection and pampering on the part of the parents, as we have noted else-where. Sometimes this is done consciously, sometimes not. A parent may shower devotion upon a child and present a constant series of obstacles and pretexts which serve to monopolize attention, for selfish purposes. The child — or grown son or daughter — may develop such a sense of dependence upon the parent that normal processes of character development and independence become atrophied. Between fathers and daughters or between mothers and sons, such relationships, however beautiful, need to be watched and kept free of harmful developments.

Everyone has a right and obligation to grow up, form independent judgments, get married, and raise a family, at least under normal circumstances. Parents die, and the next generation must be prepared to take care of itself, with laughter, maturity, and self-reliance, not with perpetual tears and unavailing grief.

For some persons, the difficulty in achieving social maturity stems from a sense of personal deficiency or from experiences of failure. Repeated experiences of this nature may produce a reaction of chronic discouragement. A scolding or nagging policy on the part of parents, teachers, or associates may result in a permanent wound. Experiences of this kind can injure persons of great talent, as well as those of meager ability. Those of sensitive temperament may be incapacitated by rough handling and inconsiderate treatment.

It should be remembered that a student who fails in one subject may be proficient in another. Not all are equally gifted along the same lines. But if there is consistent failure, in all branches, one should look for causes which may be deeper than the easy explanation of lack of brains or effort. Poor health, poor eyesight, poor hearing may be the reason. Lack of interest because of faulty motivation, an unfortunate home condition, unfair treatment on the playground, insufficient sleep, or bad sex habits may account for the trouble.

Intelligent parents and considerate teachers and counselors

will investigate these possibilities and take positive corrective measures, rather than scold and threaten children, or hold up to them hateful comparison with model students and others who are made to appear as shining examples of success. The individual who is striving for maturity in his own character must find it within himself and on a positive basis.

6

For most people, social maturity and poise come from favorable and friendly association with others. Despite the fact that we are social creatures by nature, there is within us a certain timidity and caution in the presence of our fellow men. Children, from whom much can be learned of human nature, are often like little animals in this respect. They have to be coaxed and wooed into friendship. They have a natural distrust of strangers and must have proof of friendship and reliability before they are willing to give their confidence. Unless one is accustomed to be in the company of others and has learned to deal with them in various ways, the same feeling of discomfort and insecurity may accompany one through life. The basic postulate for successful social maturity is — to repeat — respect for oneself and a willingness to be accepted by others for what one really is. The individual who is pretending to be something that he is not or who is afraid to let others get too close to him can never have a happy or successful social life. One cannot communicate a sense of comfort to others, if he does not have it himself.

Meeting people with the idea of "making an impression on them" or of sustaining relationships on our own terms is certain to end in failure. There is a kind of competition and reciprocity in all human relationships. We must be willing to give and take, to be open and fair in our dealings and to expect the same from others, even though our expectancy may be imposed upon or disappointed. By the same token a personal manner of cringing or obsequiousness is never favorably accepted by honorable people. Due respect and good manners are appropriate on all occasions, whether with our superiors or our inferiors; but a watery approach or a heavy display of humility is generally unconvincing and offensive.

One of the most important things to keep in mind in our social relationships is that maturity of mind need not be lessened by occasional blunders or mistakes. Some people are afraid of normal social intercourse because they imagine that every error will be laughed at, that every false move will be a source of humiliation, and that others are so much superior that any attempt to keep up with them would soon become ridiculous. Some persons may react in this way, but we call these people "snobs."

The ability and regular habit of making appraisals on the basis of merit, rather than of noise, display, publicity, or external rewards, as a definite evidence of personal maturity, must extend also to persons, tasks, and objects outside ourselves. Children must often be coerced into taking food, clothing themselves properly, studying their lessons, and performing their duties, with the promise of candy or some other reward or under threat of a penalty which is quite unrelated with what they are required to do. Many adults go through life under the inducement of similar expectations. They proceed in a task only if bolstered up by constant encouragement or fed with praise and recognition. Left to perform a task by themselves, they soon lose interest and heart. If progress becomes difficult, they give up in discouragement. If rightly or wrongly, the glory or the thanks is given to another, they give in to disappointment, resentment, and a sense of failure.

The mature person, while not insensible to these externals, keeps his eye on real values and continues on, with faith in himself and in his cause, after weaker souls drop by the way-side. It has been said, with much wisdom, that one of the greatest virtues is persistence. In many cases, the greatest act is survival, an objective which often calls for enduring confidence, courage, and trust.

Shakespeare has eloquently described the difference between men in this respect, with a comparison:

> But hollow men, like horses hot at hand,
> Make gallant show and promise of their mettle;
> But when they should endure the bloody spur,
> They fall their crests, and, like deceitful jades,
> Sink in the trial. . . .[1]

The mature mind is a steady mind, not turned aside by difficulty, nor sustained simply by pleasant prospects. Of course, the mature person who intends to match himself with others and endeavors to maintain his equilibrium while in association or in competition with those out of his class, will soon find himself deflated. A man of humble or moderate means who attempts to spend like a millionaire will shortly become bankrupt. The brash individual of no social acceptance who tries to break into a special group will undoubtedly receive a cold shoulder. An average bridge player who tries to beat a champion may never wish to play again. The untrained musician may feel ashamed of his performance after the exhibition of a professional.

But within one's legitimate sphere and capacities, one should not hesitate to move freely and naturally. No one is perfect. It is normal to make mistakes; and we must learn to lose occasionally, with good grace and without losing our self-confidence and social poise. Everyone likes a good loser, sometimes more than a winner. As a matter of fact, the person who wins all the time takes the fun out of the game for everyone else.

To withdraw oneself or to refuse to speak to others as the result of a difference of opinion, defeat in a game or argument, or a joke on oneself is silly. To become sullen or resentful as the result of a disappointment is likewise an injury only to oneself. We must learn to adapt ourselves to various situations and to the different personalities with whom we come in contact, and to come up smiling. It is only natural that we should feel

---

[1] *Julius Caesar,* iv, 1.

the sting of a rebuke or to react unfavorably to an embarrassing or awkward situation. But the mature person will not allow these matters to rankle in his mind. Better to forget them or to act as if they had never happened.

The mature person, called upon to deal with others in daily life, must learn also to co-operate. Teamwork is important. Even when we dislike others, we must continue to work with them on a humane and kindly basis. A friendly attitude tends to break down the resistance of others and begets a sense of respect in them, far more effectively than a display of sensitiveness and aloofness. And from this attitude of self-containment and confidence there comes a form of reassurance to others, an atmosphere of peace in which good things are done, and an inspiration for them to grow in maturity and in the enrichment of life.

With advancing years, the subject of age becomes a sensitive one with many persons. We become afraid of growing old and senile, going into a second childhood, losing our grip on life, being passed by, being left alone, neglected, and unloved. It is foolish to become obsessed with fears of this kind. There is nothing that one can do to prevent the changes that take place in the human system with the march of time. But the essential importance of the individual remains the same. One must keep hold on the basic truths and values, and not lose confidence in the meaning of life.

In a practical way, everyone can do much to keep young, yet mature, in spirit, by retaining an interest in life, pursuing useful occupations, and keeping up the appearance of one who has pride in himself or herself. We should do well also to remind ourselves that agility and physical strength are not the only evidences of vitality. Power of mind, comprehension of heart, and faith of soul are qualities far more important and enduring; and these should develop as time goes on, even to the portals of eternity.

In the words of Longfellow:

Life is real! Life is earnest!
And the grave is not the goal;
Dust thou art, to dust returnest,
Was not spoken of the soul.

Not enjoyment, and not sorrow,
Is our destined end or way;
But to act that each tomorrow
Find us further than today.[2]

---

[2] *A Psalm of Life.*

CHAPTER XVIII

The Principle of Service

I

THE secret of a healthy mind and a happy life lies in the principle of sharing with others and in building one's program on the idea of service. This is true certainly from an objective and external point of view. Something useful is always accomplished in assisting our fellow man, even if no tangible or immediate benefit results for ourselves. From a psychological viewpoint also, this external direction of interests and powers of concentration is important, for the reason that it elevates the standard of one's mental health and vigor, even though success may not crown our efforts.

One of the frequent causes of mental disorder, especially of the type known as manic depressive, is a brooding over personal problems, sorrows, and disappointments. Prolongation of such mental activity leads to habitual melancholy, loss of sleep, chronic frustration, and inability to view incidents in their objective importance or relationship. One withdraws more and more into himself and sees the world as in a conspiracy against him, from which there seems to be no escape, and for which there is no solution.

Everyone is confronted at times with situations or problems of this nature, causing mental strain, drain, and shock. It would be strange and unnatural, indeed, if one were not sensitive to grief and disappointment, or if one's interests in life were entirely impersonal. But when mental energy becomes directed exclusively toward oneself, and one's sense of values and program of life revolve entirely around one's personal grief, something is almost certain to go wrong with mental health. One begins to live, as it were, alone in a darkened room. A life devoted to concentration upon one's pains and aches presents a very dreary outlook; and the comfort which one derives from rehearsing them for others or exchanging sad symptoms with associates of similar inclinations still leaves one in the same rut.

The moment a person takes his mind off himself and applies it to the needs and welfare of others, he becomes alert, active, interested in life, and concerned with positive functioning. With this outlook, the world becomes full of real people, not merely walking shadows. We begin to have an actual investment in some of them, so that what they do or fail to do becomes vitally important for us. The situation is not unlike that of the gambler at a horse race. It makes a great difference to him whether the horse of his choice wins or not; and his whole concern is thrown into the victory of his selection. For another person, uninterested in horses, or not financially committed to any horse, it may not be of the slightest importance whether one or the other wins. This comparison is incomplete and faulty. Nevertheless, it illustrates the psychological benefits of directing our attention to an object outside ourselves and of binding that interest with a tangible risk, effort, or sacrifice.

The precise psychological reason for this instinctive reaching of the individual for comfort beyond himself is not entirely certain. The instinct of self-preservation certainly does not explain it; in some cases, the two seem incompatible. The instinct for the propagation of the race, as it is called, is almost entirely physical in character and is too limited, even in its concern for the rearing of the young, to explain the significance of the idea of service as such. The answer probably lies in the social instinct which keeps mankind together, serving as a corrective of strife and of the urgings of competition, and making it possible for people to live together in peace and progress.

The slow but steady experience of mankind has demonstrated the truth of the same proposition. Against the natural tendency of men to fear and distrust one another and to settle their differences by violence, there has gradually developed the realization that co-operation and service can produce more benefits than the elimination of potential enemies. In this way, mankind has developed from families to tribes, to cities, to nations; and, with modern advances in means, communication, and transportation, it may look forward, with some degree of hope, to a world order based upon peaceful exchange rather than on resort to force.

A recognition of the principles of kindness in human relationships, of friendliness and good will among men, of service, sharing, and sacrifice as the secret of human greatness, has been the most precious contribution of wise men through the ages. There have, of course, been individual philosophers, like Nietzsche, who held to the doctrine of the "superman" and the survival of the fittest; and in practice many persons follow a policy of extreme individualism, which is little more than "dog eat dog" under one title or the other. But even in the throes of the struggle for existence, men ardently hope for a social order in which charitable consideration and brotherly love will unite them under the fatherhood of God.

This aspiration is of the essence of Christianity and is offered as the revealed word of God in the compassionate pages of the New Testament. According to Christ, in answer to the question as to which is the greatest commandment in the law, "Thou shalt love the Lord thy God with thy whole heart, and with thy whole soul, and with thy whole mind. This is the greatest and the first commandment, and the second is like to this: Thou shalt love thy neighbor as thyself. On these two commandments dependeth the whole law and the prophets."[1] In the words of St. James, "Religion clean and undefiled before God and the Father is: to visit the fatherless and widows in their tribulation and to keep oneself unspotted from this world."[2] "Dearly beloved," wrote St. John, "let us love one another; for charity is of God. And everyone that loveth is born of God and knoweth God."[3] This idea permeates the Christian message, to such an extent that generous service of others, in God's name, represents the highest form of active sanctity, identified with the love of God Himself.

This should develop as a practical philosophy of life, as a virtue operating habitually and by instinct. And it should function, not only in the manner of co-operation when one is called upon, but upon personal initiative and planning, even before one is asked to give or to help.

2

A number of obstacles stand in the way of making this principle operative and realizing these objectives. Some arise from a native reluctance to bestir oneself more than is absolutely necessary. Others are the product of certain ideas which are suspicious of, or even hostile to, the whole principle of service. The person who is willing to try to overcome these obstacles must first examine his own conscience and study his own particular problems.

One of the most common and most easily recognizable problems is that of laziness. For many persons, great pain is attached to any kind of exertion beyond what is regarded as essential for themselves. Action on behalf of others seems a kind of remote ambition, like pushing boulders up hill. Laziness takes

---

[1] Mt. 22:36–40.
[2] James 1:27.
[3] 1 Jn. 4:7.

various forms and resorts to devious pretexts. "I'm too tired" is a favorite expression with many, the instant they are called upon to assist another. "I don't have time" is another handy device for dodging a social obligation or a friendly gesture.

In some cases, the difficulty arises from an inherent idea that one is being imposed upon and is really doing more than can be reasonably expected in helping others. Whatever is done must be coaxed. A grudging spirit accompanies every concession. Opposition is the first reaction to every suggestion or request. As the children say to one another when asked to do some menial task, "Who do you think I am, your slave?" Adults likewise, when asked to do a special favor or co-operate in a common cause, often find a battery of arguments against compliance. There are abundant reasons why someone else should do the job or why others should take care of the matter themselves.

In the face of such attitudes, many a parent has preferred to do the household chores rather than put up with the resistance and sluggish attitude of children, who assume a privileged position and refuse to do anything except with an argument and under pressure. When we encounter the same mean-spiritedness in others, we often take a similar way out of a difficult situation. But those whose habitual position is one of opposition and resentment in service usually build a wall between themselves and those who would be their friends. When the time comes for them to need and to ask for help, they may find themselves caught behind it, living in a kind of social vacuum.

No one can doubt there is such a thing as being imposed upon by inconsiderate people and of being reduced, if one is willing, to drudgery. This should be guarded against, in legitimate self-interest. One may question the prudence of some individuals who devote their time and means to public causes or to organizations to such an extent that they neglect their families and even dissipate their own energies. But while holding oneself in a position of reasonable independence, a generous spirit will never allow itself to be dominated by petty or mean considerations which block the possibility of graciousness even in refusal. There are times when one may have to say "no," but this reaction or response should come from good and valid reasons and not from a temperamentally negative position or from a habitual attitude of nonparticipation.

One of the obstacles with which most people have to contend, in one form or the other, is the idea that every service or good deed should be paid for. This idea is generated early in life and often serves as the dominating motive of action in social relationships. Children who are paid for doing the little chores that they should do under normal circumstances soon become little businessmen and women and refuse to do anything involving special effort, except for a stipulated price. I recall as a small boy being given a tip for delivering a package to a neighbor. Somehow this encouraged the idea that I should receive a similar consideration for any such service; and I began to calculate on how much I could make on such business in the course of a week. Undoubtedly, there was some merit in my commercialism, as it included the idea of saving up money for Christmas gifts. But my parents soon put a stop to this line of reasoning when it began to affect my attitude toward the chores at home.

The Boy Scout principle of doing a good deed every day — without pay — is certainly to be encouraged; and it is one which adults as well as children may do well to adopt. When we reach the point where any kind of accommodation to others requires cash payment or material reward, everyone suffers — even good business. Persons whose spirit of giving is turned on or off, depending on their bargaining position, soon find themselves in a rut of crass materialism. In this atmosphere of cold calculation and minimum performance, there is no joy for anyone.

One of the time-honored principles of merchandising is that "the customer is always right." Under this policy salespeople often have to submit to the abuse of irate and demanding customers. But in a strange reversal of the bargaining position, it

is said that a large Philadelphia store carried this sign during
World War II — "Please be kind to our clerks! They are harder
to get than customers!" During the same war, when gasoline
was rationed and motorist supplies were at a premium, many
persons noticed a corresponding letdown in related service. A
friend of mine relates that one day, after he had received his
ration of gasoline for his car, the attendant drew a cloth from
his overalls and began to wipe off the windshield. "Then," said
he, "I knew that the war was over!"

From these experiences, it is evident that any kind of service
— particularly that requiring some imagination — calls for special
effort. But one can hardly doubt that there are positive results
in improved dispositions and public relations. An actively generous mentality makes it easier for people to live with us and
do business with us. It should make living easier for ourselves.

A tendency which many persons have to watch is that of
stinginess. With some persons, the elements of miserliness and
stinginess enter into every good deed, practically nullifying the
benefits. This does not mean that we should scatter our time,
money, or efforts to the winds. Frugality is a branch of the
virtue of prudence. We must measure our giving to the extent
of our means. But it is, in general, a mistake to cut down our
service or gifts to minimum considerations. With some, every
gift or friendly gesture creaks like a rusty hinge which expects
plenty of oil. One can be certain that they will be back soon to
collect their due with a request for something larger than they
have given. Every offering they make is in the nature of a calculated risk. They judge Christmas to be a success or a failure,
depending upon whether they give or receive more gifts, and
only tolerable if they break even in the exchange.

Some are unwilling to accept favors from others, to accept
invitations, or to be on the receiving end of a social event, for
the reason that they may be expected to show some reciprocity.
There are instances, indeed, when such caution is prudent.
It may be unwise to become involved in a social obligation which

is beyond one's means or outside one's legitimate interests. One should think twice before accepting gifts which are of the nature of bribes or which have "strings" tied to them, so to speak, drawing one into a situation which one will later regret. On the other hand, a constant refusal to join with others or to accept their friendly gestures, made in good faith, simply because this may involve some expense or create a sense of obligation, is a mistake. If one's motive is pride and one's reluctance is based on the fact that one does not have a new dress or cannot afford to return the favor in like degree of lavishness, the question to be asked and answered is whether one is expected to reciprocate or go to this expense. It is flattering occasionally to think that others like us for ourselves and not for our clothes or for the expectancy of a return in kind, which we are not prepared to offer. If our reluctance or refusal is simply the evidence of a stingy and mean spirit, we need not worry about being pursued, as people will soon write us off their books.

Some are perfectly willing to accept gifts, favors, invitations, entertainment or accommodation without any fears or qualms, for the reason they do not know the meaning of the word "reciprocity." They enjoy the bounty of others and are ready to attach themselves to others, even without an invitation. They live in a mental world of constant expectancy and are prepared to draw heavily on the good nature of their friends. When it comes time for them, however, to reach for the bill, they are stricken with a strange momentary paralysis. They become engaged in a serious conversation or are suddenly called away from the table. If they make a gesture toward their wallets, it is too late or too slow to be effective. If they are asked to do a favor at a later date, they find that it is simply impossible for several reasons, none of which is genuinely valid.

There is only one way to deal with persons of this kind, and that is on a perfectly frank and business basis. If we expect them to pay when their turn comes around, we should not be hesitant in saying so. If we are perfectly willing to foot the bills on all occasions, to do all the work, and to expect no co-operation in return, then we have no right to complain if they fail to volunteer their time and money in the cause.

The discovery and treatment of stinginess in ourselves is a far more difficult matter. We can spot the disease and indicate the cure in others very easily. In ourselves, it is hidden behind good motives or so mixed up with prudent considerations that it is hardly recognizable for what it really is. Many people are stingy, not because they intend to be, but because it never occurs to them that they have an obligation to open up and share with others. It may be well for us to pause, from time to time, and take stock of favors which we have received from others and of the demands which we have put upon them. If we find ourselves on the debit side of the ledger, we should give some thought to an appropriate form in which to express our appreciation and to render a little friendly service in return. This calls for some thinking and planning if we are not to find ourselves perpetually unprepared, too busy, or forgetful until it is too late. If our problem is one of cheapness or downright evasion of social duty, we may have to wait for the lesson to be brought home to us in dramatic and painful form.

3

To break through these attitudes and to assume at least one's rightful share of giving, contributing, co-operating, and serving, we have to learn to take joy in the actions and to perform our good deeds for what they are worth in themselves. While one may reasonably look for some expression of appreciation and gratitude on the part of those benefited, this reward is not always forthcoming. If parents were to cease caring for their children for lack of appreciation, would not most of us have been starved before we reached the age of reason? If a cause is good and worth giving to, the contribution should carry its own reward. If service is one's duty, it should be done, even under difficulty and with sacrifice. I can well imagine that there are few tangible evidences of appreciation and thanks to the soldiers doing sentry or trench duties on the battle lines of the world. An old saying "It is more blessed to give than to receive" means little if giving is made contingent upon receiving in return.

As combined encouragement and admonition to those of us who require recognition for our services or who place the laurel on our own brows, Christ, the Supreme Giver, has this to say: "Take heed that you do not your justice before men, to be seen by them; otherwise you shall not have reward of your Father who is in heaven. Therefore, when thou dost an alms-deed, sound not a trumpet before thee, as the hypocrites do in the synagogues and in the streets, that they may be honored by men. . . . Amen, I say to you, they have received their reward. But when thou dost alms, let not thy left hand know what thy right hand doth, that thy alms may be in secret; and thy Father who seeth in secret will repay thee."[4]

Persons who have devoted themselves to a career or vocation which calls for service as a matter of principle must, of course, build their lives on the idea of dedication to service, if they are to do their work properly and be happy in doing it. The clergyman or religious, the doctor, the nurse, teacher, social worker, and scholar must be prepared to make great self-sacrifice, and possibly endure personal discomfort, if their missions are to be successful and they are to remain mentally healthy. To substitute another primary motive, such as notoriety, money, social position, or ease, for the avowed one of religious ministration, medical or public service, or the advancement of knowledge, is to make mockery of the calling itself and to nullify its real effectiveness.

Everyone who devotes himself to his work is entitled to a decent livelihood and possibly to some of life's comforts and graciousness. But one must make a definite choice as to one's primary objective. The scholar or scientist who burns the mid-

---

[4] Mt. 6:1–4.

night oil, the teacher who slaves day in and day out, on a meager salary, when he or she could be making fat commissions as a salesman for insurance or as an agent in a real-estate boom or as an expert for an industrial concern, can become a very unhappy person under the pressure of such meditations. The clergyman becomes a sorry figure the minute he lets social ambition and love for money or pleasure usurp his dedicated purpose of preaching the gospel and serving his flock. The mental health and even the personal ethics of one in such a dilemma may suffer serious strain.

In a very true sense, married persons should regard their married status as a vocation and ask themselves whether their lives are being built upon the principle of service to one another and to the development of a home and family. The reason many marriages fail is precisely that the individuals concerned wish to maintain their absolute independence and are unwilling to share, serve, and sacrifice, except when it contributes to their separate personal interests.

Numerous motives may be adduced to invoke the principle of service and assistance, as a reasonable and beneficial policy or as indicated in a specific case. Smart businessmen recognize that it pays them to go out of their way to take care of their customers. It is often the little extra service that makes the difference beween success and failure. In the expectancy of favors, most of us can be extra co-operative at times. Just before Christmas, when Santa Claus comes with his bag full of gifts for good children and his bundle of switches for bad ones, most little boys and girls are alert to the importance of doing what they are told, quickly and cheerfully, and of being on their best behavior. In our own way, on our own occasions, for our own purposes, we adults act pretty much the same.

But as a long-range consideration, the principle of service can be sustained only on the basis of joy in giving and doing, independently of the profit motive. From a therapeutic standpoint, the essential value of activity in the service of a person or a cause stems from the element of mental interest and the transference of attention to an object outside ourselves. Interest of a pleasurable character is derived from the fact that one likes what one is doing and is devoted, both by sentiment and by principle to the object. True friends find it easy to help each other; persons in love count no cost too great to prove their affection for the loved one. Love makes service easy and joyful. Love of God makes religion a vital reality and worship a truly divine service. Love turns human relationships from perfunctory and mechanical gestures to an outpouring of our best energies and transforms life itself into something of supreme interest.

Robert Browning expressed this thought with great eloquence, in his lines:

> Wanting is — what?
> Summer redundant,
> Blueness abundant,
> — Where is the blot?
>
> Beamy the world, yet a blank all the same,
> — Framework which waits for a picture to frame:
> What of the leafage, what of the flower?
> Roses embowering with naught they embower!
> Come then, complete incompletion, O comer.
> Pant through the blueness, perfect the summer!
>
> Breathe but one breath
> Rose beauty above,
> And all that was death
> Grows life, grows love
> Grows love!

One can be surrounded with honors, comforts, and pleasures, enjoying apparent success from every material standard, and yet live an empty life. There are many people of great wealth, living in loneliness, going regularly to a doctor for some nameless ailment or resorting to sedatives and stimulants to produce an illusion of motion and importance. If, despite a perfect setting, there is nothing in life besides pampering of self and survival, and no one or nothing of significance in it to share our love and solicitude, life is indeed empty. But with a cause to serve and with an outlook of interest, affection, and love for those about us, life thrives with a sense of purpose and direction and blooms with inspiration.

4

To activate the principle of service, it is not enough to recognize that a cause is good and worthy of support or to like people and to wish them well. One must reduce good will to specific action and must seize and even create opportunities for rendering service. To illustrate what He meant by a good neighbor, Christ related the story of the Good Samaritan who actually helped the Jew who had been waylaid by robbers, bound up his wounds, took him to an inn, and paid his expenses. The priests and other Jews who passed by without rendering assistance were undoubtedly good men and wished well to the world; but they failed to take practical action in this particular, down-to-earth situation.

Both imagination and effort must be expended. We have to be on the lookout for ways and occasions in which we can lend a helping hand. If a large number of appeals are directed to our attention, perhaps more than we can respond to, we should at least give them some attention and select for consideration those that come within our range of interest, our obligation, and our means. Too often we expend our best energies calling attention to certain needs which have become critical because nothing has been done to improve a situation. When a pointed appeal or opportunity comes our way to remedy the situation, we are too busy to consider it; or we complain that we are already "bled white" with appeals and worthy causes, and the wastebasket becomes our filing cabinet.

For many years I have been working in the field of adult education, in promoting public forums for the discussion of important topics and the formation of a cultural and intellectual consciousness of Christian principles. It has not been easy work.

The difficulty, however, has not been positive opposition, but rather a lack of awareness or sense of importance of these objects among people who should be aware and who should welcome the opportunity to support and share in the work. On occasion, people have complained to me about the lack of facilities in this field and suggested that something is urgently needed, whereupon it has become my unpleasant duty to ask them why they have never responded to the literature and appeals for support which they have received from me.

There are, of course, many people who do understand; and it is through their comprehension and generous, often self-sacrificing, support that the great public, charitable, religious, and educational causes of the world are kept alive. What many people fail to realize is that being asked to help, to serve, or to contribute, may well be regarded as a privilege and honor. To pass by the opportunity may be a mistake, even from a selfish viewpoint. A friend of mine in charge of a public charitable agency never distributes assistance to the needy without instructing them to turn some small amount back to a public or religious cause as an evidence of appreciation and responsibility. Persons of financial independence and competency have far more reason to consider public service as having a genuine claim upon their generosity.

In the realm of daily living, with our family and friends, there are so many ways in which we can bring joy and service to others and benefit richly by these acts of thoughtful remembrance.

I recall visiting some friends for dinner and arriving just as the smoke of battle was rising from the field. It seems that Mr. X had brought a box of candy as a gift to his wife, and this had given rise to a strange misunderstanding.

"What is this?" she asked.

"A box of candy, a little gift for you, my dear," he replied.

"What brings this forth?" she asked again. "What is the occasion?"

"Why don't you remember?" he said. "This is our wedding anniversary."

"Yes, I remember," she rejoined, breaking out into laughter. "But isn't it strange that this is the first time you have remembered it for at least three years? Now tell me, what mischief have you been up to?"

This pointed question was enough to exasperate him, and with one swoop he had seized the box and thrown it out the window. When I arrived, the box of candy was still lying on the outer terrace. With a settlement of truce upon my arrival, we agreed to find ways and means of retrieving the gift, and peace was restored.

Certainly, there was no ill will in any of this performance. It all boiled down to the fact that, despite this man's love for his wife, he had allowed a busy life to interfere with the observance of an important event in their lives. Tardy remembrance now appeared almost ridiculous, at least for the moment.

Several years ago, Gelett Burgess wrote an essay entitled "The Educated Heart," which I have frequently had cause to remember. In substance, he called attention to the little things that are of such great importance that they make the difference between joyous living and a taken-for-granted existence that leaves many people with the feeling of neglect and loneliness. It is possible to keep one's nose too close to the grindstone of business routine, to concentrate too much on one's personal interests, and to lose sight of one's family and one's friends to whom we owe much. If one cannot easily remember birthdays, one should secure a birthday book and jot them down. If we do not know what constitutes an appropriate remembrance, we should inquire. The time, effort, and expense involved in these considerations are all a wonderful investment. We should never wait to be asked, shamed, or forced to bring cheer and reassurance into the lives of those we love. We must not take their affection for granted or assume that our silence is sufficient evidence of our satisfaction and our love. If roses may be considered an acceptable tribute when laid upon a grave, they are far more beautiful and fragrant when received during life.

I once read this sign in the office of a business executive who headed a remarkably successful organization: "He serves himself best, who serves others well." Persons who are striving to maintain a solid mental balance and to enjoy the thrill of creating an atmosphere of friendliness as well as of achievement in their work and daily lives should adopt that motto as a sure guide.

CHAPTER XIX

The Power of the Will

I

A PRIME moving force of principled character and of mental health is the power of the free will. According to an ancient formula, character is the compound of habits; and habits are formed by repeated acts. The repetition of acts, particularly those with a calculated purpose, requires determination, or a sustained and repeated act of the will. Under the direction of the will, the individual gains mastery of himself. Action responds to deliberation, rather than to impulse; and the will, rather than emotion, remains in a position of independence and command.

For centuries, men have struggled and died for freedom. The political, social, and religious history of nations can be written in terms of the desire of individuals and of groups for self-determination and for that liberty of action which is more precious than gold. In the slow growth of mankind toward a democratic society, the great problem has been to demonstrate that men can cope with the responsibility of freedom through the orderly processes of law rather than through recourse, like animals, to violence in the achievement of their objectives. The same fundamental problem faces every individual in his development toward maturity as an independent and responsible person.

Certain psychologists, particularly those of the materialistic school, who regard the mind as only a chemical compound, deny the freedom of the will. For them, human action is simply a response to external stimuli, in the same class as animal instinct. According to this theory the brain or the imagination is aroused so as to stir emotional responses, and these in turn determine a line of action. The good things that we do, it is maintained, correspond to instinctive necessity, not differing essentially from those things which are designated as evil. Thus, the saint is an individual who has been fortunate in environment or adaptation; the criminal is the victim of his surroundings or of faulty education. Both respond to emotional pressures and physical necessity. According to this standard, there is no inherent merit in virtue apart from desirable relationships between the individual and society, or from the advantages which may accrue to the person who is happily impelled to actions which are classified as good. The sinner, the profligate, and the criminal, being only apparently responsible for their misdeeds, should not be censured or punished, but rather should be isolated, protected, and readjusted.

It is true that large spheres of human activity are strictly organic, with no reference to deliberation or to free choice and decision. The beating of the heart, the circulatory and digestive system, and most responses of the nervous and sensory organization in the body and the brain function without reference to any conscious plan or desire on the part of the individual. Physical growth, the healing of wounds, and the struggle of blood corpuscles against bacterial viruses have been so arranged by the Creator of nature as to proceed independently of any guidance or command of the human intelligence.

There is also a tremendous field of activity, outside organic processes, subject to control but generally instinctive in character and performed without conscious advertence. Women often scream at the sight of a mouse. We all groan with pain. A mosquito bite, an itch, or nervous twinge is almost automatically scratched. One does not have to do these things, but the action responds to an impulse so readily, that to avoid doing so requires great self-control.

The same observation may be made in the whole realm of what are called reflex actions. Some of these are almost muscular in nature, like the automatic lowering of the eyelids or the raising of the hand to avert an object that appears to be coming toward the face. Others are acquired through habit, to such a point that they operate, without argument or delay, the instant certain conditions are placed. The trained typist, for example, does not have to examine the alphabet on her machine each time she wishes to strike a letter. The ability to perform any kind of work which requires both skill and speed depends upon the formation of reflexes which respond without specific consciousness or deliberation.

It should be noted also that, even in the order of human conduct or action which does not come within the definition of instinct or reflexes, there are different degrees of freedom. Under some conditions, there is no choice, and one is impelled to give consent which normally would not be given were one entirely free. In explaining such action, people say, "There was nothing else I could do under the circumstances." Whether they acted freely or not may be questioned. In such cases, the motive has to be examined. If the action was performed from considerations of self-interest, and not merely from external compulsion, the act was at least partially free. The sailor who jettisons his cargo to save the ship in a storm would not have done so in calm weather; but he cannot say he did not perform a free act, however distasteful it might have been or how great the loss. On the other hand, the man who hands over his purse to a robber at the point of a gun could refuse to do so and suffer the consequences; but he could very well argue that his act was an unwilling one and not free in the proper sense of the word.

Freedom of action may be reduced, even to the vanishing point, by factors or agencies which affect the mind or disturb the will. Under the strain of extreme fatigue or emotional disturbance, the mental faculties lose their sharpness, so that the powers of the will become reduced and even nullified. Under pressure of intensive questioning, badgering, and threatening, a person may become so confused as to admit to a damaging falsehood or agree to a course of action which he would never follow while in the full possession of his powers. When the normal powers of consciousness are suspended, except for activity of the imagination, as in sleep, one can hardly be held accountable for what he does or says or imagines. Similarly, under hypnosis, the subject loses the exercise of his free will and performs mechanically the actions that are suggested to him.

Whatever disturbs the mind has a corresponding effect upon the will. Excessive use of intoxicating liquor has the effect of reducing mental co-ordination and even of blotting out all self-control. The same results follow indulgence in narcotics, such as opium derivatives or marijuana. This effect upon the mind and the will, however, cannot exonerate a person from responsibility for his actions, even those performed in a mental blur, if he has foreseen what would happen as a result of his indulgence; and his responsibility may be even greater if he uses these stimulants or narcotics as a spur to the acts which he had in mind.

In other words, there is a vast difference between *external* force, fear, and intimidation, which render a person incapable of performing a free human act, and *internal* obstacles to free functioning which a person may put in his own way. Fatigue, emotion, mental panic, and intoxication do not necessarily remove the condition for free action, although they may reduce it; but, in their effects, they emphasize the importance of safeguarding the will as a sensitive instrument, which can be blunted, distorted, and deceived. When man loses his freedom of choice and determination, particularly through his own mismanagement or abuse, he is reduced to the level of the beast. He can no longer discharge his duties as a person; nor can he exercise his rights in more than a passive sense.

2

These principles must be kept operative in any sound program of mental health. To a large extent, mental health is the product of controls over instinct, impulse, appetite, and emotion. Mental balance is maintained by the processes of deliberation and decision. Mental poise, like character, is developed from habits formed by persistent action. Mental mastery is founded upon the principle of selectivity and self-determination.

The growth of a child, from infancy to maturity, should be accompanied by a careful training in which recognition of values gradually takes the place of instinctive reactions. The child must learn to eat not merely sweets and other foods which appeal to the eye and the taste, but also those other foods which make for a balanced diet. He must learn to wash himself and to keep his appearance neat, even though the effort may be a source of annoyance. He must learn to share, even though his animal instincts may tend toward selfishness. The same process must continue in the adult, so that one acts independently upon judgment, not simply on the spur of an impulse, and examines the motives for action before making a choice.

The free act, as incorporating a deliberate choice, must search for a reasonable motive, if it is to be performed consciously. The mature person, who is master of himself, learns to act on his own initiative and discipline, without the necessity of external force or intimidation or simply first instinct to guide the course of his conduct.

The will always moves toward that which is good under some guise or aspect. But there are different kinds of good, various aspects of the same object, and alternatives of choice, even in the consequences. The disciplined will makes its choice only after careful consideration. One learns to be cautious of first impressions and to be on his guard against the lure of easy pleasure and ready gain. The important thing to keep in mind is what is really good, better, or best in the long run. This calls for a disciplining of the will, so that it can say "no" to apparently attractive objects as well as "yes" to those which may not be so appealing or desirable on the surface. The value of the slogan "Stop, look, and listen" can be tested in many places besides a railroad crossing.

It is said that in the presence of absolute goodness, as in the direct and full vision of God which is described in the Gospels as the joy of heaven, the will moves freely but always toward the same completely satisfying object of desire. St. Augustine describes this free but uniform motion in his famous lines on the love of God: "I have tasted Thee, and now do hunger and thirst after Thee: Thou didst touch me, and I even burn again to enjoy Thy peace."[1]

In the present life, however, goodness, beauty, and desirability appear only in fragments and in limited or imperfect forms. Evil is often wrapped and concealed under attractive forms.

In the words of Bassanio:

> So may the outward shows be least themselves;
> The world is still deceived with ornament.
> In law, what plea so tainted and corrupt
> But, being seasoned with a gracious voice,
> Obscures the show of evil? In religion,
> What damned error, but some sober brow
> Will bless it and approve it with a text,
> Hiding the grossness with fair ornament?
> There is no vice so simple, but assumes
> Some mark of virtue on his outward parts.[2]

Hence the importance of analyzing and deliberating before reaching any important decision. Hence also the need of a strong will to direct and sustain one's better judgment.

---

[1] *Confessions*, Book X, Chap. 27.
[2] William Shakespeare, *The Merchant of Venice*, iii, 2.

3

A strong and functioning will must not be confused with a stubborn spirit, with an attitude of resistance, or with a mistaken sense of independence which is nothing more than mulish contrariness. It is rather the faculty of acting with persistence and constancy of purpose, subject to the light of reason and in command over one's natural appetites and emotions. In its development, it proceeds from the virtue of obedience and from guidance by others to a position of self-discipline and command.

The training, disciplining, and strengthening of the will involve a number of considerations. Both principle and practice are necessary. Instruction in what is true, good, or right is not sufficient to make a wise man, a good man, or a man of strong will. This education must be reduced to the development of genuine convictions, of strong faith, and of practiced virtue. It is not enough that the will act under external command, direction, or obedience. It must become accustomed to function readily and correctly in the service and on the initiative of the individual himself.

The first step in the education of the will is the establishment of the principle that one is going to live intelligently and seriously. This should be a guiding principle through life. Many people do not abide by it. Instead, they make an exhibition of themselves by impulsive action and silly performance. When called upon to give an explanation of their behavior, they reply, "I couldn't help it." For them nothing is serious, calculated, or planned in advance. One never knows just what they may do under given circumstances. Their reactions are filled with confusion, frustration, and resentment because of awkward and disappointing situations for which they have only themselves to blame. Life is serious. Even in its lighter moments, people are expected to act intelligently and consistently.

Intelligent action does not require intellectual genius. But it calls for the spirit of reflection and for the application of common sense to the problem in hand. There is no doubt that persons who are troubled with a nervous disorder can do much to help themselves and to steady their nerves by giving some thought to the cause of their disturbance. If the cause is over-work, tension, worry, high blood pressure, dissipation, or a nerv-ous temperament, the intelligent person will take steps to quiet rather than to aggravate the system. Persons with a quick or "uncontrollable" temper can control themselves by taking an objective and intelligent view of the circumstances which cause emotional agitation and by being on their guard against the first symptoms of trouble. Those whose imaginations run riot-ously and out of bounds can learn to suppress their madness by deliberately avoiding the sources of difficulty and by taking up a definite employment. If one is disturbed by strong appe-tites and emotions, he can bring them under control if he is willing to take an intelligent view of his problem and to discipline himself accordingly.

The argument that one cannot help what he is doing is usually a subterfuge, substituting the gratification of some appe-tite in place of intelligent action which might indicate self-denial. The individual under doctor's orders, who goes off his diet to satisfy an urge of hunger or taste, cannot honestly say that he is not free. He has simply declared himself as choosing a foolish risk or of acting contrary to the rules of health for the sake of a temporary pleasure. The alcoholic may realize the folly and harm of his vice; but he chooses the bottle rather than temperance or abstinence because he likes liquor. His strength of will may become impaired as the poison of the alcohol takes hold of his system, but the first and most decisive injury to his will took place when he began to turn his back on the warnings of intelligence. The couple who commit forni-cation or adultery do so, not because they wish to do something bad. Under the pressure of emotion they may even regard their act as something wonderful and noble; or they may argue that they have been pulled along by natural forces of instinct which

numbed their free will. But if suddenly surprised or if caught
in the consequences of their act, they may come to realize that
their first offense was against intelligence and intelligent
reflection.

These examples may possibly be regarded as extreme; but
similar observations can be culled from the daily experience of
nearly everyone. The will cannot function as an active agent
in the best interests of a person, until one makes up his mind
to take a serious, intelligent, and mature view of himself and
of his problems. "With desolation is all the land made desolate,"
said the prophet, "because there is none that considereth in his
heart."³ The individual who is governed by fancy, sudden impulse, appetite, or external suggestion can hardly be depended
upon, either by himself or by others. It is only when one settles
down to take a clear and honest measurement of oneself and
of one's problems that the will can step in and be of positive
assistance.

If given even a half chance, the will can support the intellect, step by step, in its progress toward truth and reality. It
has been truly said that "the wish is father to the thought." This
can be taken to mean that desire colors one's thinking; but it
can also be understood to signify that with some pressure from
the will, the mind can get down to serious and straight thinking.

The next step in clearing the way for a functioning will is
to establish a positive notion of duty. Duty may be defined as
the moral obligation of doing something. It is a moral obligation, rather than a physical one, for the reason that it springs
from the conception of the relationships of the natural law and
also because it is fulfilled freely, not as the result of physical
force or compulsion. One has certain duties to himself, such as
reasonable care of his life and health; to others, such as justice
and fair dealing; and to God, such as worship. These duties
are set forth in the Ten Commandments, in the principles of

---

³ Jer. 12:11.

Christian living, in the laws of the Church and the State, and in the usages established by civilized, cultured society. The impact of these principles upon the will depends upon the personalizing of duty as a sufficient motive or adequate reason for action.

To go to church on Sunday, to pay one's taxes, to perform the work for which one is paid, to fulfill one's promises, to discharge one's debts, and to provide for one's family may not be easy at times. For the will to function in the right direction, instead of taking the easier path of evasion or escape, it is necessary for one to have a distinct and vigorous conception of duty, in the concrete, as a moral obligation and as a solid basis for decision and action.

Akin to duty, is the conception of rights, which implements duties and makes possible their fulfillment. Rights may be described as the moral power of doing or of possessing something, which others must respect. Rights are also rooted in the natural law, established by the Creator as the correct norm for human relations and behavior, conforming to the constitution of human nature in itself and in its relations to society and God. Basic rights are generally understood by human intelligence without the necessity of legal formulation, by positive law of the State, or by special organizations and institutions.

The American Declaration of Independence correctly summarizes these truths when it states that man is endowed by his Creator with certain inalienable rights, among which are listed "life, liberty and the pursuit of happiness." Under certain circumstances, it may be difficult to respect the rights of others, particularly those which limit spheres of action or which require the conquering of forms of prejudice and personal intolerance. Nevertheless, for orderly living and for social security in the basic sense, it is imperative that respect for the rights, and even for the duly established privileges of others, form the motive and pattern for voluntary action.

The idea of duties and of rights, and indeed in this order of logic, forms the code of moral right and wrong. To the extent that one makes this code effective in forming judgments and arriving at decisions, he may be characterized as a person of principle. The path of duty and decision in line with sound principle often calls for self-denial and self-sacrifice. Nevertheless, it is of the essence of orderly living, of personal dependability, and of mental health upon which one can rely. With a strong sense of principle, we can apply the power of the will to overcome obstacles of discomfort and to pursue a course of action with a sense of purpose and finality. Basic conviction and principle provide a stabilizing and strengthening force, a sense of direction and security in life — a motive power and a rudder to the ship that we call human personality.

4

The practical application of these standards, to achieve a genuine self-mastery and a functioning mental health, requires considerably more than a recognition of the truth. The will itself, as a free agent, must be exercised and strengthened through action. Reading a book about swimming will never teach one to swim. It is necessary to get into the water and to apply the principles. The water may be cold; one may fear drowning; the exertion may leave one out of breath. The actual experience may be considerably different from the pleasurable anticipation. But if one wishes to swim, he must not give up the attempt. Similarly, with any action involving the will, one must be prepared to stand fast by reasonable judgment and execute the decision, whether it be hard or easy. To withdraw or falter because of discomfort or opposition is to make progress difficult, not to say impossible.

To achieve strength of will, certain practices of self-denial may be recommended, quite apart from their intrinsic significance or importance. A person who is addicted to overindulgence in food or drink will do well, from time to time, to put aside an attractive dessert, to refuse a drink, and to adopt certain Lenten resolutions and penances for their disciplinary value. Persons of lazy and disorderly habits should set a goal of certain routines for themselves to be performed punctually, including, for example, time for prompt rising in the morning. Excitable persons may profitably require themselves to sit and relax for a period of five minutes to a half hour in the morning or afternoon as an exercise in self-composure. Persons who are inclined to pamper themselves and to feel unhappy unless they are constantly gratified and served may, with advantage to their own character, determine upon some act of kindness or self-sacrifice every day. Even the dropping of a penny in the poor box advances one on the road to self-control and strength of will. A will which has become accustomed to impose disciplinary action with facility in small matters is more likely to prove reliable under critical circumstances, to prevent mental panic under confusion and discouragement or collapse under fear and temptation.

To a large extent, a carefully disciplined will can be made to serve as a faithful watchdog, warning a person of impending danger and giving one time to take appropriate action for one's safety. Individuals with strong emotions, highly strung and sensitive nervous disposition, or dangerous tendencies and appetites should learn that the time to control themselves is before the impulse becomes too strong. To repeat, the will must learn to say "no" as well as "yes" to the various proposals and suggestions which are offered to it. The time to say "no" to a dangerous suggestion is with the first signal and not after the onrush of disaster.

The man who cannot drink without going to excess and making a beast of himself must say "no" to the first drink; he may not be able to render a similar decision with the second. Moral theologians refer to "remote" and "proximate occasions of sin"; and they explain that those who play with fire are almost certain to get burned. If association with certain persons stirs personal lust, the rational will must counsel avoidance or the establishment of social defenses against the onrush of demoralizing emotions. If concentration on certain subjects is likely to upset one's mental peace and stir to violent action, the will must step in at the beginning and change the trend of thought.

It must be recognized that after a certain point of gathering strength, the emotions, particularly those of a sexual or choleric nature, produce definite changes in the brain and in the physical system. For lack of a more scientific expression, we may say that certain valves are opened and others are closed in the brain, and certain glandular activities are set up within the body, which no amount of will power can change until the physical or psychological cycle has been completed. Something happens comparable to the chain reaction of an atom bomb, which, when it is detonated, proceeds irresistibly to its destructive explosion.

The person with genuine and intelligent confidence in the power of his will cannot fail to recognize its limitations. To a large extent, his strength lies in his ability within the limits of safety, where the mind can function with clear perception and the will can still command his actions. To maintain an even keel in one's mind and activity, one must look ahead and take a larger view of interests and values than that of immediate excitement and gratification. The other alternative is a life strewn with uncertainties and regrets.

This means that the strong person must be a humble person. Pride goeth before a fall. In the formation of character and in the strengthening of one's spiritual powers for a life of competence, peace, and achievement, no one can do better than to call upon almighty God for guidance in the direction of the will and grace to strengthen it in sustaining responsibility and in pursuing the path of righteousness.

CHAPTER XX

Religion and Mental Health

I

ONE of the first questions formulated by the human mind, from the dawn of reason in childhood, relative to practically everything in life, is expressed in the word "Why?" From the vast assembly of "whys," ranging from the most elemental observations about nature to the demand for an explanation of why one must do this or that, comes the greatest of all questions. "Why do I exist?" Upon the answer to this question, with its various subdivisions, is built our program of life, our sense of values, and our grading of the relative importance of our conscious activities.

An endless number of explanations can be given for intermediate activities, some of them apparently interlocking, like the old epigram, "I eat to live; I live to eat." Some of these answers satisfy, at least for the time being; others lead on to a further inquiry. It is of the nature of the human mind to push on for a logical and adequate concept, not only of the nature of the world and its component parts, but also of what lies back of it in the order of causality. The child takes an alarm clock apart to find what makes it tick and ring. The inquiring human mind pushes on from clocks to more personal problems, and from these to the final cause of all existence and the particular place that the individual holds in the general plan.

With the development of the physical sciences, which study natural appearances and activities, in an endeavor to extend the frontiers of knowledge, there has appeared a type of thinking which goes no further in its conclusions than to say, "Something has happened." Many scientists, cautious in their procedure and fearful of overstating their observations or discoveries, are willing to say, "When a given set of factors are arranged or placed in motion, something happens which can be predicted." But they are unwilling to describe these factors and their sequel, in terms of *cause* and *effect*. This is one of the principal reasons why some scientists reduce the activities of the mind to a series of molecular activities capable of making observations but not of arriving at any conclusions beyond those of physical appearances.

With this limited point of view, many eminent scientists have become agnostics, so far as religion is concerned; that is to say, they do not regard it as within the competence of the human mind to rise above considerations of a completely material kind. Within the past century particularly, it has become an accepted position in many circles to deride the idea of metaphysics, or of a philosophy of explanations which leads through the notion of permanent principles and of causes to a First Principle and a Final Cause.

The effect of this kind of thinking upon the modern mind has yet to be fully appreciated. But there are good reasons for believing that, instead of liberating mankind from the "fanaticism" and darkness of the past, as some of the new prophets maintain, this materialistic and shortsighted view may lead to mass frustration and brutality of the worst description. Despite its many inconsistencies, the entire Marxist system of thought, which has developed into crusading communism, profoundly influences the thought of many individuals and intellectuals who would deny being communists. This involves a denial of any but material forces blindly forcing mankind into some kind of an upward thrust. Where these blind natural forces do not seem to be acting with sufficient energy and speed, it becomes the mission of political communism to prod along the process by stimulating class warfare, international dissension, and the ridicule and persecution of religion.

Much of the madness of the world in which we live can be attributed to these tendencies of thought and forced action. The resulting confusion has reached deep into the lives of countless people and produced a profound uneasiness and uncertainty about fundamental principles, bound to affect mental health. Two courses of action are open to the inquiring and disturbed mind. One is to close the mind or to endeavor to close it, upon the meaning of life and to attach no more significance to the world or to human activity than that of chemical or physical arrangements and rearrangements which cannot be explained. The other is to accept the principle of causality, to recognize the existence of an intelligent God as the First Cause, and to shape the pattern of one's life in accordance with the idea of purpose and finality. This latter is the foundation of religion.

The customs and literature of mankind from the earliest beginnings bear witness to the religious aspirations of mankind. The monuments of prehistoric times, surviving after the other evidences of lost races and civilizations have disappeared — in Asia, Africa, and the New World — testify to the same fact. The almost universal report of findings by anthropologists working among primitive peoples, from the inhabitants of Tierra del Fuego at the tip of South America to the pygmy tribes of inner Africa, likewise records the existence of belief, not only in a Supreme Being or equivalent divinities responsible for the creation of the world and for the maintenance of its powers, but also in the immortality of the human soul.

It has been argued that, just as men have been in error for long periods of time about other matters, so they may be in error on these points. One might also argue that hunger has driven men to eat poisonous foods by mistake or that the human appetite in various climates and ages has differed widely. But this could not gainsay the fact that the universal character of hunger indicates that food must be eaten if life is to be sustained. The fact is that on the subject of religious belief, mankind has held a wide variety of conceptions, some of them demonstrably false and many of them now definitely abandoned, like the system of gods and goddesses developed by the Greeks and the Romans. But with the allowance for a wide measure of error in details of conception, the deep-rooted character and universal persistence of religious faith clearly indicate that the human mind, by natural impulse, moves toward the recognition of a Supreme Being and of the moral obligations which this fact places upon the individual and society.

On this subject, the eminent psychologist and psychiatrist Dr. C. G. Jung testifies that of the hundreds of patients who have consulted him, in every case above 35 years of age the problem was "that of finding a religious outlook on life." And he states that not one of them has found a real cure "who did not regain his religious outlook."[1]

As this is not a theological disquisition, our only purpose in offering these considerations is to show, if it is necessary to show, that religion is a vital factor in mental health. By "religion," we understand the relations which bind man to God, in recognition of the existence of God, in worship, in responsibility for the observance of a moral law, and in aspiring for perfect happiness in a future life of the soul beyond the grave. One can attempt to ignore these relations or to regard them as the outworn remnants of primitive thought; but they constantly return into consciousness as an inspiring or disturbing force, up to one's last breath.

If one does not regard God, the first and absolute Source of

---

[1] *Modern Man in Search of a Soul* (New York: Harcourt, Brace, 1939), p. 264.

everything that exists, as an intelligent being, then it is impossible to explain the development of order in the universe, or the emergence of intelligence in man. But with this recognition of God as an independent, necessarily existing, and therefore infinite being, intelligent and good, the world and the universe fit into a logical place as creation; and man assumes a position of intelligence, with rights and duties and a destiny. In this order of being, the mind of man can express itself, not to a blind cosmic clod or mass of chemical and physical forces, but to the mind of an all-understanding God, with the positive assurance of being heard and dealt with justly. The soul, as a spiritual and immortal being, faces the responsibilities of life in the expectation, not merely of immediate results, but of an eternal accountability and judgment with God. With this understanding, suffering finds a meaning, and the triumph of virtue over the trials of this existence in the flesh becomes essentially different from a molecular agitation.

It is sometimes said that a man can be truly religious without admitting the existence of God, simply by maintaining a respectful attitude toward the forces of nature and performing his services to humanity in a generous spirit. But, however noble this attitude or generous these services, they fall short of genuine religion. From the standpoint of mental satisfaction, they leave much to be desired. As man is obviously made from a certain pattern, the atheist or agnostic is at a complete loss to say what that pattern may be or how it originated. The truly religious man recognizes that man is made "to the image and likeness of God," and while this description applies in a broad sense to the whole man who has been created, the specific reference is to his soul, spiritual in character, endowed with intelligence and a free will, directed toward the true and the good. God is a personal God, not because He has a material body (which He has not), but because He has a mind and a will, just as man is a person, not because he has a body (which any animal likewise possesses), but because he has an intelligence and will.

With this understanding of God and of religion, one can give with complete logic and satisfaction the answer to the meaning of life: "God has created me to know Him, to love Him, and to serve Him in this life, and to be happy with Him forever in the next." This is wisdom which any normal child can absorb and enunciate, and which is adequate as a guiding philosophy of life for the most profound sage and scholar.

Of course, this is founded on acceptance of the principle that there are realities besides those which we can touch or see or hear. A man depends upon his feet and solid ground upon which to walk. But the steadying influence of God and of religion upon the mind and all the faculties of the soul is no less certain because of the fact that neither God nor the soul is visible or touchable by human senses or instruments.

2

The attitude of psychologists and psychiatrists relative to religion, when dealing with mental problems and patients, differs widely, depending upon the personal beliefs of the practitioner and of the client. Except for those who are bitterly opposed to the concept of religion or who see all mental disturbance as directly related to sex, most competent workers in this field are prepared to recognize the therapeutic value of religion in cases of mental disturbance or confusion, where the patient has at least a residual religion or faith. Faith in God is recognized as having a steadying influence and of producing comfort, particularly under stress of grief and suffering. Prayer is recommended as inducing peace and strength of decision. Persons who have neglected or abandoned the practice of their religion are often urged to return to their church and resume those practices which they have associated with spiritual expression and guidance.

Recognition of these values in religion is of the utmost importance, not merely because of their suggestive or symbolic character, but also and principally because they are rooted in fact. A child who has lost his faith in Santa Claus can never regain it, for the simple reason that Santa Claus does not exist. He can, of course, transfer this faith to something else, such as the spirit of Christmas or the joy of giving and sharing. But a person who has faith in God can never completely lose that faith, for the reason that God exists in reality; and if that faith has grown dim, its rekindling should serve the purpose of bringing back into focus a truer perspective on life and a reconciliation of self with truth, upon which mental health is founded.

The process of restoring religious faith and of reconciling oneself with God is not always an easy task. Various factors enter into the loss of religious faith or the severance of active membership in the Church; and reconciliation may involve severe wounding of one's pride and the admission of unpleasant facts which one has taken years to wall up and forget. Conscience is a potent force; and most people are afraid of it.

Persons with a guilty conscience may take various ways of solving their problem. They may argue with themselves that what they have done, contrary to their religious and moral convictions, was the human, the sensible thing to do under the circumstances. If blame is involved, the fault must lie with society or perhaps with religion itself. Under such conditions, the logical course seems to be a more independent attitude and a cutting away from the outmoded forms of religion and law, which appear as so much unreasonable red tape or heartless regulations. If the problem is very serious, it may be solved by denying the existence of God and of the future life, so that there need be no concern about spiritual accountability.

Rationalization of this kind goes on in the minds of many people, year after year. Social success, material prosperity, intellectual independence, all seem to wipe out the vestiges of an act or a decision, or of a series of commitments, which put an end to early religious sentiment and practice. But the gnawing of the conscience goes on just the same. Every clergyman knows of many instances where persons "absolutely without any remnants of religion or desire" have cried out on their deathbeds for spiritual ministration. Scoffing at religion, bitter criticisms of the shortcomings of clergymen, and general concentration on the earthly aspects — the feet of clay — of the Church are often no more than an attempt to salve one's conscience and to postpone the day of reckoning, when one must admit one's guilt before God and do penance for one's sins with a contrite heart.

In dealing with problems of mental health, whether they be of one's own or those of others, one cannot afford to overlook this matter of conscience. The idea that guilt can be eradicated simply by bringing unhappy experiences to the surface of consciousness is deceptive and shortsighted. Moral guilt is removed, not by rationalization, but by honest acknowledgment with sorrow and a plea for God's mercy. The moral law is not a figment of the imagination, but represents a relationship between God and man. If it has been violated, the conscience, which may be described as the finger of God, becomes aware of the fact and indicates what must be done to re-establish God's friendship. Psychiatric treatment as such cannot substitute for contrition. In commenting upon the sacramental confession of the Catholic Church, some writers have scoffed at the idea as simply a glossing over of offenses and an easy way of getting a fresh start to commit the same old offenses over again. But this conception completely misses the point. Sacramental confession serves no purpose unless it is accompanied by sincere sorrow and determination to amend one's ways. Employed honestly and sincerely, it serves a therapeutic value as well as a religious one; used as an instrument of deception, it is as ineffectual as a psychiatric treatment which ends with probing, and it simply increases one's torment. One cannot lie to God with impunity.

In some cases, where conscience is oversensitive or erroneous in its judgments, competent guidance at the hands of a mature, understanding director or confessor may be indicated. Some persons are inclined to make a serious case of every peccadillo or to live under a cloud of fear lest their contrition for sins has been incomplete or imperfect. An overscrupulous conscience may develop from a number of causes. It may be the product of overrigorous training or of false emphasis on the motives of fear; or it may spring from personal notions. Many adults are unable to settle their minds or to secure peace through finality of decision. In some cases, the difficulty arises from a physical condition, flowing over into the nervous system and disturbing one's power of judgment. The torture of a falsely burdened conscience can be as great as that of a bad one; both types call for humble and frank submission to a better judge than self.

3

Unfortunately, religion often fails to serve its rightful purpose, for the reason that it has been represented or conceived in a false light. The association of religion with bigotry has done incalculable harm. Some people thrive on this kind of thing, and many have become rich and powerful by exploiting religious differences and stirring up hostility. Intolerance of a kind which represents other denominations as devil worshipers, given over to all kinds of immorality and subversion, and deserving of foul treatment, is a phenomenon which appears regularly even in civilized communities; it should be sternly resisted by decent citizens of all religious faiths. Tendencies toward bigotry and meanness should be subject to careful scrutiny in the mind of everyone; and strenuous endeavors should be made to replace them with acts of genuine charity.

Much harm has been done also by circulation of the idea that all who do not share our religious faith are doomed to hell and cannot be saved. An authoritative statement of the Catholic Church, which has always regarded itself as the custodian of Christian truth, is particularly interesting in this connection. In answer to the question, "What do we mean when we say, 'Outside the Church there is no salvation'?" the Baltimore Catechism replies: "When we say, 'Outside the Church there is no salvation,' we mean that those who through their own grave fault do not know the Catholic Church is the true Church or, knowing it, refuse to join it, cannot be saved."

In answer to the question, "Can they be saved who remain outside the Catholic Church because they do not know it is the true Church?" the same authority states: "They who remain outside the Catholic Church through no grave fault of their own and do not know it is the true Church, can be saved by making use of the graces which God gives them."

The great values of religion for orderly and happy living and for peace of mind are sometimes lost through the imposition of a gloomy or technical spirit that drives people away from worship or dries up their spiritual perceptions. Religion, as the relation between God and man, should foster the spirit of love as between parent and children. God is our Father, not a tyrannical taskmaster. His message is that of light and cheer and charity, not of a bluenosed fanaticism. The worship of God should bring joy, comfort, and inspiration, not resentment, fear, and repression. The ritual of religion should be a beautiful symbolism, not a deadly bore or a bare-bones technicality. The preachments of authentic religion are toward happier living, success in one's legitimate enterprises, and the beauty and blessing of God. A shriveled existence, terrorized by a constant blast of "thou shalt nots," haunted by the constant specter of hell-fire, and irritated by picayunish thrusts at the pleasures of social living, was never the picture of religion as presented by Christ. If religion does not serve to strengthen mental health, it is not authentic religion.

It is sometimes alleged that religion, far from creating or restoring mental health, has the effect of driving people crazy. It is a fact that many persons become mentally unbalanced on the subject of religion. But it is by no means certain that their dementia has been caused by religion. A person might become insane through remorse or the torment of an unregulated conscience; but the fault, if any, could hardly be ascribed to religion. In most cases on record, at least, religion is entirely incidental to the unfortunate condition. A mental break, under the given circumstances, would have occurred with any other obsession as well.

I once came upon a man who imagined that he was a disembodied spirit. "I am not really here," he assured me. "You may think that you see me, but that is only a delusion." It so happened that he was a deeply religious man and used the language of a philosopher. But there was no evidence to show that either religion or philosophy was responsible for his mental and nervous breakdown.

Intellectually and emotionally, of course, religion may present serious problems which call for personal adjustment and self-discipline. Some individuals are of such intense nature that they are carried away by every enthusiasm and so influenced by a sense of obligation in certain respects that all other obligations and considerations are put out of focus. A wave of religious fervor sometimes has the effect of sweeping people from the moorings of common sense and of inducing them to change their homes, careers, and everything for which they are really prepared, to lead a religious crusade of some kind. Such people would do well to realize that God is served in all walks of life, and that he serves God best who does his work, whatever it may be, to the best of his ability and with an unselfish, spiritual motive. As a general rule, sudden gusts of religious fervor are to be distrusted. A solid appreciation and regular fulfillment of daily duties, well seasoned with the practical love of one's neighbor, as St. James indicated, is "religion pure and undefiled."[2]

4

On the other hand, even the most religious of people are sometimes tempted to abandon their religious affiliations and practices and to throw their religion overboard. This temptation may arise from a variety of sources. A long train of misfortunes,

---

[2] James 1:27.

disappointment in prayer, or the repeated experience of witnessing unfairness in fortunes, with the evil emerging as the apparent victors and the good as the losers — any one of these may cause a person to doubt whether God is really interested or whether religion offers anything effective in solving the problems of life. The boredom of religious services poorly conducted, or mediocre sermons, or of an irritating approach on the part of one's pastor may make one speculate whether it might not be better to stay away from Church. Dissatisfaction with the way one's Church is conducted, a personal dispute with, or rebuke from, the clergy, an unfortunate or disedifying example in a particular instance, may have the effect of causing one to doubt the truth and efficacy of the Church.

There is no simple or easy answer to these problems, which may be highly personal and extremely disturbing. In general, however, it should be noted that the basic values of religion remain steady and permanent, no matter what a particular experience may be. In prayer, we petition God; we do not command Him. It is important that we recognize His superior wisdom, since He sees the panorama of all mankind and will do what is best for us, even though we are unable to understand this at any particular moment or crisis. The spirit of faith and confidence in God pays deep and abiding rewards; the spirit of rebellion accomplishes nothing except to provide rash judgment and regrettable decisions.

With respect to the defects which we see, or think we see, in the ministry of religion, we can comfort ourselves with the thought that anything entrusted to human hands is almost certain of bad handling from time to time. If we can overlook human weakness or make such adjustments as will remove or relieve the tension, we should endeavor to do so. But it is always a mistake to reject something substantially good, simply because we do not understand it or because of an accidental or secondary feature which causes trouble. I do not understand electricity, but I should be foolish to discard its use for that reason. I have become poisoned by food on several occasions; but I do not propose for that reason to stop eating.

The religious faith of many persons has been profoundly shaken and even lost in these times for other reasons, which touch upon the reconciliation of science with revealed religion, or which arise from problems of a historical or social character. In the field of anthropology, the age and evolution of man, and in the field of geology, the formation of the universe, have appeared to offer insurmountable difficulties when taken against the literal text of the Bible. The existence of numerous religions of conflicting origins and teachings, in various parts of the world, throws many an inquiring mind into confusion and distress. The historical problems and claims of the divergent bodies within Christianity itself have served to bring weakness and loss of faith to many and have given origin to several generations of intellectuals in open attack upon all forms of institutional religion.

Yet, from all this one can conclude that religion and science are both striving and supplementing each other in a fuller understanding of the greatness of God and the mysteries of His creation. For one to abandon the worship of God or the practice of his religion, simply because the discoveries of science have pushed back the age of man far beyond the 5000 years which our predecessors thought was the limit placed by Holy Scripture, or because the Buddhists and the Mohammedans have different conceptions of Divine Revelation than the Christians, is like throwing away one's compass and other instruments of direction and sailing an uncharted sea with no particular objective in sight or in mind.

For one to say that truly religious men and women are never troubled with wonder or doubts as to details of their faith would be to ignore the facts. It is indeed a stupid or smug individual who never has cause to take the measure of his knowledge and to find it limited. There are mysteries of religion just as there are mysteries of science, and it is probable that they will never be completely explored or solved by the mind of man in this life. But the fundamentals of faith can be grasped by all, and the details of religion can be understood sufficiently by the uneducated as well as the educated. The faith of simple and humble people is often as profound as that of the learned and sometimes is more penetrating than that of those whose learning has simply produced confusion and disorder and loss of wisdom.

"Learn of Me," said Christ, "for I am meek and humble of heart."[3]

"Unless you become as little children, you shall not enter the kingdom of heaven."[4]

The man or woman of humble faith in God, of daily prayer and consultation with God, of devotion to his or her religious duties, as God has given light to see them, has the assurance of a full perspective on life, health of mind, peace of soul, and a view of time in the light of eternity.

---

[3] Mt. 11:29.
[4] Mt. 18:3.

Index

Adaptation, 253
Addison, Joseph, on Thomas More, 163
Age, old, 25, 56, 57, 254
Alcoholism, see Drinking
Allergy, personal, 120
Ambition, lack of, 98
Anger, 108
Anniversaries, 270
Antagonism, 21
Apology, 114; value of, 119, 120
Appearance, significance of, 205, 206; in surroundings, 209–211
Appreciation, defined, 80
Autosuggestion, 11

"Bad thoughts," 134, 135
Benzedrine, use of, 32
Bible, literal text of, 297
Bills, payment of, 224
Blood pressure, 22
Borrowing, 224, 225
Boy Scout principle, 261
Brain, collaboration with intellect, 11, 12; functions of, 7–9; injuries to, 12
Brooks, Phillips, on humor, 162
Browning, Elizabeth, 228
Browning, Robert, on cheerfulness, 27; on love, 267; on old age, 25
Burgess, Gelett, 270
Burlesque, 168
Burns, Robert, on humor, 173

Career, selection of, 94, 95
Carnegie, Dale, 19
Catholic Church, confession, 292; on salvation, 293, 294

Causality, 285, 286
Censorship, 143
Charity, gifts to, 225, 226; obstacles to, 259–262
Children, training of, 58
Christ, Jesus, on almsgiving, 265; on cleanness of heart, 144; on Divine Providence, 30, 60; on enjoyment, 234; on forgiveness, 113; on Good Samaritan, 268; and the Good Thief, 159; on humility, 298; on love, 258, 259; on Mammon, 219; redemption by, 158; on relaxation, 38; on riches, 214, 215; on suffering, 148; on talents, 198; on wine, 153
Cicero, on oratory, 161
Claustrophobia, 56
Cleanliness, 206, 207; education in, 210
Clothing, propriety in, 203–205; selection of, 202
Cobb, Irwin, 101, 102
"Comic" cartoons, 164
Communism, 286, 287
Companionship, 58
Competition, 191
Complaining, 65–69, 88
Confession, 75; sacramental, 292
Confusion, sources of, 3, 4
Conscience, 13, 47, 48, 60, 291; treatment of, 292, 293
Co-operation, 195, 196, 254, 258
Counseling, 139; qualifications, 181; value of, 91, 95
Courtesy, 211, 212
Courtship, 133
Crabb, George, on humor, 164, 165